Mery Christmas
1991
Dad & Chip

Also by Gary Sick

All Fall Down:
America's Tragic
Encounter With Iran

OCTOBER SURPRISE

OCTOBER SURPRISE

America's Hostages in Iran and the Election of Ronald Reagan

GARY SICK

TIMES BOOKS

RANDOM HOUSE

To Lois Anna Gordon Sick
and the memory of my father,
Ralph Sick

Grateful acknowledgment is made to WGBH Educational Foundation for permission
to reprint portions from *FRONTLINE: The Election Held Hostage*, broadcast on
April 16, 1991. Copyright © 1991 by WGBH Educational Foundation. All rights
reserved. Reprinted by permission.

Support for Gary Sick's research into U.S. policy
in the Persian Gulf was provided by the Twentieth Century
Fund, a nonprofit, nonpartisan research foundation.

Library of Congress Cataloging-in-Publication Data

Sick, Gary
    October surprise : America's hostages in Iran and the election of
Ronald Reagan / Gary Sick.
      p.   cm.
    Includes index.
    ISBN 0-8129-1989-0
    1. Presidents—United States—Election—1980. 2. Iran Hostage
Crisis, 1979–1981. 3. Reagan, Ronald. I. Title.
E875.S48   1991
973.926—dc20   91-50608
                                       CIP

CONTENTS

If circumstances lead me, I will find
Where truth is hid, though it were hid indeed
Within the centre.

—SHAKESPEARE, *Hamlet*

When you have eliminated the impossible,
whatever remains, however improbable, must
be the truth.

—SIR ARTHUR CONAN DOYLE

OCTOBER SURPRISE

INTRODUCTION

This book was never supposed to have been written. It unearths a political deception that was thought to be forever buried, a mystery never intended to be solved. The shards of evidence that have been discovered to date, while incomplete, tell a story of political intrigue on an international scale that challenges our understanding of an important moment in American history.

When Jimmy Carter was defeated by Ronald Reagan in the presidential election of 1980, one of the reasons for the electoral landslide was Carter's inability to secure the release of the fifty-two American hostages who had been seized at the U.S. Embassy in Tehran on November 4, 1979. The uncertainties of the hostage crisis loomed over the American landscape during the entire election year, and Carter's political fate seemed to be at the mercy of the caprice and personal vindictiveness of Ayatollah Ruhollah Khomeini. There was, however, more to it than that. There was a hidden reality behind those events that began to work its way to the surface in the years that followed, a dark counterpoint to the accepted facts.

We all construct history in our minds at every moment. Historians and

3

ordinary citizens alike try to weave coherent patterns that help explain the past and make sense of the present. The process of remembrance and reconstruction is notoriously difficult and inherently faulty, but even a partly true, or at least convincing, version of the past is usually to be preferred to no explanation at all. Although we can never know the entire truth about any complex series of human acts, we can strive for enough truth to reasonably satisfy both our curiosity and our hunger to understand the peculiar path history has taken. There are times, though, when the partial truth we have fashioned proves to be not only inadequate but grossly incorrect. We discover that things are not as they seemed, that there is another, more compelling explanation lurking behind the reality we thought we had known. Such a discovery may be entertaining when encountered in fiction, but in real life it is unsettling, as if the earth had shifted beneath our feet.

This book, for me, required just such a shift. A reality that I thought I knew well turned out to be little more than a façade. I had to utterly reevaluate whole constellations of events, even those that I had experienced personally. Indeed, almost everything I had lived through had to be considered in a new light. As the principal White House aide for Iranian affairs during the Carter administration, I was personally involved in the efforts to free the hostages, and I rode the emotional roller coaster, along with all other Americans, from the time they were captured through the eventful year of 1980 until they were finally released on January 20, 1981. I was in the Oval Office on the morning of the Reagan inaugural when the final agreements were cabled to Algeria, completing the terms of release. I was in the Situation Room as the hours dragged on, until Iran formally accepted the terms exactly five minutes after Ronald Reagan was sworn in as president.

The curious timing of the release gave rise to rumors of a secret deal between the Republicans and the Iranians to delay the release of the hostages until after the presidential election. The pact was struck, it was said, in order to deny President Carter an opportunity to use the hostage issue to promote his bid for reelection. I had refused to believe such rumors. I thought the Iranians were quite capable of holding the hostages a few extra hours merely to heap further humiliation on the president. In 1985, I published a book, *All Fall Down: America's Tragic Encounter with*

Iran, that examined in detail the Iran hostage negotiations as seen from my position at the White House. I made no mention of the rumors of a secret deal which had continued to circulate.

In the years that followed, I was approached from time to time by journalists asking for my comment on these allegations. My answer was always the same: The events of 1980 could be explained adequately without resort to what I considered to be a conspiracy theory based on little more than a coincidence of timing. To be sure, there were parts of the story that remained mysterious, but I thought I understood fairly well what had happened.

As time went on, seemingly inexplicable fragments of information began to appear. My experience was not unlike that of a medieval scholar discovering traces of a hidden text beneath the script on an old parchment. In my case, however, it was others who were peering through the text at the faintly discernible writing underneath and drawing it to my attention. I was reluctant to look too closely. After all, much of the main text was my own work and there was a real prospect that to get at the hidden layer it would be necessary to erase or alter substantial portions of my own research. I was not enthusiastic at the prospect, so I listened and would occasionally jot down some notes, but I regarded this line of inquiry as little more than a diversion. It was intriguing to construct alternative hypotheses, but the basic facts, I thought, were too firmly established to be challenged.

The puzzle, however, kept gnawing away at the corner of my mind, refusing to leave me alone. Part of its fascination was the sheer magnitude of the charge. If only a few of the allegations were true, this was one of the most extraordinary political events of our time. In the past, other opposition leaders have made contacts with foreign leaders, but almost always with the knowledge of the president. If a deal had been made by Reagan's team, bartering the freedom and conceivably the safety of fifty-two Americans for political gain, the very legitimacy of the Reagan presidency was put into question. Certainly, the allegations invited a much more thorough examination of the pattern of covert political actions sponsored by William J. Casey, Reagan's campaign manager, during his tenure as director of the Central Intelligence Agency. In short, if the accusations proved true, the basic history of the period would need to be reexamined and rewritten.

I also found the story irresistible for a much more mundane and personal reason: curiosity. I felt as if I were wandering into a spy novel. The backgrounds and activities of some of the individuals who were emerging from the shadows of this operation seemed to come out of fiction, and yet they were real. I had read my share of spy novels, and most of my professional life had been spent as an analyst of political and military intelligence. I knew that there were operatives for hire, ready to skirt the law for money, perhaps out of habit or duty, or simply for the thrill and sense of power illegal acts conveyed. But it was nonetheless a shock to meet them, to listen to the well-rehearsed and frequently exaggerated accounts of their exploits, to discover that they had wives and lovers and tax problems, and to learn that they worried about their children's problems with school and drugs. The conjunction of the exotic and the banal had an allure all its own.

Finally, the story was a puzzle, an immensely complicated mystery with most of the clues missing. I am an analyst by vocation, and the challenge of assembling the accumulating bits of information into a coherent picture was irresistible. As the story unfolded, one character would enter and another, briefly in the spotlight, would fade in importance; a promising lead would peter out, a chance conversation would confirm some story that had, until that moment, had no second source.

Bit by bit, pieces fell together. A single sentence in a brief article buried in *The New York Times* established the fact that Casey had been out of the country at the very time several sources said he had been meeting with Iranians in Madrid. This contradicted the assertions of Casey's associates that he had been in the United States on the dates in question. A single date in an affidavit suggested an effort by the Reagan administration to cover its tracks immediately after the inauguration. A succession of small triumphs, interspersed by many dead ends, slowly combined to reveal the contours of a hidden landscape whose existence I had never suspected.

Although the sources in this affair deserve to be treated with caution, when the facts bear them out they should be given their due. The researching of this story has been exasperating, at times even infuriating. Sources were hard to locate, difficult to contact, reluctant to talk openly, and wrong often enough to make tedious replowing of the same ground unavoidable. Many of the sources evinced genuine fear when they first started talking

about the subject; they had to be coaxed and cultivated over time. But in
the end, the bits and pieces of the mosaic that they contributed began to
add up to a remarkable picture. New information appeared even as I was
writing this book, and it is certain that other information will appear in the
future that may alter our understanding of exactly what happened and how.
There are dozens of lapses in the story, and scores of dangling loose ends.
Some of these may be resolved in time, others may never be explained.
This complicated story does not lend itself to brief news reports or thirty-
second sound bites. It requires a book.

This book is not a lawyer's brief, to be carried into court. There is not
enough evidence at this point to launch a prosecution of any individual,
much less to be assured of a conviction beyond a shadow of a doubt. There
is enough evidence, however, to raise serious questions about what happened during 1980 and to justify bringing those questions to public attention. If the evidence presented in this book means what it seems to mean,
we must conclude that in 1980 a deception was inflicted on the hostages,
the government, and the American people that has few if any parallels in
our history. That evidence is not easily dismissed.

I spent twenty-four years of my life as an intelligence officer in the U.S.
Navy, analyzing political and military affairs. Nearly all of my professional
training and experience involved solving complex puzzles, usually on the
basis of fragmentary information. As a young naval officer, I used a few
hard intelligence reports and a wealth of circumstantial evidence to trace
the development of a Soviet surface-to-air naval missile program. Later,
while stationed in Egypt, I constructed a detailed table of organization for
the Egyptian navy, relying mostly on sources that were publicly available.
In another job, I examined patterns of Soviet submarine operations in the
Mediterranean, after creating composite maps of all known sightings and
contacts. When my career took me to the Pentagon in 1973 and to the
White House in 1976, the scope of my work widened to include more
political and less narrowly military issues. I studied the U.S.-Soviet political and military rivalry in the Indian Ocean—a longstanding interest that
grew out of my Ph.D. dissertation at Columbia University. After the fall of

the shah, I delved into the rivalries among political factions in revolutionary Iran.

I discovered, as any analyst discovers, that the subject matter of the investigation may change, but the analytical process remains very much the same. Certain iron rules apply whether one is studying the habits of birds or the behavior of nations. The first—and the most inflexible—of these rules is that you never have enough evidence. So you begin by accumulating every possible scrap of information from any source and arranging this unwieldy mass of data into some kind of order, looking for patterns and clues to guide subsequent research.

This study was plagued by the absence of hard information. Any deal between a U.S. political party and a hostile foreign power was by definition a covert political action, and the participants could be expected to do everything in their power to conceal their footprints. The purpose of a covert action is to manipulate events and the perception of events in such a way that the desired outcome is achieved while the participants remain unaware that they have been manipulated, or, if they suspect, to ensure that the truth can plausibly be denied.

A visitor to Iran in 1953 recalled going to bed one evening with crowds milling in the street outside shouting "Down with the shah!" When he awoke the next morning, crowds were swirling in the streets, but now they were shouting "Long live the shah!" Something, he gathered, had happened. What had happened was a political covert action that mobilized pro-shah forces and threw anti-shah forces into disarray. Everything was done by Iranians and no foreign troops appeared in the streets. Although many people in Iran and elsewhere rightly suspected U.S. and British involvement, the fiction was successfully maintained for years that this was a spontaneous Iranian uprising on behalf of the shah. Many other covert actions pass totally unobserved. That is an important measure of success.

According to many accounts, the deal between the Reagan-Bush campaign and Iran over the hostages was carried out with professional assistance—either from former CIA officers with long experience in covert actions, or from CIA officers who were still on active duty. William Casey, himself a spymaster in World War II, had directed secret operations behind German lines. These individuals took some pains to clean up any obvious trail of evidence and to preserve deniability. Hard evidence was scanty and circumstantial evidence was often ambiguous. In the end, the operation was discovered only because a few men who were either involved in the operation or had knowledge of it chose to tell what they knew.

A second iron law, partially offsetting the first, is the coherence and internal logic of a sequence of events. It is possible to invent fanciful bridges to connect almost any sequence of political events. But those inventive connections, the speciality of the conspiracy theorist, cannot withstand close scrutiny. Facts do not exist in a vacuum; they grow out of events and, if they are part of a human scheme, they are rooted in some underlying logic. At the beginning of an investigation, particularly one as complex as this, theories abound; but as the body of data grows, the facts crowd out one theory after another until only a few remain, and those can increasingly be tested. If the sequence of events was simply random or coincidental, that should become evident rather quickly as contradictions and internal inconsistencies appear. If, however, new facts tend to confirm or explain previous bits of information that originally seemed puzzling or unlikely, then confidence may grow. That is what happened in this case. The strength and internal consistency of the story increased as new evidence accumulated, often from the most diverse or unlikely sources.

Sources were a special problem. Covert actions cannot be carried out without a lot of help. Inevitably, many people learn something about the operation. For those conducting a covert action, there are three layers of protection against disclosure. First, there is the culture of secrecy surrounding such operations. People are sworn to silence, and they take their oaths with the utmost seriousness. In this case, even those who later became disillusioned and decided to talk were extremely guarded and evasive. Many feared for their physical safety. Second, there is compartmentalization. Ideally, in a political covert action almost no one should have the whole picture. Especially those at a lower level should have as little information as possible about any activities except those required to fulfill their mission. "Need to know" is the rule, and if it is rigorously observed, even a disgruntled operative will only be able to reveal one tiny dimension of the operation. If the operative is also a suspect character, which is typically the case, then deniability is even easier to maintain, since he can easily be discredited by the "respectable" people who planned the operation. The third layer of protection is culpability. If the covert operation involved criminal actions, the source will be reluctant to subject himself to possible prosecution. That inhibition is greatly strengthened if those he is accusing happen to be in positions of great political power.

In this case, all three layers of protection applied. Under the circumstances, I am frankly surprised that my colleagues and I were able to make as much progress as we did in unearthing this mystery. In the course of this book, I make a number of disparaging remarks about some of the sources who have spoken to me or others on this subject. Let me be clear at the outset: Some of these men may have had ulterior motives and some may have embellished the truth, but each of them in his own way demonstrated a greater measure of courage than any of us who merely assembled and corroborated their stories. They had less to gain and more to lose.

Corroboration, however, was essential. The allegations were so serious and the implications so grave that no important element of the story could be permitted to rest on the unsubstantiated word of any one source. For the same reason, I have used anonymous sources only sparingly, usually to reinforce information provided by named sources. As a result, many anecdotes and suggestive leads had to be omitted, but that proved to be less of a problem than might have been supposed. Key elements of the story were affirmed by two or more independent sources. The reader, however, will be the ultimate judge.

This research was a form of political archaeology, and the evidence was fragmentary, with many blank spots. In the welter of details, dates, allegations, and personalities associated with this account, it is useful to step back and look at the broad structure of events. Like a mosaic that has been partially reconstructed, the overall effect can only be appreciated from a certain distance. What are the essential questions that need to be answered? The following are some of the fundamental problems that puzzled me and drew me back to the evidence over and over in an effort—not always successful—to tease out an answer.

■ *Where and how did the story begin?* The antecedents of the illicit Republican contacts with Iran in 1980 can be traced to the taking of the hostages in November 1979, or to the overthrow of the shah earlier that year, or even to the nature of the shah's regime and his relations with Israel and the United States. The secret dealings were the product of strategic

interests, political rivalries and personal ambitions in three different countries: the United States, Iran, and Israel. It was, however, the dynamics of
the U.S. presidential race that led William Casey to initiate contact with
two Iranian intermediaries, Cyrus and Jamshid Hashemi, early in 1980.

▪ *Why would the Republicans run such a risk?* We will probably never
have a firsthand answer to that question. The evidence suggests that Casey
and others may have seen possible manipulation of the hostage crisis by
Carter as a more serious threat to their election plans than the risk of being
caught in secret dealings with Iran. There was genuine and widespread
concern within the Reagan-Bush campaign that Carter would launch an
"October surprise" that would win him the election.

▪ *Where and when did the key meetings take place?* According to many
sources, the major meetings involving Casey and high-level Iranians were
in Madrid in July and August, where the outline of an agreement was
struck, and again in Paris in October, where the terms were made final.
There were probably a number of other meetings in Europe involving arms
dealers, Americans, and Israelis between the August and October sessions.
There are detailed accounts of a few of these meetings; most, however,
have been described only in general terms.

▪ *What was the nature of the agreement?* It evolved over time, but the
essence of the arrangement from the start was for Iran to hand the hostages
over to the Republicans (rather than to Jimmy Carter) in return for some
arms immediately (via Israel) plus the promise of future arms and political
benefits once the Reagan administration came into office. There seems to
have been considerable doubt, at least on the part of Iran, whether the
hostages would be released immediately after the election on November 4
or on Inauguration Day, January 20, 1981. Casey reportedly insisted on the
latter.

▪ *Was the Carter administration aware of these contacts?* No. In retrospect, there was evidence that something was afoot, but it never occurred
to White House officials that a party out of power would attempt to undercut the legitimate government in an important negotiation affecting the
lives of fifty-two Americans.

▪ *Was the bargain kept by both sides?* Arms began flowing to Iran from
Israel well before the election, including a planeload of badly needed tires
for Iran's U.S.-built jet fighters that was delivered in spite of protests from

the Carter administration. After agreeing at the last minute to settlement terms that were financially harmful to themselves, Iranian officials released the hostages minutes after President Reagan took the oath of office. Almost immediately thereafter, the flow of arms to Iran intensified; it apparently included matériel from U.S. military depots.

■ *Could the Iranians have negotiated a similar or better agreement with the Carter administration?* Not if their principal interest was the acquisition of arms, as appears to have been the case. Carter was prepared to unfreeze Iran's financial assets and return the military equipment that Iran had paid for under earlier contracts. He was unwilling to enter into a new arms-supply relationship with Iran or to approve Iran's purchase of U.S. arms through Israel. Iran had reason to expect that it would benefit more from a relationship with the new Reagan administration than it could from a hostile Carter administration.

The secret contacts between the Reagan-Bush campaign and the Iranians in 1980 affected real lives and real political events. The deal to delay the release of the hostages may well have been the first act in a drama that was ultimately to conclude with the Iran-Contra Affair. The evidence strongly implies that individuals within the government worked actively with members of the Reagan-Bush campaign to influence the outcome of the 1980 election. Those allegations are exceptionally grave. If true, even in part, they suggest that there was an organized cabal among individuals inside and outside the elected government of the United States to concoct an alternative and private foreign policy with Israel and Iran without the knowledge or approval of the Carter administration. To the extent that these people may have attempted to thwart the legitimate policies of the U.S. government or to manipulate the electoral process, they were engaged in nothing less than a political coup.

In writing this account, I have deliberately excluded the names of most such individuals. These accusations involve actions which, if performed, were not only strictly illegal but bordered on treason. Because of their seriousness, they deserve to be examined by a legally constituted investigative body, exercising its powers with due process of law and with full respect for the presumption of innocence.

Did Iran's failure to release the hostages before November 4, 1980, determine the outcome of the U.S. presidential election? There is no way to answer that question authoritatively. Jimmy Carter was vulnerable on many different fronts, especially the economy, and it is entirely possible that the election would have turned out the same way regardless of what happened to the hostages in Tehran. But there is no doubt that the Reagan-Bush campaign and the Carter campaign regarded the hostage issue as a pivotal factor, and both behaved as if it might well determine the outcome of the election. Whether or not they were correct to place so much emphasis on the hostage issue will never be known. The election is long since past, and history cannot be replayed.

But the question is irrelevant. The issue is not the outcome of the election but the operation of the democratic process. The intent of the Reagan-Bush campaign was unquestionably to influence the outcome, and the methods employed were beyond justification.

In the end, a book such as this can only serve as a cautionary tale. It can remind the reader that politicians and historical events are not always what they seem, that the lust for power and the seductions of ideology can overcome respect for the law, and that the fundamental political values we take for granted may not run as deep as we thought. I argue not for in- creased cynicism but for a healthy dose of skepticism among those in public life and among those of us who must rely on them to protect our basic freedoms and our well-being.

This book was a conscious effort to return to a history I thought I knew intimately and to peel back the layers of visible evidence to see if there was something faintly stirring beneath. In the process, I discovered that almost everything I thought I had known may have had a separate dimen- sion that gave an ironic twist to my earlier interpretation. What I found shocked me, for I had stumbled upon a tale of bold deception by a few powerful men who apparently calculated that political manipulation, if conducted on a sufficiently grand scale, would be essentially invisible and ultimately beyond the law.

·1·

AN ELECTION
HELD HOSTAGE

On the morning of November 4, 1979, a mob of Iranian students clambered over the gates of the United States Embassy in downtown Tehran. The embassy had been buttressed against bullets and bottles—Marine guards called the compound Fort Apache—but the students had been planning the takeover for weeks. They knew all the key nerve centers of the embassy, and they moved swiftly to capture and blindfold everyone in the compound. Most of the senior staff quickly retreated to the basement of the chancellery, and then raced up the stairs to the chargé's office on the second floor, where they sealed themselves behind heavy metal doors and frantically tried to burn mounds of official documents while they telephoned for help. Despite urgent requests from the State Department in Washington and initial promises of aid from the Iranian Foreign Ministry, no effort was made to rescue those trapped in the embassy. After several hours, with smoke and tear gas pouring in, the Americans surrendered to the mob and were taken hostage. Thus began the most devastating diplomatic incident in modern U.S. history.[1]

The Iran hostage crisis concerned the lives and welfare of a band of innocent Americans. It was a mass kidnapping on an international scale, and that made it sensational. But that fact alone could not explain the incident's immense psychological and political impact on the United States and Iran, and to a lesser degree on other countries throughout the world.

The Iranian students who carried out the attack believed that their actions were a logical continuation of the revolution that had overthrown the shah eight months earlier. From the perspective of the revolutionaries and their charismatic leader, Ayatollah Ruhollah Khomeini, the shah was merely a convenient target and rallying point for their wrath. The shah's real importance, in their view, lay in his role as an instrument through which Western influence was able to penetrate and manipulate the politics, economy, and culture of Iran.

The radicals, especially the clerics close to Khomeini, celebrated the collapse of the monarchy but regarded that as only the first step in cleansing their society of the *gharbzadegi*,[2] "Westoxication," that afflicted generations of Iranians. They hailed the hostage-taking as the "second revolution" that would sweep away U.S. influence and serve as a declaration of Iran's newly won independence.[3]

In the West, and particularly in the United States, these emotions met with little understanding and no sympathy. Even those Americans who were prepared to believe that Iran had genuine grievances against the West denounced the hostage-taking as an ill-conceived, inexcusable, and potentially destructive expression of defiance. The students' actions, and the almost immediate endorsement of those actions by the Iranian leadership, were condemned by President Carter as an outrageous example of international terrorism, and the members of the European Community issued a statement calling the seizure a "breach of international law."[4] Carter soon ordered the freezing of $12 billion worth of Iranian financial and military assets in the United States and instituted an arms embargo on the revolutionary regime.

Each side expressed itself in tones of moral indignation, and the escalation of nationalist rhetoric soon transformed the incident into a fundamental political test for both Iran and the United States. Whatever the validity of Iran's complaints about past U.S. interference in its internal political affairs, the tables were now turned. Iran's behavior played directly into the domestic political struggle shaping up in the United States. Great crowds of Iranians marched dutifully through the streets of Tehran, waving their fists at the television cameras and shouting "Death to America!" In every American living room, these images were just as dutifully replayed every night, arousing intense feelings of anger and frustration.

Typically, American presidential elections turn on domestic issues. The pocketbook issues of taxes, employment, debt, and inflation played their traditionally important roles in the 1980 contest between Jimmy Carter and Ronald Reagan, but the seizure of the American hostages just months before the presidential primaries had an exceptional political relevance. Citizens of all ages who normally paid little attention to events outside of the country sat transfixed in front of their television sets, breathlessly following each new twist and turn of events—even when not much was happening, which was usually the case. Television quickly domesticated the foreign scenes and characters by bringing them into the intimacy of our living rooms. During the first six months of the siege, about one-third of the three networks' weeknight newscast time was devoted to the hostage story. ABC went so far as to create a regular thirty-minute nightly program, *The Crisis in Iran: America Held Hostage*, which they promised to broadcast as long as the crisis lasted, and CBS anchor Walter Cronkite ended each newscast with a running count of the number of days the Americans had been held captive.[5] Americans became as familiar with the faces of Khomeini and his sometime foreign minister, Sadegh Ghotbzadeh, as they were with those of President Carter and his secretary of state, Cyrus Vance. Ordinary Americans suddenly became experts, tripping the exotic names off their tongues like old Iran hands and discussing the nuances of the latest pronouncements from Washington and Tehran.

It was a domestic crisis in another way. The hostages had relatives in the United States, and in the absence of hard news these family members were interviewed repeatedly in national and local media. Predictably in a group that size, some proved to be exceptionally articulate and telegenic. Their faces and their plight became as familiar as those of a next-door neighbor. In only a few weeks, an event playing out on the opposite side of the globe became, for most Americans, a family affair.

The sustained passion and intensity of the American people during most of the 444 days of the crisis was remarkable. Anti-Iranian demonstrations burst out in Washington, Houston, New York, and many other cities. Sales of Iranian flags went up—across the nation, Americans were burning them in the streets—and sales of Iranian caviar went down in gourmet shops like Zabar's in Manhattan. A Texas newspaper offered iron-on patches urging "Let my people go"; over 250,000 people sent Christmas cards to the hostages in Tehran. Meanwhile, Iranian-Americans faced problems that hadn't been seen since Japanese-Americans had been interned during World War II: Some were booted out of their jobs; others had their property vandalized; and their children were taunted and jeered in school.

The American people were united in a single concern as they had not been united since before the Vietnam War. For at least the first five months of the crisis, people instinctively rallied behind their president. Carter's approval rating in the Gallup poll leaped from 32 percent in early November 1979 to 61 percent in early December. Pollster George Gallup called the turnabout "stunning . . . the largest increase in the four decades the Gallup poll has made measurements."[6]

President Carter was facing a serious challenge from Senator Edward M. Kennedy, and as the primary season approached, the focus of attention on the White House and on crisis management was not unwelcome. The first week after the seizure, Carter canceled a state visit to Canada and other plans to go to Pennsylvania, Florida, and Georgia. As he later wrote, "Staying close to Washington quickly became a standard policy."[7]

By the time he formally announced his candidacy on December 4—a month after the embassy was taken over—the President said he would not engage in active campaigning or other partisan activity until the hostage crisis was resolved. Carter dropped out of a debate with Senator Kennedy and California Governor Jerry Brown to be held in January in Iowa, and let his wife, Rosalynn, and Vice President Walter F. Mondale stand in for him on the campaign trail.

Frustrated by not being able to meet head-on with Carter and jealous of his leap in popularity, many candidates denounced his decision as unfair. Senator Kennedy, who had led Carter in Gallup polls by a margin of about two to one almost consistently from the fall of 1978 up until the hostages were seized, derisively tagged Carter's refusal to campaign "the Rose Garden strategy," and the media instantly picked up the term.[8]

Nevertheless, the President, it was clear, was tangled in the cords of events and immobilized; the more he struggled, the tighter the net was drawn. The economy was running away from him. The oil shock generated by the Iranian revolution had set off a global recession compounded by a deadly combination of high interest rates and inflation. The numbers were all moving the wrong way.

Carter's considerable legislative and policy accomplishments were reduced by circumstances to the status of political liabilities. A hard-fought-for package of energy legislation, providing, among other things, public funding for research in alternative power sources, was a grim reminder of the hour-long lines at gasoline pumps. The Panama Canal Treaty, which provided for the eventual return of the canal to Panama, may have been necessary medicine, but it left a bitter taste in the mouths of many voters, who saw it as yet another symptom of the declining strength and prestige of the nation.

The SALT II arms-control treaty became a political white elephant after the Soviets launched their brutal invasion of Afghanistan in December 1979. Even Carter's ultimate triumph—the Camp David Accords and the subsequent peace treaty that he had personally brokered between Egypt's Anwar Sadat and Israel's Menachem Begin—won him little support among Jewish voters. Many of Israel's supporters in the United States were privately dismayed that a truculent Begin seemed determined to cast himself as the villain opposite Sadat, whose generosity and reason seemed nothing short of heroic, and all cheered the final peace treaty. They were nonetheless apprehensive about Carter's apparent willingness to lean on Israel, and they wondered what a second term might portend.

On April 24, 1980, at the peak of a hotly contested race for the Democratic presidential nomination, scarcely one month before the eight crucial primaries of "Super Tuesday" on June 3, Carter launched a secret mission to rescue the hostages. It failed, tragically taking the lives of eight Americans. Secretary of State Cyrus Vance, who had consistently argued for restraint and against military action and who had not been present at the crucial meeting on April 11 when Carter and the National Security Council decided to launch the rescue attempt, resigned in protest. A chorus of self-appointed strategists heaped scorn and ridicule on an administration that was already foundering politically. The President, however, behaved with great dignity. He made no excuses, he sought no scapegoats, he accepted absolute personal responsibility. But it was agony to watch.

Zbigniew Brzezinski, Carter's national security adviser, intended to do more than watch. On April 27, only forty-eight hours after the White House announced the disaster, he and the President flew by helicopter to a secret site to visit the members of the rescue team.

Colonel Charles Beckwith, the mission commander, was in tears when the President stepped off the helicopter. "Mr. President," he said, "I'm sorry we let you down!" President Carter embraced him and thanked him and his men for what they had done.

"Will you let us go back?" Beckwith asked. Carter was guarded in his reply. He very much doubted that another rescue mission would be possible, since Iran now had its guard up and was dispersing the hostages. He said that he would do everything possible to free the Americans in Tehran and he intended to bring them out. If he decided it was necessary, he would rely on Beckwith's team as before.[9]

On the trip back to Washington later that day, Brzezinski picked up Beckwith's request and pressed the President to authorize a new rescue plan. Although Carter was skeptical, he eventually yielded. At a minimum, he agreed, the United States had to be prepared to intervene if the hostages' lives were in imminent danger.[10] Soon afterward, a U.S. brigadier general was summoned to the office of General David Jones, the chairman of the Joint Chiefs of Staff, and was told that the President had approved the planning and development of a new operation to rescue the U.S. hostages in Iran. He was asked to assume responsibility as the deputy commander of the force. Since the operation was to be entirely secret, as cover, he would be expected to continue heading the U.S. Air Force's international programs office in the Pentagon. Although General James Vaught would serve as the nominal commander of the operation, the deputy would in fact exercise primary responsibility.

His name was Richard V. Secord and he was a natural choice in many ways. A twenty-four-year veteran of the air force, he had worked in special operations in Southeast Asia, focusing on Laos, where he had been known for his flamboyant and unconventional style. It was there that he became a member of the exclusive fraternity of covert-action specialists who inhabit the hidden world where the usual boundaries between the military and intelligence communities dissolve. Secord later commanded the air force mission to Iran for three years, with responsibility for a thousand officers and technicians who were assigned to train the shah's air force; after the revolution, he had excellent contacts in the Iranian exile community. His experience with international arms sales had immersed him in a lucrative and dangerous world, where boldness and the ability to deliver were highly prized and richly rewarded. He had a reputation as a man who knew how to get things done, even (or especially) when orthodox methods were inadequate or inappropriate.

Outside a few select circles, he was virtually unknown. Years later, however, when the exploits of Lieutenant Colonel Oliver North burst into the headlines, Secord would acquire an unwelcome measure of fame as a star witness and defendant in the Iran-Contra Affair.

Secord had mixed emotions about the offer. A rescue mission had just been attempted and had failed. A second mission would be far more risky and uncertain. He already had his hands full with a demanding job. Adding what promised to be a complex, clandestine, and full-time set of responsibilities would place crushing demands on his time. Nonetheless, his can-do approach had served him well throughout his career and he was confident of his ability to fashion an effective plan. Moreover, the appointment would place him very near the heart of the major foreign-policy issue of the day.

He asked for some time to think it over, and then he sketched out a plan that would rely on a quick and forceful strike to take the embassy and remove the U.S. hostages. Instead of stealth and high technology, it would rely on surprise and overwhelming local military superiority. He did a rough calculation of the forces required. They were substantial. He outlined his strategy to Secretary of Defense Harold Brown some days later. He was characteristically blunt: If he were to do the job, he said, he would need access to a variety of units from different services, in significant numbers, perhaps for prolonged periods of time. In short, he laughed, he wanted everything. Brown replied simply, "You've got it."

Secord set to work.

∎ ∎ ∎

After the inglorious failure of the rescue mission, the public reservoir of goodwill and tolerance began to run dry, and Carter's reelection campaign began to falter; it was time for the President to step out of the Rose Garden. On April 29, Mondale broached the subject with Carter. "The first couple of months I explained that you were back at the White House trying to deal with the hostage crisis and all our other problems, and people would respond warmly and sympathetically," the Vice President commented. "In the last couple of months, they just aren't buying that anymore. They're tired of seeing me pinch-hitting; they want to see their President." Hamilton Jordan, Carter's chief of staff, seconded the opinion. Carter was convinced; he left the Rose Garden.[11]

During a press conference on April 30, Carter responded to a question about his political plans: "None of these challenges are completely overcome, but I believe they are manageable enough for me to leave the White House for a limited travel schedule." White House aides winced and Ronald Reagan pounced. "If he feels freed," Reagan quipped, "I wonder if he thinks now that the hostages have now been somehow freed."

On Super Tuesday, President Carter faltered again, winning only three of the eight contests. He picked up enough delegates to guarantee his nomination in August, but there was no joy in the Democratic Party and no sense of momentum. Their candidate was already limping badly in the race to the November election, and the main event had not even begun.

Still, Carter's rivals realized that they were at a tactical disadvantage. Although Carter was vulnerable on his handling of the hostage issue, his challengers had to be cautious in their criticisms or risk being perceived as undercutting the President during a national crisis. They also lived with the knowledge that the rescue attempt, despite its spectacular failure, had demonstrated that President Carter was prepared, under certain circumstances, to take great risks to resolve the hostage crisis. They suspected that he might embark on equally perilous acts in the future to redeem his political fortunes. They worried that a sudden breakthrough in the negotiations, or some unexpected development concerning the hostages, could instantly divert public attention away from the campaign. The best-laid plans could be laid waste by a change in the hostage situation. It was the wild card in the election.

The Republicans, no doubt, wanted to ensure that the Iranian hostage issue would not be used to promote the reelection of Jimmy Carter. They were particularly worried about the possibility of an unexpected development, outside the control of the campaign, that might shift public support to the President. Such an event could take many forms, but the most obvious possibility was a sudden release of the hostages in Iran. If it should happen at a sensitive moment in the campaign, the joy and relief of the American people could allay doubts about Carter's leadership and swing many voters into the President's camp. Michael Deaver, a Reagan campaign official and close confidant, later wrote: "One of the things we had concluded early was that a Reagan victory would be nearly impossible if the hostages were released before the election. . . . There is no doubt in my mind that the euphoria of the hostage release would have rolled over the land like a tidal wave. Carter would have been a hero, and many of the complaints against him forgotten. He would have won."[12]

Thus, the Republicans adopted a comprehensive strategy to defend themselves against a possible release of the hostages prior to the election. The strategy had two prongs: intelligence and disinformation.

First, the Reagan-Bush campaign began to organize an extensive and sophisticated intelligence operation designed to penetrate key agencies of the U.S. government and to provide early-warning information to the campaign about any hostage developments. According to Robert Neumann, a former ambassador to Saudi Arabia and a senior foreign-policy adviser to the Reagan campaign, this proved to be unexpectedly easy, particularly in the national-security community.[13] Jimmy Carter had made enemies in dangerous places.

Carter had come into office vowing to clean up the CIA in the wake of the worst scandals in the history of American intelligence. Admiral Stansfield Turner, Carter's director of Central Intelligence, carried out that promise with a cool, technocratic vengeance. In the fall of 1977, in what came to be known within the agency as the "Halloween Massacre," he cut the CIA's covert-operations personnel from 1,200 to fewer than 400, notifying the hapless officers with a computerized form letter.[14] These individuals, many of whom had years of experience in undercover operations, including the clandestine manipulation of elections, suddenly found themselves unemployed. They were angry and bitter, and many volunteered to work with the Reagan-Bush campaign, especially given the added attraction of a former CIA chief as the vice-presidential candidate. "There were Reagan-Bush posters, cut off in the middle with only the right side, i.e., the George Bush side, up all over the agency," recalled a former staff member who had frequently visited the headquarters at Langley.[15]

Years later, Richard V. Allen, Reagan's chief foreign-policy adviser during the campaign, condescendingly dismissed this group as a "plane load of disgruntled former CIA" officers who moved into the Reagan-Bush campaign headquarters in Arlington, Virginia, where they were "playing cops and robbers."[16] Allen thoroughly distrusted these "nutballs," as he called them, and said they were one of the reasons he conducted the foreign-affairs activities of the campaign from his downtown office rather than at campaign headquarters.

The operations center in Arlington, which maintained a twenty-four-hour watch on news developments, was under Stefan A. Halper, who had been associated with the Bush campaign. The watch officers of the operations center were former CIA employees who had worked for the Bush primary campaign.[17]

In the Pentagon, the Carter administration's military policies had won few friends, and many high-level military and civilian officials made no secret of their opposition to Carter and their preference for a Republican administration. In some cases, these political interests were given expression more tangible than personal votes on Election Day. For example, an unidentified man contacted Richard Allen to offer him information about the plans for the highly secret second rescue mission.[18] According to Allen, this man met him on a park bench in Washington and briefed him on the rescue mission, which was one of the most sensitive and highly compartmentalized operations in the U.S. government at the time. As a result of this briefing, Allen, who held no government position, was better informed about the nature of the rescue-mission plans than were many of the most senior officials at the Department of State and the White House.

Allen later said the information from this "unsolicited source" "died with me"—but it didn't die before he told Zbigniew Brzezinski, that he "knew about the plan, but wouldn't use it." Brzezinski said he had no memory of Allen's statement. But if Allen did make it, not only would it have been a tweak to the man who had championed the second rescue plan, but it also would have been a none-too-subtle warning that the Republicans were looking over the administration's shoulder.[19]

On August 18, four days after Carter was renominated by the Democratic Party, columnist Jack Anderson published the first in a series of columns charging that the Carter administration had formulated a plan to invade Iran with "a powerful military force." Anderson wrote, "The tentative invasion date has been set suspiciously for mid-October," a few weeks before the November presidential election; the date was supposedly based on an assessment by the White House that the political consequences would be popular with the electorate. Anderson surmised that the essential purpose would be to rescue the hostages, but that the operation would also "exact military retribution." "Our armed forces plan to invade and hold portions of Iran," he asserted, and "training exercises have been initiated."[20]

White House spokesman Jody Powell termed Anderson's charges "absolutely false," and said the suggestion that the Carter administration would start hostilities "for political benefit is grotesque and totally irresponsible." The *Washington Post,* which normally carried Anderson's syndicated column on the comics page, refused to print the series of columns, as did most other major newspapers and magazines. As a consequence, although these columns became some of the hottest political topics of the day, few people had actually read them.

Anderson said he had learned of the alleged mission from unidentified experts who believed the plan was doomed to fail and who opposed its "political motivation." His columns went on to say that Carter had ordered the failed April rescue mission because his standing in public opinion had dropped, and the new plan had been devised because his poll ratings had dropped again. Three days later, in a speech to the annual convention of the Barber and Beauty Supply Institute, Anderson backed off a bit. Although Carter had not actually ordered an invasion, Anderson said, "he has started preparations for a limited invasion of Iran," and one of the three "control points" in the operation had already passed.[21]

Anderson's charges were indeed false. No invasion of Iran was planned, for October or any other time. His description of the operation, however, bore at least some resemblance to the plan for the second rescue mission.

According to Jack Anderson and Dale Van Atta, the documents describing the alleged invasion came from two sources. One was a member of the Joint Chiefs of Staff and the other was a member of the National Security Council in the Carter White House.[22] This leak may have been the first in what later became a flood, as national security officials who opposed Carter worked from the inside of the administration to attempt to sabotage it and assist in a Reagan victory.

The commanders of the mission worried that the Anderson columns, however garbled and inaccurate, would prompt the Iranian hostage-takers to take additional defensive action. The timing was critical. Only two weeks after the Anderson story appeared, Secord formally certified the mission to be combat-ready.[23]

In fact, the Iranian students did take note of Anderson's charges, and they issued a statement on August 25 threatening to kill the hostages in the event of any military action by the United States. "The 'attackers' and spies will be dispatched to hell," Tehran radio quoted the students as saying. They also announced that they had moved some hostages to new secret locations. It was a bluff. The hostages by this time had been assembled in Komiteh Prison, where they were to remain for the next two months. No new security procedures were initiated, which suggested, perhaps, that the hostage-takers were confident of their security—or, possibly, that they did not take Anderson seriously.

Others, especially those in or around the Republican campaign, made a show of taking Anderson very seriously indeed. In a speech on August 20, Reagan expressed concern that President Carter might be "tempted to take reckless actions designed to reassure Americans that our power is undiminished."[24]

There was yet another leak of the plans for the second rescue attempt. In a sworn affidavit, Allen noted a meeting on October 10, 1980, during which Seymour Weiss, an adviser to the Reagan campaign who had retired four years earlier from the State Department (where he had served as under secretary of state and then as ambassador to the Bahamas), "provided me with information concerning planning for a second hostage rescue attempt."[25]

The Republican campaign was "feeling the heat" of the second rescue mission, as a very senior official who was in the Defense Department during the 1980 campaign put it.[26] They were "thoroughly paranoid" and were doing everything possible to elicit all the information they could from their contacts within the administration. This source was aware of the second rescue mission. He believed it was going to be launched, and he was sure the Republicans believed so as well. He was convinced that a massive strike on Iran, even if it failed to get all the hostages out of the country, would have had a powerful impact on Carter's standing and indeed might have reversed the course of the election. There were also many Reagan supporters, he added, outside the Pentagon—such as Alexander Haig, the former Supreme Allied Commander in Europe, and retired Admiral Thomas Moorer, the former chairman of the Joint Chiefs of Staff—who had excellent contacts inside the defense establishment and who acquired useful bits of information simply in the course of their normal business. Haig and Moorer were both cultivating roles as special foreign-policy advisers to the Reagan-Bush campaign.

A more formal reporting network was organized by retired Admiral Robert Garrick, who had joined the Reagan-Bush campaign in August as the director for political development and research. Garrick, a garrulous man who was part of the campaign's freewheeling "California group" (there was also a more staid "Eastern group"), recalled how the operation had started: "One day I was looking at the *Washington Post,* and here was a photograph of great mounds covered in black tarps [at McGuire Air Force Base in New Jersey]. . . . The caption said it was the matériel that President Carter had embargoed, and there it sat." Garrick reasoned that a movement of transport aircraft from other bases to McGuire would signal an arms-for-hostages swap. He enlisted someone who lived near the base in New Jersey and asked him to check daily. Every day, Garrick called the lookout and asked if anything had moved. He also contacted a group of retired military officers, who made checks at three other U.S. Air Force bases across the country: Andrews, near Washington, D.C.; Norton, near San Bernardino, California; and March, near Riverside, California. Garrick's efforts were in vain: No planes flew to McGuire; no one touched the military hardware. "It was always there!" Garrick said in 1990. "It never moved! It may still be there!"[27]

Even within the White House, there were individuals who were committed to the defeat of Jimmy Carter and his replacement by Ronald Reagan. Using code names and clandestine reporting channels, they provided information about deliberations within the White House and among National Security Council staff concerning the hostages and other policy matters. One of these sources stole a copy of President Carter's briefing book, which the Republican campaign then used to prepare Reagan for his debate with Carter on October 28.[28]

In every political campaign there is a certain amount of spontaneous political enthusiasm and self-serving partisanship that shows up in the form of voluntary offers of support and information. The Reagan-Bush campaign undoubtedly had its share of what Richard Allen later called "these independent, free-lance, spontaneous, over-the-transom volunteers."[29] Nor, as he pointed out, could the campaign account for those, like the *"espontáneos* in a bullfight," who get so carried away that they just jump into the action. But there was nothing spontaneous about the intelligence activities of the Republican campaign in 1980.

By October of the election year, the Reagan-Bush campaign had organized a hostile intelligence penetration of its own government. The agents who functioned in the most sensitive areas of the government—the Pentagon, the intelligence agencies, the State Department, the White House—were providing regular intelligence reports on the most highly classified policies and operations.

Much of this activity was illegal. The theft of President Carter's briefing book before the debate was almost certainly an illegal act. The leak about the details of the second rescue mission was an egregious breach of security. When Richard Secord was informed of the leak to Allen, he said: "If it were true, it would be one of the grossest violations of operations security I've ever seen in my career."[30] Indeed, if this leak had been detected at the time, the source of the leak would surely have been subject to severe disciplinary action.

The second prong of the Republicans' strategy was disinformation. Beginning in early October and rising to a climax in the weeks before the election, mysterious news reports popped up from coast to coast asserting that military equipment was being assembled or was actually on its way to the Middle East as part of a last-minute swap for the release of the hostages. All of these reports had one thing in common. They were false.

Even Admiral Garrick was later to admit that his network of reserve officers never detected any movements toward Iran. Yet WLS-TV in Chicago began reporting in mid-October that, according to "military reserve pilots," five U.S. Navy cargo aircraft loaded with spares were due to arrive in Iran within forty-eight hours.[31] There was a string of such reports on radio and television, in newspapers, and from the wire services throughout the country. These reports were all characterized by a wealth of convincing details: dates, places, times, quantities, and the like. Since in reality nothing was moving, these reports now appear (as they did to the White House at the time) as part of a deliberate program of disinformation. They seem to have been invented out of whole cloth and fed to the media by credible but anonymous sources as part of a propaganda campaign to keep public attention focused on a possible "October surprise" by the Carter administration.

The Reagan-Bush campaign's strategy was largely successful in its primary objective of keeping the Carter administration off-balance and on the defensive. The White House was reduced to issuing constant denials that never managed to catch up with the juicy leaks springing up left and right. The strategy also probably succeeded in planting the notion in the public mind that the Carter administration was preparing a cynical maneuver to free the hostages just before the elections. But it had other effects as well.

For the U.S. public, the sense of personal identification with the hostages was deep and powerful. For most Americans, and especially for the hostages' families, this was an agonizing time of hopes repeatedly raised, only to be dashed. With their campaign of disinformation, the Republicans trifled with those emotions, playing them skillfully but cynically for the party's own tactical advantage.

These constant reports also did not go unobserved abroad. The stories of imminent arms deals were so persistent that Ayatollah Mohammed Hussein Beheshti in Iran, worried that the populace would conclude that Iranian officials were making deals with the Great Satan, had to call a press conference to announce that Iran was not receiving any arms from the United States.

Beheshti's statement was technically correct. Though official negotiations were going on, not one shipment of arms had been sent from Washington. What was left unsaid was more important: By mid-October, as we shall see, Iran had already opened an arms relationship with Israel, allegedly with the acquiescence and active assistance of the Reagan-Bush campaign, and without the knowledge or sanction of the Carter administration.

The rash of stories, presumably planted by the Republicans, obliged both Washington and Tehran to issue public denials about nonexistent secret deals, which diverted attention away from the real thing.

The disinformation campaign added gratuitous complications to an already difficult negotiating situation. In mid-October, when Iranian Prime Minister Mohammed Ali Raja'i came to the United Nations headquarters in New York, rumors multiplied that he was coming to ratify a secret arms swap with the Carter administration. As a result, the already slim chance that his visit would provide an opportunity for quiet U.S.-Iranian diplomacy was effectively eliminated.

The most avid and uncritical audience for these stories, however, was the workers and many of the officials in the Republican campaign itself. They were already inclined to believe the worst about Carter, and these stories simply enhanced their paranoia, creating a campaign atmosphere of permanent crisis that occasionally bordered on panic. Richard Allen, who claimed that he had been confident of a Reagan victory and wasn't worried about the hostages, would later recall that there were individuals, such as Michael Deaver, "who were scared to death that a rescue would win the election for Carter." These people, he caustically added, usually did not even know where Iran was.[32] It was a classic case of what is known in intelligence jargon as "blowback"—political disinformation intended for one audience that is heard, and believed, by your own people. The effect in this case was to reinforce the feeling within the Reagan campaign that drastic action had to be taken to protect against an imminent move by the Carter campaign.

Another part of this strategy was the highly publicized creation of an "October surprise committee" by the Republican campaign staff. This group, composed of ten foreign-policy experts under the direction of Richard Allen, was first announced in *The New York Times* of October 7, 1980, reportedly in anticipation that Carter would attempt "some kind of dramatic action during the next two weeks."[33] Allen invited Ambassador Robert Neumann, who had been an adviser to Bush during the primary campaign, to be the committee's "Iran-watcher." In that capacity he met almost daily with Allen.[34] The purpose of this committee, Allen later said, was to be alert for any last-minute surprises, including the possible release of the hostages, and to develop contingency plans to deal with them. The committee, however, was itself part of the contingency plan. By dramatizing the possibility of a sudden move by Carter just prior to the election, the creation of the committee planted the idea in the public mind that any such move should be viewed as a cynical political gesture. Allen said he came up with the concept of the October surprise committee almost immediately after the Republican convention in July. The idea was "to put the phrase into the press's vocabulary. It could be anything to do with the release." He was delighted with the coverage it received in the media: "It was a great success. The press swallowed it hook, line and sinker."[35]

Allen made no apologies for the publicity campaign's drawing of attention to a possible October surprise. "That is just politics," he said, "and entirely legitimate." Jody Powell, the White House press spokesman for President Carter, agreed. "We saw the flood of publicity about an October surprise as a Republican damage control exercise," Powell said later. "It was supposed to create problems for us, and to some extent it did. Fair enough. We were trying to create problems for them, too."[36]

But no one was more concerned about an "October surprise," or more prepared to do something about it, than William J. Casey, Reagan's campaign manager. A veteran of the World War II Office of Strategic Services (OSS)—the forerunner of the Central Intelligence Agency—a lawyer, a venture capitalist, and the chairman of the Securities and Exchange Commission during the Nixon administration, Casey had a reputation as a shrewd tactician who did not let small niceties stand in his way. Scandals and charges of impropriety trailed in his wake. A voracious reader with strong conservative political instincts, he made no secret of his ambition for higher public office, especially in the field of U.S. foreign policy.

Although he had had a rich and varied career, everyone who knew him agreed that his first and dominant love was intelligence. He earned a Bronze Star for his work in organizing French resistance in support of the Normandy invasion in World War II, and when the war ended he was in charge of American Secret Intelligence Operations in Europe. He was an active and enthusiastic member of VOSS, the alumni organization of Veterans of OSS, and many of his closest associates, friends, and clients were drawn from that same background. His aggressive style, which produced results even if a few eggs were broken along the way, seemed to be an extension of the buccaneer heyday of U.S. wartime intelligence.

According to a U.S. government official who watched Casey in action, he relished secret operations and displayed almost casual disregard for routine security. In his periodic meetings with senior State Department officials after he became the director of Central Intelligence, he would casually describe breathtaking operations that he had initiated in countries around the world; some of the operations were of dubious legality.[37] The purpose of this exercise seemed to be twofold. If any of these operations went sour or resulted in an international incident, Casey could legitimately say that he had signaled them in advance to the State Department. But more important, he seemed to enjoy the opportunity to display his own daring and to observe the startled reactions of his diplomatic colleagues.

Casey did not play petty games. He disdainfully refused to employ false names, even when his identification might be dangerous.[38] When he believed himself to be in "safe company," he seemed to have no inhibitions about discussing very sensitive information even with strangers. This nonchalance was part of his style, and it was one of the characteristics that won him the admiration of those who knew and worked with him.

Casey's concern to monitor the Carter administration's intentions with regard to the hostages began shortly after he was appointed as Reagan's campaign manager on February 26, 1980. A few weeks later, he would approach an Iranian go-between who was cooperating with U.S. intelligence and the Carter administration, seeking information on the administration's thinking and plans about the hostage situation.[39]

As the campaign unfolded, his concern would become an obsession. According to his biographer, Joseph E. Persico, Casey later described his apprehension as follows:

I noticed in the last days of the Wisconsin primary that Teddy Kennedy was pulling up fast on Carter. That could be the beginning of a sweep of the industrial states. Then, on the Sunday before the election, Carter notified the networks that he expected good news on the hostages—they would be taken out of the embassy and moved to safer quarters. He got up at seven o'clock on Tuesday, election day, and announced it again as the voters were going to the polls. And he scored a tremendous victory in Wisconsin over Kennedy.[40]

Participants would dispute the historical accuracy of Casey's account,[41] but his perspective was widely reflected in the media and became part of the conventional wisdom of the hostage crisis. There is no reason to doubt that Casey genuinely believed what his words implied: that Carter could and would cynically manipulate the hostage situation for his own political advantage; and that public reaction to hostage developments could dramatically influence the outcome of an election. "That was a shabby business about the Iranian hostages on the morning of the Wisconsin primary, the act of a man with no nerve," Casey told Francis X. Clines of *The New York Times.* "We expect that Carter will try everything to get re-elected. So we'll be ready for everything."[42]

Casey was an old warhorse when it came to campaigns—he had worked on Nixon's successful presidential bids in 1968 and 1972, and he had seen more than a few "dirty tricks" played. As Ronald Reagan's campaign manager, he would be remiss if he did not take steps to protect himself and his candidate from unexpected surprises that could tip the election. Casey may have regarded the risk of exposure of his secret contacts as less serious than the risk of being surprised by uncontrolled developments in the hostage crisis.

Over the ensuing months, Casey and the Republican campaign systematically constructed an elaborate and sophisticated intelligence organization targeted on their own government. By the time of the election in November, they had succeeded in penetrating every major agency in the national security complex of the U.S. government, including the White House, the Defense Department, and the Central Intelligence Agency. They had their own network of agents who kept watch on key air bases and military facilities throughout the country, and a command center staffed with former intelligence professionals. The process of penetration was made easier by the fact that President Carter was unpopular with the national security fraternity and that many of its members were formerly friends and colleagues of those organizing the campaign against him.

In fact, there may have been several different attempts to obtain information on the hostages during the primaries. In early 1980, Ronald Reagan and George Bush were in hot competition for the first spot on the Republican ticket. Each had incentive to develop potential sources of information.

Jamshid Hashemi, the Iranian intermediary whom Casey would later approach, recalled that he first met Donald Gregg in the spring of 1980 at his brother Cyrus's bank on the corner of Fifth Avenue and Fifty-seventh Street in Manhattan. Cyrus introduced Gregg to Jamshid simply as "the man from the White House."[43] At that time, Donald Gregg, a longtime CIA officer with extensive experience in the Far East, was a member of the National Security Council staff in the Carter White House, where he was responsible for intelligence coordination and East Asian affairs. The sensitive position of intelligence coordinator was traditionally filled by a professional intelligence officer, who was responsible for liaison between the White House and the entire intelligence community.[44] Although Gregg was uniformly regarded as a competent professional, there was a dimension to his background that was entirely unknown to his colleagues at the White House, and that was his acquaintance with one of the Republican frontrunners, George Bush.

Gregg had first met Bush over a dinner in Tokyo in December 1967, when Bush was a first-term U.S. congressman from Texas.[45] In 1974–75, when Bush was chief U.S. liaison officer to the People's Republic of China and Gregg was CIA chief of station in Seoul, South Korea, Gregg traveled to Beijing to brief him.[46] When Bush was the director of Central Intelligence in 1976, Gregg worked as agency liaison to Congress's Pike Committee, which was investigating alleged CIA misconduct. He remained at the NSC until the change of administration in January 1981, and in August 1982 he retired from the CIA and joined the staff of Vice President Bush as his national security adviser. In 1989 he became U.S. ambassador to South Korea.

It is not clear what Gregg might have been doing in Cyrus Hashemi's New York office in the spring of 1980. He had no official responsibility for the contacts between Cyrus Hashemi and the U.S. government. I was the NSC representative for Iran in the White House at the time, where Gregg was a colleague of mine. To the best of my knowledge, he had no responsibility for Iran policy. It is possible that he was aware of the contacts between the U.S. government and the Hashemi brothers, but all of the key participants in those contacts have denied that Gregg was involved at any level. According to Jamshid Hashemi, he and his brother had lunch with Gregg that day in the Shazan Restaurant just around the corner from Cyrus's offices and discussed the various contacts that were under way between the brothers and the U.S. government.[47] (Gregg stated in May 1991 that "I did not leak any information concerning Iran or any other topic to the Reagan-Bush campaign staff or anyone else in 1980," and that "prior to the 1980 election I had had no contact whatsoever with any member of the Reagan-Bush campaign staff.")

There were other efforts as well, and I myself may unwittingly have been a source for the information-gathering efforts of one or more of the various Republican campaigns. In mid-February 1980, while the primaries were still in progress, I was contacted by a former Iranian Cabinet minister who had been close to the shah. This man had been introduced to me by a highly respected American lawyer during the summer of 1979, when the shah was in exile in Mexico.

The Iranian was extremely concerned about his personal safety, since Iranian hit squads were trying to assassinate former high officials, so we met in a private suite at the Waldorf Towers in New York.[48] He was interested in exploring U.S. attitudes about permitting the shah to enter the country, but when I offered no encouragement he delicately changed the subject to a general discussion of Iranian politics. Our contacts ceased after the shah entered the United States for medical treatment in October and the hostages were taken on November 4.

However, in February 1980, as the primary season was entering its crucial phase, the ex–Cabinet minister's lawyer again contacted me and arranged a series of private luncheon meetings at the lawyer's home in Georgetown. We met approximately once a month for the next five months for wide-ranging discussions about U.S.-Iranian relations. I found the discussions stimulating. He had an agile and inquiring mind, and his experience with Iranian politics was vast, if slightly dated. He was in contact with Iranian exile groups, and, like many of those in the exile community, he was full of information and rumors about the latest developments in Iran. He was only one of several members of the ancien régime with whom I compared notes on a regular basis.

It was only years later, quite by chance, that I discovered that this man was working closely with Henry Kissinger. In the course of my research on the events of 1980, several sources told me that Kissinger had developed a considerable network of his own informants inside the U.S. government who reported to him on a variety of issues, including the hostage situation. A senior official at the Pentagon, for example, recounted several experiences during 1980 when his colleagues in the Defense Department would interrupt a discussion to place a call to Kissinger to inform him of something they had just learned.[49] In retrospect, it is likely that my regular discussions with my Iranian contact in the elegant setting of his lawyer's Georgetown home were also intended to elicit information about the Carter administration's thinking on the hostage issue and were reported in full.

At least in the early part of 1980, there may have been some competition among these various groups. The available evidence overwhelmingly suggests that there was widespread anxiety within Republican circles about the effect the possible release of the hostages would have on the election, and that multiple efforts were undertaken, from the earliest days of 1980, to develop information and sources about the Carter administration's plans and strategy for dealing with the dilemma. Before the year was out, what may have begun as an effort by William Casey to defend his candidate against surprises would evolve into political covert action. Unbeknownst to the Carter administration, a rival foreign policy would be concocted by representatives of an opposition political party whose higher obligations to their country would be sacrificed on the altar of ambition.

· 2 ·

THE QUEST
FOR ARMS

I t was May Day, 1980, and Colonel Charles Wesley Scott, United States
Army, was not having a good day. That morning he had lost his temper
and threatened one of his colleagues, a Foreign Service officer whose
deliberate dawdling over breakfast made both of them miss a chance for
some exercise and fresh air. He had grabbed him by the shirt and shouted
in his face. After 178 days, the strain was beginning to tell.[1]

He and the dour Foreign Service officer had been together only two
weeks. On April 15, the Iranian guards had assigned the two men to the
same sunny upstairs room in the chancellery of the American Embassy in
Tehran. His companion groused, but for Scott the move was sheer delight.
Since the November 4 invasion of the embassy, he had been beaten, threatened, interrogated, subjected to fake executions, and confined to a windowless underground cell. He had not seen the sun for five months.

His captors thought he was CIA. He was not, but it was easy to understand the mistake. He was one of the few prisoners who spoke fluent
Persian. His previous service in Iran had given him a familiarity with the
physical and cultural landscape that would be the envy of any spy, and his

military duties had led him into some sensitive security areas. Only days before the takeover, he had received a $5 million check from the Iranian minister of defense as down payment for a selective resumption of U.S. military deliveries to Iran. His expertise, Scott wryly told himself, had cost him a lot. It was better not to think about it.

Then, on April 26, Scott, the Foreign Service officer, and two other prisoners were suddenly packed up again, handcuffed and blindfolded, and shoved into the back of a stuffy van. The mini-convoy—one lead car, the van, and a trail car—sped through the night, barely braking for curves on a mountain road. There were no rest stops. The guards muttered about commandos. They seemed to be traveling for hundreds of miles. The van was climbing steadily; they must be going north, Scott thought. Then traffic and city sounds at dawn. He could hear Turkish dialect spoken on the streets. He guessed it: Tabriz.

When they finally stopped at the home of a mullah, there were two moments of great satisfaction. One was a visit to the toilet. The other was astonishing his host and alarming his guards by asking why he and the other Americans had been brought to Tabriz. Now they were sure he was a spy. Two nights later the hostages were bundled into the van and driven across town. When the blindfolds came off, he recognized the room. They were being held in the old American consulate in Tabriz. But why?

In the streets, crowds were shouting "Death to America!" "Death to the shah!" and, most immediately worrisome, "Death to the hostages!" Inside the consulate, he and the other prisoners started to settle into a new routine. Tabriz was famous for its *chello kebab*, but it looked like a steady diet of bread, tea, rice, and cheese for the American "guests." A few weeks of this, he thought, and he might even grow nostalgic for the moldy remains that had passed for meals at the embassy commissary in Tehran.

On the morning of May 1, Scott wanted to get outdoors and "eat some air," as they say in Persian. But the Foreign Service officer deliberately refused to move. Scott exploded and nearly hit him.

It was not a good day. The guard canceled the exercise period, then moved Scott into a small room with the other two prisoners—Don Sharer and Sam Gillette—leaving his former cellmate in splendid isolation. Sitting on the floor, on a Persian carpet left behind when the consulate closed hastily during the revolution, Scott tried to make sense of the past five days.

Without warning, the door opened and a familiar figure entered the ten-by-twelve-foot room, accompanied by a clutch of guards. Hojjat ol-Eslam Mohammed Ali Khamene'i, just forty years old, was one of the central figures in the Iranian revolution. He had first joined Ayatollah Khomeini as an eighteen-year-old student in the Qom seminary. When he was twenty-four, during the 1963 rebellion against the shah, he was a courier for Khomeini and was arrested twice, spending time in Tehran's Qezel Qala Prison. After Khomeini was deported in 1964, Khamene'i formed an underground group of Islamic activists, which was broken up by security police. He was imprisoned several times for his political activities between 1967 and 1969, and in 1974 he spent most of a year in the notorious Komiteh Prison.

In 1977, Khamene'i was arrested again and exiled to a small town in southeast Iran. He then returned to his hometown of Mashhad, where he led the Islamic movement, then called the Combatant Clergy Society, during the 1978 revolution. After the revolution, Khamene'i became a member of the powerful Revolutionary Council and, with Ayatollah Beheshti, founded the Islamic Republic Party, which now dominated Iranian politics.

Scott had first met Khamene'i in the fall of 1979, when the cleric was deputy minister of defense and involved in negotiations to restore the flow of U.S. military spare parts to Iran. By the time they met again in a cell in Tabriz, Khamene'i had been appointed to the immensely influential position of Friday prayer leader in Tehran, which effectively made him the public spokesman for the regime. He also had been elected to the Majles by a huge margin in the March parliamentary elections.

Though Scott recognized Khamene'i immediately—the man was wearing traditional robes and a Rolex watch—he did not stand. After an awkward moment, the cleric sat down on the floor across from the American prisoner and, snapping out a gold-filled Dunhill lighter, lit his pipe.

In the next hour or so, Scott learned a lot. Khamene'i told him that the United States had unsuccessfully attempted a rescue mission on the night of April 24. That explained the rush to Tabriz, Scott thought; with the hostages scattered all over Iran, another rescue mission would be nearly impossible.

Khamene'i went on to say that Iran had reduced its earlier demands for the release of the hostages. The leadership now sought U.S. assurances of noninterference in Iran's internal affairs, a withdrawal of U.S. military forces from the Persian Gulf, return of the shah's money, which the new government believed had been stolen from Iran, and the cancellation of all debts and claims against Iran. If those conditions were met, he said, Iran would be prepared to discuss the release of the hostages. He made no mention of what had been until that time Iran's two most important demands—the return of the shah to Iran and a formal U.S. apology for its past behavior in Iran—both of which the United States regarded as totally unacceptable.

This almost casual description of Iran's negotiating position appears more startling in retrospect than it did to Colonel Scott at the time. The conditions outlined by Khamene'i in Tabriz on May 1 were essentially the same as those that would be secretly conveyed to the White House four months later.[2] Why did Iran delay presenting these more reasonable demands to the U.S. government? Stranger still, why had Khamene'i traveled 330 miles from Tehran to Tabriz to discuss them with an imprisoned American army officer?

Khamene'i came to the point. "Let me ask you a question," he said, looking directly at Scott. "If we were to release *you*"—he spoke in Persian, knowing that the two other Americans in the room could not understand— "how long would it be before you could begin to supply us again with spare parts for our military forces?" Scott swallowed. What was going on here?

Iran was in trouble, more than Scott could have guessed. For the first time, Iran was seriously confronted with the possibility of a war with Iraq. In the initial rush of exhilaration after the overthrow of the shah, bands of clerics and other revolutionaries formed teams to export the revolution beyond their own borders. At first this was a largely spontaneous effort, relying on long-standing personal and family contacts with Muslim communities, especially Shi'i, in other countries. But over time, as they gained financial and operational support from the revolutionary government, these groups became more organized and sophisticated. Some became virtually autonomous paramilitary organizations with their own policy agendas. Others were eventually incorporated into the intelligence apparatus of the Islamic Republic.

One of the most important targets for subversion was Iraq, where Shi'ites formed a majority of the population, but the secular Baathist regime of President Saddam Hussein, himself a Sunni, treated them as second-class citizens. The two holiest shrines of Shi'i Islam, Najaf and Karbala, were in Iraq,[3] and Khomeini had lived in Najaf for nearly fourteen years after he was exiled by the shah. Not only was the ayatollah intimately familiar with the plight of his coreligionists across the border, but he also detested Saddam Hussein, who, at the height of the Iranian revolution in October 1978, had expelled him from Iraq.

That had been a frightening and bewildering experience for Khomeini. He first tried to travel overland to Kuwait but was refused permission to enter; for several hours he was trapped in the no-man's-land between the two borders. He then returned to Baghdad, flying first to Syria and then on to Paris, where his followers found him a small house in the suburb of Neauphle-le-Château.

This humiliating ejection, which Khomeini believed with good reason was engineered by the shah, proved to be a blessing in disguise. Through the media in Paris, Khomeini achieved an international influence that would have been impossible on the stony plains of Najaf. But the brooding cleric never forgave Saddam Hussein for the insult, and after the revolution Iran immediately began to mobilize the Shi'i population of Iraq in an effort to destabilize Iraq's government.

The festering dispute between Iran and Iraq erupted in April 1980. On April 1, an Iranian attempted to assassinate Tariq Aziz and Latif Nasif Jasim, two close associates of Saddam Hussein. The attempt failed, but two other Iraqis and the assailant were killed. Immediately, the Iraqis arrested Ayatollah Mohammed Baqir al-Sadr, an internationally respected Shi'i clergyman, presumably as a warning to Iran. On April 5, at a funeral procession for those killed in the earlier attack, another Iranian threw a grenade that killed an Iraqi bystander. Two days later, seventy Iraqi commandos attacked a western Iranian province with rockets and missiles, and Iraqi officials began deporting thousands of individuals of Iranian origin. On the eighth, Khomeini made a speech openly calling for the people of Iraq to "wake up and topple this corrupt regime."

At almost the same time, but unrelated to the growing Iran-Iraq tensions, President Carter finally broke diplomatic relations with Iran and called for international economic and military sanctions. In response, Italy canceled the delivery of an important helicopter contract, and Japan and the European Community withdrew their ambassadors from Tehran. Two prominent Iranian exiles, former Prime Minister Shahpour Bakhtiar and General Gholam Ali Oveissi, arrived in Baghdad to confer with Saddam Hussein about the possibility of a military operation against Khomeini.

On April 15, reports that the Iraqis had executed Ayatollah Baqir al-Sadr and his sister set off emotional shock waves in Iran and in Shi'i circles around the world. On April 22, Khomeini declared three days of mourning. Before the mourning period was over, the United States launched its attempted rescue mission.

Iran was scarcely ready for a war with Iraq, let alone a confrontation with a superpower. Its army was still in shock, demoralized after its collapse during the revolution and weakened by purges. The new Revolutionary Guards Corps was little more than a ragtag band of zealous, inexperienced youths. Abol Hassan Bani-Sadr, who had been president and nominal commander-in-chief of the armed forces for only three months, later characterized the status of Iran's military-supply system as an "indescribable mess."[4] Iran possessed vast quantities of military equipment that had been purchased under the old regime. However, nobody knew where to find these supplies without access to the computerized inventory system that the United States had been in the process of preparing for the shah.

So Khamene'i went to Tabriz to see Colonel Scott, the only American on Iranian soil who was familiar with the military supply system. The offer was simple and tempting. Iran, Khamene'i suggested, would release Scott to return to the United States and act as an advocate for restoring U.S. military deliveries, presumably in return for the release of the other hostages. It was an improbable scenario, but almost everything about the hostage situation was improbable.

"You're asking the wrong man," Scott replied, reminding Khamene'i that he had been out of touch with the U.S. government for five months and could not predict the reaction. "Frankly, my guess is that it will be a long time before you'll get any cooperation on spare parts from America, after what you've done and continue to do to us." Still, he added, if Iran would release all the hostages, normal relations might be restored and military supplies might be available.

Khamene'i did not pursue Scott's suggestion.

"Have you been getting some good Tabriz *chello kebab*?" Khamene'i asked.

"We are pretty much living on rice and bread," Scott replied.

Khamene'i gave a hard look at the guards. They had obviously been pocketing the money they received to feed the prisoners.

"Your diet will improve," he said, looking at his watch. Then he was gone.

Scott would never see him again. A few weeks later, Khamene'i was named Khomeini's personal representative to the Supreme Defense Council, the top coordinating body for Iranian security policy. He went on to become the president of Iran for eight years and, when Khomeini died in June 1989, he was named as Khomeini's successor as Iran's spiritual leader, the ultimate position of power in the country.

As for Scott, in the nearly nine months of captivity that followed, he would have more than enough time to replay this scene in his mind. Had Khamene'i been making him an offer he thought Scott could not refuse? Had it all been an elaborate ruse? Had he been a fool to turn it down?

One thing was utterly clear. Iran's leaders were growing anxious about the country's military plight, and at least some were willing to consider unorthodox methods to reestablish the U.S. military supply line.

It was a deal waiting to be made.

Iran after the fall of the shah was a gold mine for hustlers and entrepreneurs of all kinds, especially those who had good contacts with the emerging clerical rulers. Businessmen who were quick on their feet and who had the proper contacts could make a fortune. Some found immense opportunities for theft, embezzlement, and bribery. Others, who were perhaps squeamish, on the wrong side politically, or simply slow to adapt to the new realities of theocratic dominance, lost everything.

For Ahmed Heidari, the revolution was initially a disaster, then a business opportunity, and finally a chance to make himself exceedingly rich at the expense of the new system. During the final years of the shah's reign,

Heidari was an unprepossessing bureaucrat at the Iranian Defense Ministry. Iran had become the world's most lucrative arms bazaar. The dramatic increase in the price of oil after the Arab-Israeli war of 1973 meant a windfall of ready cash for Iran. This vast wealth, combined with the shah's seemingly inexhaustible appetite for sophisticated armaments, transformed Tehran into the Mecca of the arms trade. Representatives and agents from every country and company that produced military equipment lined up at the procurement office of the Ministry of Defense, waiting to meet General Hassan Toufanian. Toufanian was the vice minister of defense for procurement, and although he was junior to the military chief of staff or minister of defense, he may have had greater influence than any other political or military figure in Iran, save the shah himself. As Toufanian put it, "I had the power."[5]

Toufanian, a slight man with a gentlemanly air, combined all of the characteristics necessary for longevity under the shah's jealous and suspicious eye. He was a loyal and devoted follower, showed no signs of personal political ambition, and knew how to get things done. He gave the shah honest advice about the relative merits of the various weapons systems under consideration, but when his king made decisions contrary to his own counsel, he accepted gracefully and set to work to carry them out as effectively as possible. He was self-effacing and efficient, and displayed the successful courtier's passion for anonymity. In a business awash in corruption and easy money, he maintained a certain reputation for probity. His proudest achievement, in his own estimation, was his absolute refusal to pay fees to the army of agents who attempted to act as brokers between the Iranian government and the defense companies. If the companies wished to use agents, he said, that was their business; but the percentage of the profits that these fixers demanded—and which often translated into fat bribes and kickbacks—could not be passed on to the government. The general became a moderately wealthy man, but he avoided both the excesses and the venality that were so common among some of his colleagues in the military and the court.

Nonetheless, the procurement office at the Iranian Ministry of Defense in the 1970s offered exceptional opportunities for anyone who wanted to master some of the arcane secrets of the arms trade and high finance. Ahmed Heidari, then in his mid-thirties, with a passable French education and a taste for business, regarded his job under Toufanian as a unique postgraduate course in how to make money.

The era of massive arms purchases and fat profits, however, came to an explosive end in September 1978, with the first of the massive demonstrations that undermined and eventually destroyed the shah's regime. General Toufanian played a crucial role to the very end. On February 2, 1979, the day after Khomeini flew back to Iran from his exile in Paris and some two weeks after the shah's departure, General Toufanian signed a memorandum of understanding with Eric Von Marbod, a representative of the U.S. Department of Defense. This document effectively gave the United States power of attorney to act on Iran's behalf in terminating Iran's vast array of military contracts. It was indispensable for the United States: initially to manage the complex network of contracts and deliveries in the absence of any responsible authority in Tehran; then to handle Iran's frozen military assets during the hostage crisis; and finally to resolve the disputed claims of the two parties at the special tribunal established at The Hague in 1981 as part of the negotiated agreement for the release of the hostages.

Seven days after the memorandum of understanding was signed, units of the elite Imperial Guard unsuccessfully tried to smash a rebellion of prorevolution air force cadets and technicians. Other armed groups joined in the fighting and started attacking police stations and army bases. Hundreds of people were killed, and after two days, senior military commanders ordered their troops—demoralized and in disarray—back to the barracks. Faced with an ad hoc band of revolutionaries, the supposedly invincible Imperial Guard had effectively been defeated, and the shah's elaborate and expensive security organization simply dissolved.

Immediately, bands of revolutionary students and pro-Khomeini military men, leftists, and others began hunting down members of the ancien régime. Some were executed on the spot, others were subjected to torture and mock trials before being shot, some went to prison. Others, who were quick on their feet, managed to escape, including Toufanian, who went underground and spent nine months in hiding before escaping across the border to Turkey.[6] Heidari, less lucky or less nimble, was arrested and sent to jail.

He was soon released, however, through the efforts of Ayatollah Mohammed Hussein Beheshti, one of the most powerful figures in the revolution.

Heidari's relationship with Beheshti may have originated with Major General Nasser Moqaddam, who was the father of a schoolmate from Paris and who had befriended Heidari.[7] At the time of the revolution, Moqaddam was the chief of SAVAK, the feared Iranian secret police. (SAVAK is the Persian acronym for National Intelligence and Security Organization.) He was the most important point of contact between the political and military authorities and the revolutionaries, including Beheshti. Many Iranian exiles regarded Moqaddam as a traitor who betrayed the shah and paved the way for the clerics' takeover. Though he denied the charges, he was later permitted to leave Iran for Europe, where he lived in seclusion.

Whatever the reason for Heidari's release, once he was out of jail he immediately went to work for Beheshti, practicing some of the skills he had learned while working for Toufanian and the shah. Thus Heidari was associated, almost from the start, with one of the most powerful factions emerging from the political chaos of postrevolutionary Iran.

The most important and enduring dividing line in postrevolutionary Iranian politics was between the clerics—men with formal religious training —and the nonclerics. The clerics wore beards, turbans, and religious robes; most had known each other for years, dating back to their days in the seminary; and most were closely associated with a senior religious leader, such as Khomeini, who was their teacher and patron. Although they would stick together when challenged from the outside, the clerics did have their differences. Many religious figures, including some of the most senior ayatollahs and their followers, remained aloof from politics; some objected strongly to Khomeini's leadership and his notion of a theocratic state. Among those who were politically active, some had remained in Iran through the prerevolutionary years and had often endured long prison terms under the shah. Others had been with Khomeini during his years in exile in Iraq or had spent most of those crucial years outside the country. Evidence of commitment and sacrifice during the shah's regime and the revolution became important qualifications for high office in the new Islamic Republic, so there was no shortage of exaggerated sufferings and apocryphal exploits. In all, probably a couple of dozen clerics with extensive revolutionary credentials constituted the central core of the new theocratic elite.

Ayatollah Beheshti was one of the most prominent members of this group, and certainly the most intellectual. A former student of Khomeini, he had studied traditional Islamic doctrine at the Qom seminary. A small, plump man, always wearing a cloak and turban, he cultivated a reputation for being very strict, an advocate of the eye-for-an-eye school of justice. But he also held a degree in theology from Tehran University, where he had been exposed to more secular and "modernist" influences.[8] He was a committed revolutionary, one of the handful of Khomeini's trusted associates who organized and directed the movement in Iran after Khomeini was exiled in 1964, and he was probably involved in plotting the assassination of Prime Minister Hassan Ali Mansur in January 1965. Yet he stayed out of jail and even held a position with the Ministry of Education, preparing Islamic texts for Iranian schools. Within the provincial circles of the mullahs, most of whom had only a traditional religious education, he stood out as unusually worldly. He spoke English and German, and the shah's regime approved his appointment as prayer leader in the mosque in Hamburg from 1965 to 1971. One acquaintance recalled that when Beheshti would return to Iran from his mosque in Germany, other clerics would whisper behind his back that he was becoming too Westernized.[9]

Even at the height of the revolution, Beheshti maintained his contacts abroad. In late 1978, he flew to the United States to meet with Islamic leaders and student groups. He had a long meeting in Houston with Ibrahim Yazdi, Khomeini's representative in the United States. He also met with various chapters of the Islamic Students Association, including a small group in California whose membership included an engineering student named Mohammed Hashemi Rafsanjani, who was the younger brother of the future president of Iran and would himself become the director of Iranian radio and television, and a Stanford graduate student in economics named Ali Reza Nobari, who went on to become the governor of the Central Bank under Abol Hassan Bani-Sadr, the Islamic republic's first president.

The purpose of Beheshti's visit apparently was to recruit members for the new political party he planned to form. He told the students and others that this new party would accept good Muslim revolutionaries as members, but the leadership would remain in the hands of the clergy.[10] Later, the secularists would claim that the revolution was "stolen" by Khomeini and the clergy, but they had been fairly warned. The theft, if that is what it was, was premeditated and carefully planned in advance by Beheshti and others.

In fact, Beheshti often led others to believe he was on their side in order to achieve his own goals. A turbaned Machiavelli, he had secret contacts during the last days of the revolution with William Sullivan, the U.S. ambassador in Tehran, about plans to deport two hundred top Iranian military leaders. At the same time, Beheshti was carrying on daily negotiations with the Iranian military leaders through the chief of the shah's intelligence service.[11]

These many contradictions lent a well-deserved aura of mystery to Beheshti. Was he secretly cooperating with SAVAK? Was he preparing a power play of his own? Whatever the truth, it was obvious that he was a man who coveted power and understood how to use it. He was cynical and shrewd, and he was remarkably successful in covering his tracks. Despite his daring connections to all sides, he apparently never lost Khomeini's confidence, and he never fell prey to the vicious internal politics that wounded so many around him.

Beheshti seemed to care more for power than for ideology. He carefully maintained his reputation as a radical, but that may have been little more than protective coloration. The path to power in revolutionary politics is not to be found in moderation. Despite his embrace of radical positions, one close observer noted that Beheshti was "extremely pragmatic, much more than the image he liked to portray in public."[12]

Beheshti did not inspire affection. He never established the kind of warm personal relationship with Khomeini that characterized the ayatollah's rapport with some of his other followers. In fact, Beheshti seemed to have few real friends. After his death in 1981, he was seldom memorialized in the emotional terms that were applied to other major revolutionary figures. But for his purposes, it was perhaps better to be feared than loved.

In early 1979, Beheshti was just beginning to build his new political structure. He realized that, to have any power independent of the official government, he had to have his own procurement agency for equipment and arms. Ahmed Heidari was just the man to set things in motion.

After being released from jail through Beheshti's good offices, Heidari set up a company named Interparts with Karim Minachi, the brother of an influential cleric.[13] Beheshti was, in effect, a silent partner, and with his support, Interparts soon secured its first contract, for about $200 million, to purchase locomotives and spare parts from General Motors in Canada, thus bypassing the U.S. market that was closed to Iran.

The deal was so lucrative that Musa Kalantari, the minister of roads and transport, purchased a share of the company. They were soon joined by a fourth partner, Colonel K. Dehqan, chief of logistics and procurement for the Iranian army, who had arranged a $600 million contract to purchase weapons. But before they could draw any funds, Heidari and his partners needed two authorizations: one from the minister of defense, and the other from Ayatollah Beheshti, representing the clerical "shadow government."

As an arms procurer, Interparts was remarkably ineffective. During its two-year life span, the company arranged only a few significant shipments of military equipment. But the partners understood very well how to make money. Their powerful patrons kept them supplied with a steady flow of contracts and protected them from even the casual fiscal oversight of the chaotic revolutionary administration. The partners had access to very large sums of money subject to only the most cursory bookkeeping constraints, and it took little effort to generate lucrative commissions and fees. As Heidari would remark years later in a plush Monte Carlo casino, "The revolution was terribly unfair. Some people lost everything, others became rich. I became rich."[14]

Another Iranian who profited from the revolution was Cyrus Hashemi. Born in Tehran on December 27, 1938, he was the youngest of three sons in the well-to-do family of an Iranian oil-company executive. Cyrus and his brothers all went to England for their college education.

As a young man in the 1960s, he took government jobs with the Iranian oil consortium and the Water Ministry before going into business for himself. The 1960s was a decade of great turmoil, as Mohammed Reza Shah Pahlavi attempted to impose his own vision of a modernized Iran—the White Revolution—on a reluctant and sullen populace. The Shi'i clergy, who saw the shah's land-reform and modernization program as a direct attack on their own wealth and influence, were at the center of the opposition movement.

Demonstrations in 1963 and 1964, led by Ruhollah Khomeini, brought

Iran to the brink of revolution, but the shah's forces quashed the rebellion, killing several hundred people in the process.[15] Khomeini was arrested repeatedly and finally exiled to Turkey in 1964. In 1965 he moved to Iraq, where he lived for almost fourteen years, plotting his revenge—a second revolution that would succeed in toppling the shah.

The Hashemi brothers, like many of their peers, identified with the anti-shah protest movement. Jamshid Hashemi said he was imprisoned on several occasions under the shah.[16] In 1968, Cyrus Hashemi left Iran to join a trading firm in Geneva. Four years later, his company opened a branch office in North America, which he visited frequently. In 1976, Cyrus resigned as chief executive officer and moved to New York, where he established himself as an independent merchant banker and trader. Operating from New York, Paris, and London, he maintained commercial and political contacts in Iran as the revolution swelled to its climax in February 1979.[17]

After the fall of the shah, Cyrus Hashemi was well placed to deal with the new revolutionary government, thanks to his international financial experience and anti-shah credentials. He even claimed in later years that he declined a position in the provisional government of Mehdi Bazargan after the fall of the shah in 1979. Although that claim was probably little more than self-promotion, it is true that he and his brothers worked closely with Rear Admiral Ahmad Madani, the first minister of defense of the new Islamic Republic of Iran.

The Cabinet assembled by Bazargan in the days immediately after the revolution included many men of stature and sophistication. These men were practicing Muslims, with deep respect for the Islamic traditions that the shah had attempted to eradicate in his drive for modernization. Most of them were also secular politicians, whose political roots ran back to the nationalist movements of the 1950s, personified by then–Prime Minister Mohammed Mosaddeq. They had participated in Mosaddeq's effort to wrest control of Iran's oil from the British, and they had experienced the pain and disillusion of his government's collapse when the United States and Great Britain intervened covertly in 1953 to restore full control to the shah.[18]

Staunchly dedicated to Iran's independence from Western political intervention and manipulation, the men of Bazargan's Cabinet were at the same time committed to democratic values and human rights. They had joined forces with Khomeini and the clergy during the revolution in the belief that these values would be reflected in a post-shah government, but they were dismayed when Khomeini instituted a theocratic regime, shunting aside anyone who stood in his way. Within two years, Khomeini and his followers would revile these men as "liberals" and remove them from office. Many would be forced to flee for their lives.

Admiral Madani was one of the most attractive and charismatic members of this group. A dapper, well-dressed man who kept himself in excellent shape, he also liked to talk, to the point of being garrulous, and would spin stories in Persian or heavily accented English. Even his flight from Iran did not seem to cramp his style. He remained an active and appealing figure, dividing his time among residences in Paris, New York, and Denver.

In 1970, because of his outspoken anti-shah sentiments, he had been forced out of a senior position with the Iranian navy on the pretext of corruption. Madani, who already had an economics degree, went on and took a doctorate in political science. He remained politically active in the anti-shah movement, teaching and speaking out against the shah at a series of provincial universities, constantly harassed by the shah's authorities.[19]

Immediately after the revolution in February 1979, Admiral Madani accepted the dual posts of defense minister and commander of the navy. He attempted to restore some order within the demoralized Iranian military and to reopen supply channels of military spare parts that had been interrupted by the chaos of the revolution. However, he found himself in constant conflict with the religious overseers who interfered in every aspect of government activity, and he resigned as defense minister in April, after only two months in office. He nevertheless retained his position as commander of the navy and, with Khomeini's approval, he was appointed governor general of the strategic Khuzistan Province. This southwestern province has always been critical to Iran's security because of vast oil deposits, extensive naval facilities on the Shatt al-Arab waterway, access to the Persian Gulf, and a long border with Iraq.

When Admiral Madani went to Khuzistan in the spring of 1979, he asked a number of former navy colleagues and personal friends for help in managing his many political and military responsibilities. Among the latter were the Hashemi brothers, who, as the sons of a former neighbor in Tehran, were longtime family acquaintances. The two elder brothers, Jamshid and Reza, joined Madani in Khuzistan; Cyrus maintained contact by telephone from Europe and the United States.

When the U.S. hostages were taken on November 4, an American lawyer in Paris who represented Cyrus Hashemi called an associate in Washington, suggesting that Hashemi had good contacts in Iran and might be useful. The Washington attorney wrote a letter to Deputy Secretary of State Warren Christopher, who passed the information along to Harold Saunders, the assistant secretary of state for Near Eastern and South Asian affairs. Saunders did a quick check and concluded that Hashemi was indeed an interesting contact.

On December 3, Hashemi flew to New York for a series of meetings to establish his bona fides. He met briefly with Donald McHenry, the U.S. ambassador to the United Nations, and with Ramsey Clark, the former U.S. attorney general, who was familiar with and trusted by the anti-shah opposition in Iran because of his civil-rights practice. Clark had returned only a few weeks earlier from a mission on behalf of President Carter to the Middle East, where he had unsuccessfully attempted to arrange the release of the hostages.[20]

Cyrus Hashemi quickly demonstrated that he had access to a number of high-level officials in the Iranian revolutionary government, most notably the governor-general of Khuzistan but also individuals within Khomeini's own family. He clearly understood the politics and internal decision-making within the still-mysterious Revolutionary Council, which had assumed supreme authority in the nation. (Bazargan had resigned in protest over the seizure of the hostages.) Hashemi insisted, with vigor and credibility, that he, too, was personally opposed to a policy of hostage-taking. And, he claimed, he was a cousin of Ali Akbar Hashemi Rafsanjani, a revolutionary leader who was emerging as a key policymaker in Khomeini's inner circle.

There was, however, a darker side to Hashemi. The Carter administration quickly determined that he was no ordinary banker. On the contrary, he was a member of that loose confederation of international deal-makers who operate on the fringes of international finance and arms sales. The exact nature of his business activities was always murky, and it was no coincidence that it was a lawyer who identified him to the U.S. government, for his business activities regularly attracted the attention of legal authorities in the countries where he operated. He lived by his wits, always on the lookout for a deal and a quick profit, and he was not unduly scrupulous about the people he did business with or about the nature of the transaction.

Like other members of this freewheeling profession, Hashemi maintained an impressive front. Whether he had money or not, he managed to live in high style, keeping a Rolls-Royce and driver in London and a limousine in New York, staying in the finest hotels, and eating at the most exclusive restaurants. He was, in every sense, a high roller: At the time of his death in 1986, his gambling debts alone totaled nearly $5 million.

Impetuous and daring, Cyrus Hashemi relied on his own judgment, improvising his way out of trouble and apparently savoring the risk as much as the reward. Like other men in his business, he promised whatever was necessary to get the deal, then started to work to see how to make it happen. Breaking one's promises was occasionally dangerous, but once a client was hooked he could usually be kept in play with stories of unavoidable difficulties and with new promises that replaced the old. Confidence men understand this, and arms dealers operate by the same rules, often outrageously bilking their supposedly tough clients, relying on nothing more than a combination of smooth talk, improvisation, and chutzpah.

Image-making was a valued tool of Hashemi's trade. The lavish life-style was merely part of a systematic exaggeration of his own importance, and particularly of how much he knew and what he could produce. That image of omniscience and power opened doors, elicited information from the unwary, and kept his options open when things got tough. A classic example was his unfounded claim to be a relative of Rafsanjani. Although the two men shared the name "Hashemi"—a relatively common one in Iran— they were not related.[21] Still, Cyrus Hashemi knew that the casual assertion enhanced his appeal as a source and that it was unlikely to be challenged in view of the sprawling interconnections of Iranian families. (In fact it was not challenged, and to this day the myth of his family ties to Rafsanjani is preserved in books, articles, court documents, and U.S. government files.)

Hashemi became a regular contact for the U.S. government for information about what was happening inside Iran. His importance, however, should not be overestimated. Many private individuals provided information about political developments in Tehran during the hostage crisis, supplementing the burgeoning output of the regular intelligence services. These private "volunteers" were always treated with caution, since it was understood that they often had their own agendas and special interests that might affect the reliability of their information. But from time to time, they provided valuable insights. That was particularly true of Cyrus Hashemi.

Fearful of being tagged as a CIA agent, Hashemi almost never talked directly to anyone in the U.S. government. Instead, he relayed his observations and analyses of political developments in Iran to an American intermediary, who passed them along by telephone to the Department of State.[22] These commentaries, which he provided once or twice a week throughout 1980, proved to be quite accurate. There was no doubt whatsoever that he was able to contact individuals in Tehran political circles, and the modern Iranian direct-dial telephone system (installed by American technicians for the shah) permitted him to stay in touch on a regular basis.

His information was mostly insider political gossip of the sort that circulates in any capital city, but such gossip can be useful. Over time, his reports came to be accepted as valid pieces of the mosaic that was constantly being assembled about the political climate and mood in Tehran.

At the end of 1979, Admiral Madani resigned his posts in order to run in the first presidential elections in Iran. He was not alone: 124 Iranians announced their intentions to run for the office. The race, however, narrowed rather quickly to three principal candidates: Abol Hassan Bani-Sadr, the finance minister; Jalal el-Din Farsi, the candidate of the clerical forces in the Islamic Republic Party; and Admiral Madani. To the consternation of the clerical "shadow government," Farsi, who had been regarded as Khomeini's favorite, was disqualified in mid-January when it was revealed that his father was an Afghan. Since the constitution required all presidential candidates to be Iranian by birth, he was hastily replaced by a substitute candidate, Hasan Habibi, but it was too late.[23] The contest effectively narrowed to a choice between Bani-Sadr and Madani.

The Hashemi brothers were elated. They were personally devoted to

Madani, who was an independent-minded secularist running on a strong law-and-order platform. In his candidacy, the Hashemis saw an opportunity to advance a personal friend, a centrist policy built around a strong military, and their own fortunes.

The Madani campaign, in their view, faced only one formidable obstacle. Bani-Sadr was a popular figure, who had been close to Khomeini during the revolution. His tracts on Islamic economics, written from exile in Paris, had earned him a position as one of the philosophical progenitors of the new Islamic order. To defeat Bani-Sadr, it was necessary to get Madani and his message to the people. That meant money.

Cyrus Hashemi had understood from the very beginning that the Madani connection was a potential gold mine. When Madani became minister of defense in early 1979, Cyrus had contacted his brother Jamshid with a proposition. Why not deposit all the defense ministry funds in his bank? Jamshid raised this question with a group of senior military men who were gathered at his house one evening. After some discussion, they concluded there was no objection to such a scheme in principle, but they wondered what they had to gain from such a transfer. Jamshid called his brother Cyrus in their presence, and Cyrus agreed over the phone that if they used his bank he would guarantee that 5 percent of the interest on this very large sum of money (the ministry's funds amounted to several hundred million dollars) would be set aside for them. They agreed.

When Madani decided to run for president, his supporters concluded that he would need about $15 million to mount an effective campaign, and they decided to use their 5 percent commission for that purpose. With the exception of Jamshid, who was moderately wealthy, most of these men were military officers who lacked independent financial resources. Jamshid asked Cyrus urgently for the money, but Cyrus was evasive. He would not confirm that he actually had the money, but he hinted that he had other sources that might be willing to help.

The campaign period was very short, and time was running out: The election would be held on January 25, 1980. So on January 1, Jamshid Hashemi flew to New York to sort out the problem of the missing 5 percent with his brother and to seek funding for the Madani campaign. He planned to be gone for two weeks; in fact, he was never to return to Iran again.[24]

To Jamshid's dismay, Cyrus was either unwilling or unable to provide the needed funds. In good con-man fashion, however, he had a tempting alternative to offer. He had established some contacts with the U.S. government, he said, who might be prepared to pony up some financial support for the Madani campaign. Jamshid ultimately failed to locate the necessary funding, and Madani lost the election to Bani-Sadr in a landslide.[25] But Jamshid took the bait dangled by his brother, pursuing contacts in the United States and thus setting in motion a sequence of events that would reverberate throughout both American and Iranian politics.

Meanwhile, the Iranian desire for arms continued to grow. The problem of spare parts was particularly acute. There was, for example, the problem of tires for American-built F-4 fighter aircraft in the Iranian inventory. When the shah assembled his formidable air force, he was conscious of the need for a large inventory of spare parts. After the revolution, this extensive inventory was inherited by Iran's new rulers but they lacked the military specification lists that matched specific parts to particular weapons systems. Moreover, because the computerized tracking system that the United States was designing for the shah had never been completed, the new Iranian regime was unable in many cases to determine just what they had in the way of spare parts or to use effectively those items they had been able to locate and identify.

Much of the spare-parts inventory involved sophisticated avionics and key electronic items that might be needed in an emergency. It did not include an adequate supply of expendable items such as tires. Iran, like other countries that purchase U.S. weapons systems, was part of a worldwide integrated supply system that routinely provided deliveries of expendables as they were needed. It was neither feasible nor efficient for a country to lay in a lifetime store of mundane items such as tires, since it was always assumed that the U.S. supply line would continue to function even in cases of national emergency.

Ironically, it is often easier for an embargoed country to locate and purchase, on the international black market, a sophisticated radar or a self-contained weapons system such as a TOW missile, than it is to find prosaic items such as tires that are routinely provided through national logistics systems. This was Iran's problem in 1980. It had enough spare parts to keep its F-4 fighters in the air, but landing them was something else: Tires were in short supply. Israel, however, had a huge fleet of F-4 aircraft and vast stores of spares. It also manufactured its own tires and wheel assemblies for the F-4, which meant that it did not need U.S. permission to sell these items to a third country.[26]

Almost immediately after Ahmed Heidari created Interparts in 1979, he was contacted by a man he believed to be an Israeli agent, who expressed interest in the new company and offered to introduce him to arms sources in Europe. Heidari described the circumstances:

When I started Interparts with Minachi, in Tehran the first contact I had was an Iranian-Israeli person who contacted us. He said "Let me help you; let me give you some addresses." We started like that. Our first connection was through this man, who was working for Mossad. The first appointment I had at the Israeli embassy in Paris was through him. And later I was in direct contact with Tel Aviv and with the Israeli embassy in Paris.[27]

Heidari did not know it, but that discreet overture was only a small part of Israel's campaign to resurrect a longtime secret relationship with Iran. Nonetheless, Heidari clearly understood the Israeli purpose:

Israel was very, very interested to be in contact—directly—with the religious leadership, not through somebody else. The deal with them was that every time they had a direct contact [with the mullahs] they would give something at a very, very low price—even half the price. I believe I was the first person to have put Iranian mullahs into direct contact with them, outside the country. After these arrangements started, it became very easy for Iranian Jews to get out of the country.[28]

In time, Heidari would meet with individuals in Israel to discuss undercover trade and possible sales to Iran. He would also arrange meetings in Europe between Israelis and a number of important clerics, including several who are still prominent in Iran. These meetings would lay the groundwork for a truly remarkable renaissance of an old Iran-Israel connection.

· 3 ·

THE DOCTRINE OF
THE PERIPHERY

The furtive triangular alliance linking Iran, Ronald Reagan's campaign, and Israel probably owed its origins more to coincidence than design. At least at the start, the conspirators knew little about each other and probably cared even less. In the spring of 1980 each was preoccupied with its own narrow interests; each was a political system that traditionally regarded outsiders with suspicion, if not hostility. Yet, before the year was out, their interests would converge in a secret agreement that carried the promise of significant benefits at the price of mutual dependence and vulnerability.

That bargain surely would not have recommended itself to any of them as they were first examining their political options. Iran would have reason to fear the contamination of intimate contact with the two "satanic" powers that topped the revolution's list of enemies. American politicians of any stripe or ideological conviction would have to beware of dealing behind their government's back on an issue as emotionally explosive as the hostages. Israelis would have to be wary of any actions that could subject them to charges of meddling in American domestic politics. So why do it?

The answer, presumably, was that each of the three parties badly wanted something that they could get only with the collaboration and assistance of the other two. Iran wanted to get back the money that had been frozen in U.S. banks at the start of the hostage crisis and to find an assured supply of arms, both of which could be provided by a friendly administration in Washington. The Republican strategists wanted to rid themselves of the specter of an "October surprise" by President Carter that might, in their view, unfairly tip the election away from their candidates. But why did either party need Israel—and why did Israel agree to participate?

Simply put, only Israel had both the capacity and the incentive to make the agreement work. Israel possessed large stores of American military equipment and spare parts, and its leaders knew how to arrange confidential arms deliveries in politically sensitive circumstances. Moreover, such deliveries to Iran would be consistent with Israel's own perceived strategic interests.

Israel's willingness to cooperate with the Republicans might be explained in two ways. First, the Israelis had undoubtedly read the most recent polls in July and August, which indicated a steady rise in Ronald Reagan's popularity and the increasing likelihood of a Republican victory in the fall; they might reasonably have concluded that a bit of discreet cooperation during the campaign could serve them well once the Republicans came to power. Second, and perhaps more important, Israel's almost frantic efforts to reopen an arms relationship with Iran were being thwarted by President Carter, who stubbornly refused to acquiesce to even token Israeli arms shipments until the hostages were free. But Israel was so determined to pursue its arms-sale policy with Iran that it was willing to risk seriously offending Washington, to the point of delivering military equipment to Iran without the knowledge or approval of the Carter administration.

Cooperative and friendly relations between Iranians and Jews had ancient origins. When Cyrus the Great conquered Babylon in 538 B.C., he freed the captive Jews and assisted them in returning to Jerusalem.[1] This pattern was repeated almost precisely after the creation of the state of Israel in 1948, when the shah and his government permitted the Jews of Iraq, the site of ancient Babylonia, to flee to Israel via Iran. As part of that effort, Israeli intelligence agents were permitted to operate in Iran, and in 1950 Iran established de facto relations with Israel in return for a $400,000 bribe paid by the fledgling state to the Iranian prime minister.[2]

At the same time, Prime Minister David Ben-Gurion of Israel propounded the "Doctrine of the Periphery," which has since become a touchstone for Israeli foreign policy. This doctrine was predicated on the belief that while Israel was destined to be surrounded permanently by a ring of hostile Arab states, just outside this hostile ring there were non-Arab states such as Turkey, Ethiopia and Iran that were themselves frequently at odds with the Arabs and therefore potential allies of Israel. It was a classic case of the old maxim, "The enemy of my enemy is my friend," raised to the level of international policy.[3]

Ben-Gurion and his successors perceived that the long-term security of Israel required taking whatever steps were necessary to maintain good (if often clandestine) relations with the three states of the "periphery" and to prevent them from allying with the Arabs, whatever their current governments or politics might be. The doctrine was so thoroughly ingrained among Israeli officials that even the Marxist revolution in Ethiopia in 1974 was regarded as little more than a temporary setback in an otherwise successful strategy.

And its successes were indeed considerable. The relationship with Iran, in particular, became an invaluable political, economic, and strategic asset. Although Iran and Israel never established formal diplomatic relations, Israel maintained a senior diplomat in Tehran who was more active and influential than most accredited ambassadors. Israel provided large-scale technical assistance in agriculture, water management, oil production, and other areas of development. For example, Israel trained some ten thousand Iranian agricultural experts, according to Arieh Eliav, a Labor member of the Knesset, who spent two years in Iran in the early 1960s.[4] But over time it was in military and strategic affairs that Israeli-Iranian cooperation became most intimate and indispensable.

After the Suez crisis of 1956, during which the Suez Canal was briefly closed to all shipping, Iran helped finance the construction of a pipeline across Israel from Eilat on the Gulf of Aqaba to the Mediterranean port of Haifa, as an alternative route for Iranian oil to bypass the strategically vulnerable Suez Canal without requiring a lengthy trip around Africa. In return, Iran secretly agreed to provide Israel with crude oil. When the Suez Canal was closed again in the 1967 war, Iran and Israel built a second, much larger pipeline stretching from Eilat to the port of Ashkelon. These pipelines earned transit fees for Israel and provided a steady supply of oil for Israel's refineries and its growing domestic consumption.[5]

In March 1960, Israel sent Colonel Ya'acov Nimrodi as its first military attaché to Tehran, an act that marked the beginning of a deepening collaboration on military affairs. In subsequent years, almost all senior Israeli military officials visited Iran, and many high-level Iranian military officials paid visits to Israel.[6] Hundreds of Iranian officers came to Israel for special training, including members of the shah's secret police, SAVAK, who were instructed by the Israeli intelligence services as well as by the U.S. Central Intelligence Agency.[7] Prime Minister Ben-Gurion visited Iran secretly in 1961, setting a precedent for all successive Israeli prime ministers until the Iranian revolution.

Ben-Gurion's doctrine also included cooperation with non-Arab minorities in the Middle East, and Israel began in the early 1960s to provide support for the Kurds in northeastern Iraq. The Kurdish people were one of the largest and most fiercely independent minority groups in the region, and Israeli assistance (in the form of money, training, and medical supplies) was funneled through Iran with the tacit cooperation of the shah and his government. Although the shah had a Kurdish minority of his own, he was willing to permit limited aid to the rebellious Kurds in Iraq as a means of keeping the Iraqi government off-balance and so preoccupied with its internal problems that it had no opportunity to focus its aggressions on Iran.

The Kurdish secret war was greatly intensified after the visit to Tehran by President Richard Nixon and National Security Adviser Henry Kissinger in May 1972. For the first time, the United States joined with Iran and Israel in their "Kurdish strategy," designed to put military pressure on the Baathist regime in Baghdad and its strongman, Saddam Hussein. This covert action proved surprisingly effective, at least from the shah's perspective. In March 1975, Saddam Hussein met with the shah in Algiers and signed a far-reaching border agreement that called for each side to refrain from any further interference in the other's internal affairs. In re-

turn, Saddam Hussein agreed to divide control of the Shatt al-Arab waterway in the south, a longstanding territorial objective of Iran.

Having achieved his political goals, the shah abruptly terminated all
support for the Iraqi Kurds, including his toleration of American and Israeli assistance, and the rebellion collapsed. For the Kurds it was a stunning and costly betrayal. The legendary Kurdish leader Mulla Mustafa
Barzani was forced to flee the country; he ultimately settled in McLean,
Virginia, not far from CIA headquarters, where he lived in obscurity until
his death in 1979.[8]

In 1966, Iran and Israel signed their first major arms contracts. Though
regarded as substantial at the time, these contracts would be dwarfed by
the volume of trade in arms and other commodities in the years that followed. The huge increase in oil prices in the mid-1970s that triggered
Iran's buying spree of arms from the United States had a similar effect on
its dealings with Israel. Neither country released figures on its arms trade,
but by 1978, Iran had become one of Israel's best customers for defense
goods.

The high point of this military cooperation between Israel and Iran
occurred when the two nations concluded a secret agreement on technological cooperation in 1977. Iran was to provide funding for a number of
sensitive research-and-development projects in Israel, including development of a surface-to-surface missile capable of carrying a nuclear warhead.
The test firings were to be conducted in Iran. According to General Hassan
Toufanian, the Iranian vice minister of defense for procurement, his nation's motivation for the missile project was Iraq's acquisition of Soviet
Scud missiles and the American refusal to sell Lance missiles to Iran.
Israel, in turn, had been unable to persuade the United States to provide
funding for projects that had nuclear implications. The two countries therefore secretly agreed to pursue nuclear-oriented research in tandem, without
informing the Carter administration.[9]

Until the revolution, Iran continued to make regular payments to Israel
for these projects, by means of secret deliveries of oil to a Swiss broker,
who sold it and then transferred the money to Israel. The transactions were
supervised by Meir Ezri, an Israeli who had been born in Iran and who

returned to Tehran, where he acted as Israel's representative for twelve years.[10]

But in the end, Iran got nothing from its substantial investment. The final payment of $260 million worth of oil was made by General Toufanian shortly before the shah's regime collapsed, yet Iran "never received a single screw."[11] Toufanian was so concerned with maintaining the secrecy of the program that he packed up all the files during the final days of the revolution and sent them to Israel on one of the last El Al flights out of Tehran. When the revolutionaries took over the government, they learned the general outline of the program but none of the details.

The collapse of the shah's regime was potentially a disaster for Israel, no less than for the United States, for Israel was at risk of losing the entire investment that it had made in Iran over a quarter of a century. The policy that had begun as a political effort to break out of the Arab encirclement of Israel had blossomed into the fields of energy, trade, development, intelligence, arms sales, military training and exchanges, and eventually joint research and development on the most sensitive defense projects. The relationship with Iran had become a crucial element of Israel's regional strategy. It was too important to let it go without a fight.

Israel had developed an elaborate network of contacts at all levels of Iranian society and was exceptionally well positioned to sense the collapse of support for the shah long before this phenomenon was recognized by most other governments. When Israeli Foreign Minister Moshe Dayan paid a secret visit to Iran early in 1978, he was informed by Israeli intelligence on his arrival that the shah had been behaving strangely, that he was distracted and uncertain, and that he had reportedly broken down and wept during a meeting with some of his advisers.[12] Several months later, the unofficial Israeli ambassador to Tehran, Uri Lubrani, sent a cable to Jerusalem in which he warned that the shah might not survive more than a few more years. During this same period, the U.S. Embassy was reporting that the shah had the situation firmly under control.[13]

During the last days of the shah, while mobs were raging in the streets of Tehran, the Israeli mission was working frantically to adapt its extensive network of sources and contacts to operate in the hostile environment that was expected to prevail after an Islamic victory. Israel had some unique advantages in this salvage operation. First, Israel, like the United States, is a nation of immigrants, so it could draw on the services of Israeli citizens who were born and raised in Iran or who were second generation. These individuals possessed the cultural experience and language skills that enabled them to operate easily within Iran with only a minimum of training. And since most of them had come to Israel by choice, they tended to be highly motivated and patriotic.

The second great advantage, which the government of Israel prefers not to discuss for obvious reasons, was the Jewish diaspora in Iran, which, like its counterpart in the United States, was reasonably prosperous, well educated, and generally well integrated into the local society. Jewish communities outside Israel are usually sympathetic to Israel's plight and are inclined to be helpful. The prospect of making a direct contribution to Israel's security, even if it entails some risk, may be attractive.

Israel is extremely sensitive to the damaging charge of dual loyalty. If Jews are suspected of placing their affection for Israel above loyalty to their own country, they are more likely to be subject to the kind of discrimination and anti-Semitism that Israel is dedicated to eliminating. There is an exceedingly fine line between the security interests of the state of Israel and the welfare of the world Jewish community, and walking that line is often an agonizing and perilous process.

In order to avoid some of the more obvious pitfalls, a number of rules have been adopted in Israel's relations with other states where there is a substantial Jewish minority.[14] One of these is that Jewish citizens of other countries will not normally be employed as active intelligence agents. Admittedly, it may not always be easy to distinguish between the activities of a well-meaning volunteer and those of an agent, at least for the outside observer. Moreover, the injunction is not always honored, as in the notorious case of the U.S. Navy civilian analyst Jonathan Pollard.[15] There is no injunction, however, about the use of non-Israeli Jews as voluntary assistants to provide logistical and other support for Mossad operations. These volunteers, or *sayanim,* are citizens of the target country with legitimate businesses, access, or skills that are entirely independent of any intelligence organization. In that sense, their "cover" is perfect: They are exactly what they appear to be.

Each Mossad station maintains a register of willing volunteers who can be called upon as necessary, with no questions asked. These individuals may provide a useful piece of information or donate support facilities, often on very short notice. Thus, the string of apartments and "safe houses" in a foreign city that are needed for intelligence operations would typically be identified, rented, and maintained by a local *sayan* housing agent as part of his normal activities. Similarly, if a business front were needed for an operation, a volunteer might permit the use of his offices on a temporary basis.

As a result of this arrangement, the Mossad has been able to maintain an extraordinarily streamlined international operation. The availability of the *sayanim*, together with the ultra-professionalism and high motivation of the handful of experienced Mossad agents, meant that the Mossad, with relatively few people and a limited budget, could often match or surpass the performance of intelligence services many times its size.[16] In many cases, money could not buy the kind of operational flexibility and cover that the Mossad enjoyed through the services of its unacknowledged brigades of willing volunteers. The object of the Israeli intelligence effort during the final months of the Iranian revolution was to establish contact with individuals who had lines into the revolutionary leadership and the clerical establishment and who could continue to function once the shah's regime was no longer in place.

But in February 1979, as the shah's regime crumbled, and angry crowds demonstrated in the streets of Tehran, Israel closed its mission and evacuated its employees. In a symbolic demonstration of defiance, Ayatollah Khomeini's forces turned the Israeli mission over to the Palestine Liberation Organization. For most of 1979, it appeared that the Doctrine of the Periphery and Israel's twenty-eight years of careful cultivation of Iran had come to naught. Iran was caught up in the exhilaration and chaos of assembling a radical new order, while Israel was preoccupied with the politics of the peace treaty signed with Egypt in March.

When the U.S. hostages were taken in November, an action followed by the freezing of Iranian assets and a limited international embargo, Iran began to seek outside help. Ironically, the hostage crisis and Iran's growing isolation and vulnerability provided Israel the opening it needed to begin to cultivate ties with the clerical regime in Tehran.

■ ■ ■

In many ways, the contours of the Israeli intelligence effort in Iran during the revolution and hostage crisis can be discerned through the activities of one man, Ari Ben-Menashe.[17]

Ari's father, Gourdji Ben-Menashe, was an Iraqi Jew who grew up in Baghdad, attended the Alliance Française school, and completed his education in Paris, before becoming a businessman with international interests that often took him abroad. During World War II, Gourdji Ben-Menashe visited Palestine, where there was Jewish resistance against the British Mandate. There, according to the family, he participated in some activities of the underground Lehi group, better known as the Stern Gang, which was responsible for terrorist acts during and after the independence struggle. (The head of the Lehi, Yitzhak Yezernitzki, later changed his surname to Shamir and eventually became prime minister of Israel. Many other members of the organization found their way into intelligence work after Israeli independence.) Because of his activities, Gourdji Ben-Menashe was placed on a wanted list by the British authorities.

In 1945, as the war ended, he returned to Baghdad, where he met his future wife, Khatoun (or "Katie," as she later chose to be called). Shortly thereafter, they resettled in Iran, a refuge for Iraqi Jews in those unsettled times, where Gourdji Ben-Menashe acquired a profitable dealership in Mercedes-Benz spare parts and began raising a family. Ariel, his only son, was born in Tehran on December 4, 1951.

Ari Ben-Menashe grew up in the Iranian capital and got his early education at the American School, where he was known to his classmates as Fouad Menashi. (Like many Israelis, Ben-Menashe adopted a Hebrew name when he immigrated.) In 1966, at age fifteen, he insisted on going off to Israel, which he did, while his mother, father, and three sisters remained in Tehran.

This was a dramatic statement by the young teenager. Leaving home at that age was unusual enough, but moving to Israel just before the 1967 war was even more unusual. Young Iraqi Jews living in Iran at that time were largely uninterested in Israel. For the most part, they were prosperous, and they lived in a relatively tolerant environment, unlike many of their fellow Jews in the Arab states of the Middle East who were the victims of turmoil and persecution in those early years after Israel's independence. If they chose to emigrate, as many did, they typically went to the United States or Canada, almost never to Israel.

Ari completed his secondary education at the American School in Israel and entered the religiously orthodox Bar Ilan University in 1969. The rest of the family joined him in Israel in 1970. During these formative years, he had two unpleasant encounters with Israeli authorities, which had a profound influence on him.

As part of his effort to find out as much as possible about his new country, he spent some time on Kibbutz Mishmar Hasharon in the Sharon Valley between Haifa and Tel Aviv. The secular creed of communal life and manual labor close to the land was entirely foreign to his experience and beliefs, but it gave him an introduction to the European Zionist ethos. While there, he shared a room with two fundamentalist Christians. One of them was an Australian who thought God had ordered him to return to the Holy Land for a higher purpose. Unbeknownst to Ben-Menashe, that "higher purpose" turned out to be the bombing of the Dome of the Rock, one of the holiest sites in Islam.[18] When he realized what his roommate had done, Ben-Menashe went to the police and was himself subjected to severe interrogation. He discovered that the Israeli police were less interested in the whole truth than in covering up the Australian's link with an Israeli boy, as well as what Ben-Menashe believed were financial links to the extremist Jewish Defense League (an allegation which has never been proved). It was his first realization, as he put it, that "the law could be manipulated."[19]

Later, while studying at the university, Ben-Menashe began teaching English on a volunteer basis at an Arab school. He was soon summoned for an interview by the Shin Bet, the Israeli domestic intelligence agency. They asked him to act as an informer and offered him a deal: Instead of reporting for military service, he could remain at the school to develop contacts with the Palestinian Arabs. He declined, and shortly thereafter he was drafted into the army.

These two episodes, though minor, left a lasting impression on the idealistic young Israeli, who thereafter took a more cynical attitude toward authority.

He reported for military service in late 1973, just after the Yom Kippur

War. Although he went through the requisite basic training with the Golani Brigade, a tough combat unit, it was clear from the start that Ari Ben-Menashe was not going to have the career of a normal recruit. He had some unusual and valuable skills: His family spoke Arabic at home, and he had studied written Arabic at college; he had grown up in Iran, and Persian was one of his native tongues; he had attended American schools for most of his education and was completely fluent in English; and by this time he was, of course, fluent in Hebrew. He was adventurous and restless, with an intense curiosity about politics. In short, he was a natural for the intelligence services.

Even before he started his basic military training, he was given an introductory course in cryptography. He was then assigned to Signals Intelligence Unit 8-200, where he helped break a code used for sensitive Iranian diplomatic communications. In his off hours, he attended graduate classes in history at Tel Aviv University, not far from his unit in Herzliya.

Soon after his tour of duty ended in 1977, Ben-Menashe joined the "External Relations Department" (Intelligence) of the Israeli Defense Forces. He was assigned to the "Foreign Flow" desk, which was responsible for liaison with other national intelligence services on military issues.

Most intelligence services have exchange relationships with their counterparts in friendly countries. These are eminently practical arrangements. By trading some of its own information, a country can obtain in return information that would be difficult, expensive, or even impossible to obtain through its own resources. In the late 1970s, for example, Israel was developing a main battle tank and wanted to obtain the physical characteristics of a special armored segment used by the British army. The British were uncooperative, but they did sell their tanks to Iran. So the Israelis, through their exchange relations with Iran under the shah, were able to acquire the desired part, which in time appeared on the Israeli Merkava tank.[20]

Liaison work requires travel, so Ben-Menashe almost immediately began what was to be more than a decade of incessant air travel to every corner of the globe. For an ambitious young man of twenty-five, the glamour and excitement were intoxicating.

One of his most frequent stops was Tehran. Ben-Menashe's entry into the Israeli intelligence community came at the high-water mark of Israeli-Iranian relations, in the last two years of the shah's reign. During this period he traveled to Iran approximately once a month for routine contact with Iranian officials through the Israeli unofficial embassy. The frequency of his trips accelerated as the momentum of the Iranian revolution quickened in 1978.

Although Ben-Menashe was in military intelligence and dealt with the Iranians through the assistant military attaché, he soon began widening his scope of activity. He could pass as Iranian, he had many local friends and acquaintances, and he was incurably inquisitive and audacious. As the political situation in Iran unraveled, his presence in Tehran made him a most useful asset to the Israelis.

Ben-Menashe managed to establish at least informal connections at universities wherever he went. Usually he would strike up a relationship with a professor by asking for advice about a research project and dropping in on classes. His quick, inquiring mind, engaging manner, and youthful appearance enabled him to blend easily into student settings. In Tehran, where he was in contact with a well-organized group of *sayanim*,[21] he focused much of his attention on the university, which was a hotbed of anti-shah politics. He began dropping in at Tehran University during his regular visits to the city; he was working on a paper about the politics of the Tudeh (Communist) Party in Iran, and he contacted a professor at the university who was willing to advise him on his research. At the same time, he became acquainted with a number of student leaders on the campus, most notably Ahmed Kashani, a young student who was a teaching assistant in a university seminar. He had been arrested under the shah and was active in the revolutionary politics of the day. Ben-Menashe began dropping into his class from time to time.

Kashani was the youngest son of Ayatollah Abol Qassem Kashani, a charismatic religious leader with a huge following during the turbulent early 1950s. He was a key clerical supporter of Mosaddeq's struggle to nationalize Iranian oil, and was an early exemplar of the kind of Muslim populist leader that Ayatollah Khomeini would come to personify a quarter-century later.

In 1953, the elder Kashani broke with Mosaddeq and shifted his support to the monarchy, a devastating blow for the nationalists. The change of allegiance proved devastating to Ayatollah Kashani as well; he soon faded into obscurity, reviled by his detractors as a paid turncoat who had aided the U.S.-British "countercoup" that restored the shah to the throne.[22]

In the revolutionary environment of Tehran in 1978, Ahmed Kashani was an interesting figure. He was a man with a famous name, whose family retained some political power and had its own network of influence. But his father's history placed the young Kashani somewhat outside the mainstream of either the nationalist or the clerical revolutionary camp. According to Ben-Menashe, Kashani always used the first name Mehdi in their dealings, further blurring his identity.[23] From an intelligence perspective, Kashani was an intriguing prospect, and Ari Ben-Menashe soon befriended him.

Shortly after the hostages were taken, Israel put out new feelers in Iran, quietly offering assistance in circumventing the U.S. embargo, in return for political access. As we have seen, among those who accepted the offer was Ahmed Heidari of Interparts. Another was Ahmed Kashani.

According to Ben-Menashe, in early 1980 Kashani left Iran to visit Israel, the first important Iranian to do so after the revolution. There had been prior meetings in Europe between Israeli representatives and Iranians, but going to Tel Aviv "took a lot of courage" and—for political reasons—a false passport.

Kashani may have been among the first to visit Israel after the revolution, but other channels between Israel and Iran were functioning long before he arrived. Even at the height of revolutionary fervor, Israel's ties to the Iranian military had never been entirely erased, and some contacts had been quietly restored as early as the summer of 1979. Some of these contacts involved unfinished military business dating from before the revolution. For example, before the shah fell Iran had sent an American tank to Israel to be upgraded. Only months after the revolution, Iran's military authorities contacted Israel and asked that the tank be returned, and it was secretly shipped back to Iran. Other loose ends relating to the extensive Israel-Iran military relationship also had to be tidied up; some of these involved military shipments. According to several authoritative Israeli sources, these deliveries had been largely completed by early 1980.[24]

After checking into the Tel Aviv Hilton, Kashani met with Israeli military-intelligence officials. The young man stressed that he had come to Israel as a "concerned private citizen" of Iran to discuss matters of mutual concern to both Iran and Israel. One of those concerns, he was quick to point out, was the Iraqi nuclear-development program. As we shall see, these initial contacts may have resulted in Israeli intelligence support for an unsuccessful Iranian air force strike against the Iraqi reactor.

As a result of Kashani's visit to Israel, an initial shipment of approximately three hundred tires for F-4 fighter aircraft was arranged as a demonstration of good faith. In March or April 1980, these tires were flown on a regularly scheduled El Al flight to Vienna, where the cargo was transferred to a commercial Iran Air flight to Tehran.[25] This relatively small transaction was the first arms sale by Israel to Iran since the fall of the shah, and within Israel it was regarded as something of a breakthrough.

According to Ben-Menashe, the shipment had to be approved by Prime Minister Menachem Begin because of its great political sensitivity. The nature and dollar value of the shipment were unexceptional, but the delivery was being made without the knowledge of the U.S. government and it was a direct violation of the U.S. embargo on arms sales to Iran.

This incident shows clearly that the Israeli government was prepared to pursue its own interests in Iran regardless of the possible adverse reaction in the United States. That response would have been swift and vehement, for it is likely that the American public would have viewed Israel's actions as aiding Iran while American soldiers were dying in the desert. Ben-Menashe never forgot the reaction of a young couple in Brooklyn whom he was visiting in April 1980. It was a very emotional time for all Americans as they learned of the failed rescue mission and watched televised pictures of the charred helicopters and the desecration of the bodies by Hojjat ol-Eslam Sadegh Khalkhali, Iran's infamous hanging judge. When Ben-Menashe told his hosts, who were Jewish, that Israel had shipped arms to Iran behind the back of the U.S. government, the young woman was so outraged that she declared she would never want to live in Israel.[26]

When Begin visited Washington on April 13, 1980, he told President Carter that Israel had some useful contacts in Iran and that those contacts could be further developed if Israel was willing to provide military equipment. Begin said that he thought Israel's contacts might be helpful in negotiations about the American hostages in Tehran, but that the United States would have to authorize Israel to sell military equipment to Iran on a covert basis. President Carter rejected the offer and asked for Begin's assurance that Israel would observe the arms embargo. Begin agreed and withdrew his suggestion.[27] Moreover, upon his return to Jerusalem, Begin issued strict instructions to the Ministry of Defense and to the chief of staff of the Israeli Defense Forces, ordering them to stop selling Iran "everything—not even shoelaces."[28]

But Begin did not wear Carter's shackles gladly. Indeed, according to an American who was meeting with the prime minister ten days later, when the news arrived of the failure of the U.S. rescue mission, Begin reacted with a measure of grim satisfaction, saying simply, "Jimmy Carter is finished."[29]

·4·

THE DIE IS CAST

T his campaign is ours," a Reagan campaign aide noted after the Republican National Convention, "but it's ours to throw away, too. . . . If [Carter] does something with the hostages, or pulls something else out of the hat, as only an incumbent president can, we're in big trouble." [1] That mixture of triumph and nagging uncertainty would dominate Republican campaign strategy for all three months of the presidential race. The Republican National Convention convened in Detroit on July 14, 1980, and three days later nominated Ronald Reagan as its presidential candidate in a remarkable show of unity and confidence.

Standing behind a podium decorated with red and white stripes of geraniums and emblazoned with the phrase, all in capital letters, "TOGETHER . . . A NEW BEGINNING," Reagan graciously received the wild cheers of the delegates and then moved to the attack. "Adversaries large and small test our will and seek to confound our resolve," he told them. "But we are given weakness when we need strength, vacillation when the times demand firmness." As President, he would lead the country away from its recent past to a "new beginning."[2]

The hostages were an invisible presence at the Republican convention. The party leaders decided from the start that they would not make a political issue of the hostages, and their injunction was admirably respected. Though there were few direct references to the crisis, the hostages stood just behind the rhetoric in speech after speech—all of which had to be cleared personally by William Casey. On the second day of the convention, Henry Kissinger invoked the hostages with his declaration that "a new administration will show that blackmail does not work, that our friendship has benefits while hostility to us involves penalties."[3] The proceedings opened each morning with a minute of silent prayer on behalf of the hostages.

But prayers were not sufficient for everyone. Immediately after the convention, a series of contacts with foreign officials was initiated by staunch supporters of the Reagan candidacy, most of whom were not officially involved in the campaign.

A man described as "one of Reagan's closest friends and a major financial contributor to the campaign," who "kept referring to him as Ronnie," contacted Bassam Abu Sharif, who later became chief adviser for Palestine Liberation Organization leader Yasir Arafat. According to Abu Sharif, they met in Beirut in the period after the Republican convention. Reagan's friend "said he wanted the PLO to use its influence to delay the release of the American hostages from the embassy in Tehran until after the election," Abu Sharif recalled, adding that the man asked him to contact Arafat with the request. "We were told that if the hostages were held, the PLO would be given recognition as the legitimate representative of the Palestinian people and the White House door would be open for us."[4] On another occasion, Abu Sharif said: "It seems it was important for Reagan not to have the hostages released during the remaining days of President Carter. . . . He was interested in having the hostages released afterwards. Of course, blocking the release of the hostages for Reagan would mean in one way or the other some sort of discredit to Carter."[5]

Asking the PLO to act as middleman in the hostage affair was politically risky, but it was not capricious. The PLO had been received triumphantly in Tehran after the revolution, and its representatives had moved into the former Israeli mission. The PLO had trained many of the Iranian revolutionaries in Lebanon in the years prior to the revolution, and PLO operatives provided communications, security, and other technical services and support for the new regime. After the takeover of the U.S. Embassy, the PLO assisted the captors in organizing security for the sprawling embassy compound. The PLO also sent three of its top officials to Iran for intensive hostage negotiations in November 1979. This initiative, which had the support and encouragement of Secretary of State Cyrus Vance on behalf of the Carter administration, resulted in the release later that month of thirteen women and blacks who had been taken prisoner in the attack.[6]

By the summer of 1980, the PLO no longer enjoyed the close relationship with Iran that it had in the early days of the revolution, but it still had access and credibility. Abu Sharif said that the PLO was still, at that time, interested in trying to help free the hostages, and that all efforts to prolong the hostage crisis were rejected, including the approach from Reagan's friend.

Abu Sharif adamantly refused to name his contact in the Reagan camp, for fear that such a move would be viewed by the Bush administration as "blackmail." "You know very well that some of the people who were working closely with President Reagan are still working closely with President Bush," he said. The PLO later learned, according to Abu Sharif, that the same proposition was made to others in Iran who accepted it.[7]

Another extraordinary effort to deal with the hostage problem involved former President Richard Nixon, who traveled to London approximately a week after the Republican convention. During his visit, a British political notable helped him to arrange a meeting with Alan Bristow, the chairman of Bristow Helicopters. Bristow had operated a helicopter service in Iran for twenty years during the shah's era, and his firm had extensive flying experience in the country. After the 1979 revolution, Bristow had planned a mission in which former British Special Air Service (SAS) officers— paratroops—would retrieve the company's helicopter fleet that the revolutionary government was threatening to impound. Iran eventually released the helicopters, and the plan was never implemented.

Bristow met with Nixon at the U.S. Embassy in London in an office that had been made available to the former President as a courtesy during his London visit. Nixon's objective, he said, was to explore the possibility of organizing a raid, with Bristow's assistance, to rescue the hostages in Iran. "Nixon was absolutely serious," Bristow recalled. "We had a long and detailed discussion about the chances of success of a second strike. I told him it could be done, but the strike force would suffer at least 30 percent casualties. . . . Mr. Nixon was certain that President Carter's shame over the [first rescue] operation would ensure that he would not try again before the election. . . . Nixon kept repeating that something had to be done."[8]

It was never clear to Bristow whether the mission was being considered as an independent effort to free the hostages before the presidential election or as part of a contingency plan that a future Reagan administration might use after coming to office. The timing of the visit, however, coming as it did almost immediately after the Republican National Convention, together with Nixon's apparent sense of urgency and his decision to consult a private firm outside the United States, would make it unlikely that this was contingency planning for a new administration that was at least six months away.

But without access to the military and intelligence resources of a government, the possibility of a successful rescue mission was almost nil, and the idea was finally dropped. The significance of the Nixon initiative was that it reveals the apparent willingness of very senior figures in the Republican Party to consider extraordinary measures to deal with the hostage dilemma. If Nixon's overture had been a unique occurrence, it might be regarded as nothing more than a curious aberration. Instead, it appears to have been only one of several exploratory efforts by senior Republicans seeking various ways to influence the nature and timing of the hostage release. There was at least one other attempt. And it produced dramatic results.

During the course of a visit to Washington, D.C., in March 1980, Jamshid Hashemi was in his room in the stately Mayflower Hotel, just four blocks from the White House, when there was a knock at the door. He opened the door to find two men standing in the softly lit corridor. According to Hashemi, one of the men introduced himself as Roy Furmark, an American businessman who had met Jamshid's brother Cyrus in 1979 in the Bahamas where they were looking at business opportunities. The other man said he was William Casey.[9]

According to Jamshid Hashemi, Casey was all business. He said he was aware of Hashemi's contacts in Iran and with the U.S. government, and he wanted to talk about the U.S. hostages in Iran. The Iranian was startled and more than a little alarmed. How had this man located him? What did he have to do with the hostages? Was this a setup by U.S. intelligence?

While Furmark waited outside (he has since denied that he was even present at this meeting),[10] Jamshid called his brother in New York and told him what was going on. Cyrus assured Jamshid that William Casey was a very important figure in Republican politics and that the contact could be worthwhile. After a brief discussion, Cyrus asked to talk to Casey directly. Casey took the phone and spoke with Cyrus for several minutes, during which time they arranged to meet in New York. Casey then thanked Jamshid and left as abruptly and as mysteriously as he had arrived. Jamshid said the meeting was quite brief: "The whole conversation lasted only about twelve minutes."

In fact, Jamshid was in Washington for meetings with his intelligence contact in the U.S. government, and he reported that he had been contacted unexpectedly by William Casey. Jamshid said he was told to "disregard the meeting" and not to meet with Casey again.

A few days later, however, Cyrus proposed a different course of action. The Hashemi brothers and their families had assembled at Cyrus's home in Wilton, Connecticut, on March 21 to celebrate *Now Ruz*, the Iranian New Year. It was the first time Jamshid had seen Cyrus since the mysterious meeting with Casey in the Mayflower Hotel, and as was often the case in their dealings, he looked to his younger brother for some explanation as to just what was going on. Cyrus, in typical fashion, did not give him a straight answer, but instead circled around the subject. There was a very good chance, he told Jamshid, that the Republicans might win the next presidential election. If so, it would be useful to the brothers and to their friends in Iran to have some contacts on that side as well. Casey was an important figure in the Republican campaign, and an old friend of John Shaheen, a businessman with whom Cyrus had worked on several projects. (The most ambitious of these was an oil refinery that Shaheen built in Newfoundland, and which was to receive its supply of crude from Iran. The refinery turned out to be a spectacular failure, one of the largest bankruptcies in Canadian history.) Shaheen was an oil man and a promoter who had invented the concept of flight insurance purchased from vending machines in airports. (He was also Roy Furmark's former employer.) He came to know Casey while serving as a naval officer attached to the Office of Strategic Services (OSS) during World War II, and he was a childhood acquaintance of Ronald Reagan.[11] This was an opportunity, Cyrus advised, that they should not overlook.

Thus it was, in the course of a family picnic celebrating the Iranian New Year, on the grounds of Cyrus's spacious home in Connecticut, that the Hashemi brothers became, in Jamshid's words, "double agents." They were perfectly positioned. Both of them by this time were in regular contact with members of the Carter administration, and their participation in promoting Admiral Madani's candidacy had demonstrated an exceptional degree of access to political developments inside Iran. Throughout 1980 they would cooperate actively and apparently sincerely with the Carter administration in its efforts to free the hostages—they were, for example, consulted by U.S. intelligence in advance of the April rescue mission—while at the same time sharing with the Republicans their insights on the administration's thinking and plans about the hostage situation. It was a dangerous game, but they were confident that they could pull it off, and they knew that if they were successful the rewards were potentially enormous, regardless of the U.S. election outcome.

That spring, the Hashemi brothers informed Madani that they had established contact with Casey and the Republican campaign. He warned them of the danger of playing both sides, but they were not dissuaded. Madani would later remark with a sigh that the Hashemis were energetic and well-meaning, but "they did not always exercise the best judgment."[12]

Before the *Now Ruz* picnic, Casey had asked Cyrus to arrange a meeting for him with a senior Iranian official, someone who would be in a position to speak authoritatively about the hostages.[13] Unlike the abortive Nixon visit to London and the attempted contact through the PLO, Casey's contacts with Cyrus Hashemi would result in a series of important meetings between individuals in the Republican campaign and high-level Iranians.

The Hashemis went to work immediately after Casey made his request. Jamshid had two Iranian candidates in mind who would fit Casey's description of an authoritative spokesman on the hostages and on current political developments. Not surprisingly, these two represented the two opposing factions that were battling for control of Iran.

One of these was a relative of Ayatollah Khomeini. In the course of his political work for Admiral Madani, Jamshid had developed relations with some individuals who were very close to Khomeini's family but who were more moderate than Ayatollah Beheshti and his circle. During the election, these individuals had become effective supporters of President Bani-Sadr, and they occasionally acted as a communications bridge between Bani-Sadr and the ayatollah. Jamshid and Cyrus were well acquainted with one man in this group who was about their age and who could provide a line of contact directly with Bani-Sadr and, through his family connections, with Khomeini himself. Jamshid Hashemi approached this man and confirmed that he would be willing to meet with the Americans if his identity and political safety could be protected.

The other possibility was Hojjat ol-Eslam Mehdi Karrubi, a man who represented the Beheshti faction of clerics who opposed Bani-Sadr. Karrubi was then forty-three years old and one of the clerics in Khomeini's inner circle. He had joined Khomeini's movement in 1962 and had spent six months with Khomeini during his exile in Iraq. His revolutionary credentials were impeccable. He had been imprisoned by the shah's police at least six times between the 1963 uprising and the successful overthrow of the shah in 1979. After the revolution, he was appointed head of the Shahid (Martyrs') Foundation, the successor of the shah's lavishly endowed Pahlavi Foundation, which disbursed more funds than many of Iran's government ministries.[14] Jamshid Hashemi had become acquainted with Mehdi Karrubi when the two of them had headed the operation of *komiteh imdad,* the committee created immediately after the revolution to monitor the operations of Iran's radio stations.

Each of these men had certain things to offer. One provided a reliable channel to the legitimate government of Iran. The other represented the powerful shadow government of the clerics. Both were well known personally to the Hashemis. They decided to explore both channels.

Beginning in early May, only a few weeks after the failed hostage-rescue mission, they offered these two possible contacts to Casey. Astonishingly, and apparently in keeping with their equal-opportunity policy, they also offered the same contacts to the Carter administration. On May 8, Cyrus

Hashemi raised the name of Mehdi Karrubi with the Carter administration and reported that both Karrubi and the Khomeini relative would be willing to come out of the country for a meeting.

The offer came in a telephone call from the American who acted as an intermediary between Cyrus and the U.S. government. Cyrus, he said, had told him that a senior cleric would be willing to come out of the country. Ayatollah Karrubi, he added, could also come out of the country for a meeting. Karrubi was largely unknown at the time, and Cyrus identified him as a member of the Majles who was close to Khomeini's son Ahmed and had been a student of Khomeini's for fifteen years. Cyrus stressed that Karrubi would be willing to participate in a meeting.[15]

That telephone conversation was regarded as particularly important since it resulted two months later in a meeting between the Khomeini relative and an American representative in Madrid, as part of the Carter administration's efforts to develop reliable lines of communication into Tehran. Cyrus obviously did not inform the Carter administration that he had made the same offer to Casey and the Reagan campaign, but the timing, the names, and the purpose were totally consistent with Jamshid Hashemi's account more than ten years later. That telephone conversation confirms that by May 8, 1980, Cyrus Hashemi had established contact with two key figures in the Iranian leadership and that each had agreed to make a trip out of Iran for a meeting.

On the basis of my own personal knowledge of that time, I can confirm that the relative of Khomeini did in fact come out of Iran and meet with an authorized representative of the Carter administration in Madrid on Wednesday, July 2, 1980. The meeting was arranged by Cyrus Hashemi and was held at the Ritz Hotel. Cyrus Hashemi and the American representative flew from London to Madrid that morning, met with the Iranian, and returned to London the same evening.[16]

That meeting produced no breakthrough, but it did result in a new U.S. initiative to open a more productive dialogue with Iran over the hostages. Specifically, Secretary of State Edmund S. Muskie sent a confidential letter to Bani-Sadr on September 3, timed to correspond to the establishment of a new Cabinet in Iran. This message was confirmed separately in the memoirs of both Bani-Sadr and Jimmy Carter. Bani-Sadr reported that "on September 3, the ambassador of the Federal Republic of Germany handed me an offer from Jimmy Carter, which to me seemed very favorable."[17] One week later Carter noted in his diary, "Muskie important message via [West German Foreign Minister Hans-Dietrich] Genscher, responded affirmatively."[18] Within the Carter administration, this sequence of events was seen as the genesis for secret negotiations that would be initiated by Iran later that month.

The July 2 Madrid meeting was also important in other ways. It demonstrated beyond any doubt that the Hashemis were capable of organizing a clandestine meeting between Iranian clerics and Americans. It also showed that it was possible to have breakfast in London, lunch in Madrid, and dinner back in London—all on the same day. For all practical purposes, it was a dress rehearsal for the series of meetings in Madrid that would take place between Ronald Reagan's campaign manager and a different group of Iranians a few weeks later.

Although Mehdi Karrubi had agreed as early as May 8 to meet secretly with an American delegation in Europe, the meetings with Casey did not take place until the last week in July.[19] The dates of the meetings were probably chosen by Casey to coincide with a long-scheduled trip to London, where he was to present a paper on World War II intelligence operations to the Anglo-American Conference on the History of the Second World War, held at the Imperial War Museum. The meeting provided a perfect excuse for the busy campaign manager to be out of the country. Casey's records show that he was absent from July 26 to July 30. He made an appearance at the London conference on the evening of the twenty-eighth and the morning of the twenty-ninth. Since the travel time between London and Madrid permitted a round trip and a meeting in one day, there was ample room in his schedule for the reported meetings in Madrid. And on his first night back in Washington, he had dinner with George Bush at the Alibi Club, a private establishment that was perfectly named for the occasion.[20]

The choice of Madrid as the meeting site was probably made for Karrubi's convenience. In those days, Madrid was a favorite destination for Iranians traveling to Europe, because there were direct Iran Air flights from Tehran on Tuesdays and Fridays and because Spain did not require a visa for Iranians to enter the country. Since no entry or exit visas were required, there would be no record of the visit. Many years later, Mehdi Karrubi denied that he had ever visited Spain.[21] The evidence, however, suggests otherwise.

A few days before the meetings, Jamshid was at the Madrid airport to greet the delegation from Tehran. Iranian Ambassador Ali Asghar Behnam was also there with the embassy limousine, but the Hashemis had been warned in advance that the ambassador was unaware of the purpose of the visit. The meetings with Casey were not to be discussed in his presence.[22]

Mehdi Karrubi and his brother Hassan arrived in their clerical robes but without their usual turbans. They were accompanied by two Iranian Revolutionary Guards. The ambassador greeted Mehdi, and they sped off to the ambassador's residence. Another limousine, reserved by Cyrus for their exclusive use during the meetings, took Jamshid and Hassan to the Plaza Hotel near the Plaza de España, where they registered under disguised names.

Hassan Karrubi, although not as prominent as his brother, was an interesting figure in his own right. He never held any official government position, but he served as an important link between the tight little circle of influential advisers around Khomeini and the less savory worlds of intelligence operatives and arms dealers. In covert operations, there is often a respectable front man and another behind-the-scenes figure who carries out the dirty work. In the Madrid meetings in 1980, Mehdi Karrubi played the former role while Hassan, who was widely suspected of intelligence associations, neatly filled the latter. His presence in Madrid to talk about the hostages was particularly ironic, since he was reputed to have been one of those involved in planning the takeover of the U.S. Embassy in Tehran.[23]

The meetings began, possibly as early as Sunday morning, July 27, at the five-star Hotel Ritz, a sumptuous Belle Epoque structure just a few blocks away from the Prado Museum. Cyrus, who was a valued customer, had reserved a suite for the meetings.[24] William Casey and his party arrived promptly, as did the Hashemis and Hassan Karrubi. Mehdi Karrubi was last to arrive—a pattern that he maintained throughout the meetings, often showing up thirty minutes or more after the others had assembled.

The American delegation consisted of Casey and two other individuals.

Casey characteristically made no secret of his identity, using his own name. His two colleagues, however, used aliases. One of them was unknown to Jamshid, the other he claimed to recognize as the White House official whom he had met previously in his brother's office in New York, Donald Gregg. (Gregg, however, has denied any contact whatsoever with the Reagan-Bush campaign staff in 1980 and any involvement in secret negotiations with the Iranians at that time.)

The meeting was conducted in Persian and English, with the Hashemi brothers alternating as translators. Mehdi Karrubi, with his gray beard and stern eyes peering through his glasses, was clearly in charge on the Iranian side; his brother remained silent throughout the meeting, occasionally passing a note to Jamshid asking for clarification of certain points he didn't want to raise specifically with Casey. Casey was definitely in charge on the American side and did most of the talking. His two colleagues reportedly said very little, though at one point, according to Jamshid, Gregg referred to some specific events in internal Iranian politics that the Iranians felt could have been known only by an insider. The other American was consulted from time to time by Casey, apparently on specific technical points.

The conversation was interrupted twice, when hotel waiters arrived to serve coffee. While the waiters were in the room, all discussion stopped and the participants sat awkwardly waiting for them to leave.

Mehdi Karrubi opened the meeting with a tirade against the United States, its past involvement with the shah, and the actions of the Carter administration. This speech, which was the pro forma soliloquy any good Iranian revolutionary would deliver upon meeting a high-level American, went on for perhaps thirty minutes. Throughout this set speech, Casey remained perfectly cool, betraying no hint of emotion, showing neither agreement nor disagreement.

When Karrubi was finished, Casey did not respond to his charges. Instead, he presented a lengthy and well-informed history of U.S.-Iranian relations. The theme of his presentation was that relations between the two countries were good when Republicans were in the White House but deteriorated when Democrats were in power. Iran, he said, was in no position to fight the United States, and it would be better advised to come to terms. Ronald Reagan was going to win the presidential election, he claimed, and once in office the new administration would not only be willing to give back to Iran the financial assets that had been frozen at the time of the embassy takeover, but would also return all of Iran's confiscated military equipment after the hostages were released.

In his presentation, Casey demonstrated that he was fully aware of the contacts that had been established between Cyrus Hashemi and the U.S. government. He was also familiar with the details of the contacts between the Carter administration and Iran during the previous nine months.

What, Casey asked Karrubi, were Iran's intentions about the hostages? Karrubi replied that the Islamic Republic had tried to make some deals with the Carter administration, but, he stressed, these efforts had been undertaken *without* Khomeini's approval.[25]

On that ambiguous note, the first meeting adjourned for lunch, with an agreement to meet again. That evening the ambassador gave a dinner for the Iranian delegation at the embassy. In the course of the dinner, Mehdi Karrubi asked Jamshid Hashemi what was going on. What was the purpose of this meeting? Jamshid said he did not know.

When the two delegations reassembled, Mehdi Karrubi opened the discussion by asking Casey the same question point-blank. What was the purpose of this meeting? Casey replied with a question of his own. Was the Islamic Republic ready to deal with the Republicans? It was impossible to establish good relations between the two countries, he said, as long as the hostages were there.

Karrubi asked if the U.S. government would be willing on its part to return Iran's financial and military assets. Casey said that would be impossible at this time since the Republicans were not in power, but it could be done after they came into office. As for arms, perhaps that could be done through a third country.

Could Iran confirm, Casey asked, that the hostages would be well treated until the moment of their release? If Iran could give that assurance, and if the hostages were released as a "gift" to the new administration, the Republicans would be most grateful and "would give Iran its strength back."

Karrubi said he had no authority to make such a commitment. He would have to return to Tehran and seek instructions from Khomeini. Casey said the Reagan team had no objection if Iran continued to deal with the present U.S. administration, but he personally had washed his hands of President Carter. According to Jamshid Hashemi, Casey's remarks played on Khomeini's extreme personal hatred for Carter and elicited a positive reaction from Karrubi.

Although no decision was taken at the meeting, the atmosphere was cordial and the meeting reportedly ended with handshakes and smiles all around. At the end Karrubi remarked in Persian, which was not translated for the Americans, "I think we are now opening a new era. I am talking to someone who knows how to do business."

It was understood that Mehdi Karrubi would fly back to Iran to discuss what he had heard and would be back in touch at a later date. Hassan Karrubi, however, did not return to Iran immediately. Instead, he and Jamshid Hashemi traveled together to Germany, Denmark, and back to Germany trying to drum up military equipment for Iran.

Five other sources have independently confirmed that these meetings took place and that Jamshid Hashemi's account with respect to the content of the Casey-Karrubi talks is substantially accurate:

- Admiral Ahmad Madani, the former Iranian minister of defense and candidate for the presidency of Iran, was in touch with the Hashemis throughout 1980. He was aware of the Hashemis' contacts with William Casey starting in early 1980 and of the Madrid meetings.[26]
- Ari Ben-Menashe revealed in 1990 that he had read Israeli intelligence reports describing these meetings, and he volunteered significant details that independently confirmed Hashemi's account.[27]
- Arif Durrani, a Pakistani arms dealer who was deeply involved with Iranian arms purchases in the early 1980s, said in January 1991 that he was informed of these meetings by Mohsen Rafiqdust, the head of Iran's Revolutionary Guard.[28]
- Heinrich Rupp, a contract pilot, reported in November 1990 that he was involved in several flights to Spain in the summer of 1980, two of which were to Madrid for secret contacts between Casey and the Iranians.[29]
- Richard Babayan, an American arms dealer with ties to U.S. intelligence, said in June 1991 that he had been visited in Paris in mid-August 1980 by an Iranian intelligence official who said he had

just come from Madrid, where he had attended meetings between Karrubi and Casey.[30]

On August 4, about five days after the first set of meetings had concluded in Madrid, there was a debate in the Iranian parliament, the Majles, over the hostage issue. During the debate, Speaker Rafsanjani remarked in passing that the "United States organized this hostage problem for their elections."[31] Rafsanjani was an excellent political strategist; at a minimum, his comment suggested that by this time he and the top clerical leaders in Iran were fully conscious of the importance of the hostage issue in the coming presidential elections in the United States.

During those same days, the clouds of war were rapidly building. On August 5, Saddam Hussein, who had just officially become the president of Iraq, paid the first visit by an Iraqi head of state to Saudi Arabia. This may have been part of his strategy to coordinate action by the regional Arab states in preparation for the war he would launch against Iran six weeks later.[32]

At about the same time, former Iranian Premier Shahpour Bakhtiar announced in Paris that he was forming a national resistance front to overthrow the Khomeini government. Bakhtiar had just returned from his second visit to Baghdad, where he had discussed a coordinated military and political strategy with Iraqi officials.

In Iran, President Bani-Sadr warned in a speech that the Iranian military was "sick" and badly in need of spare parts that were being denied because of the U.S. embargo. The pressure on Iran to find a solution to its military weakness was growing intense.

It was against this backdrop of events that Mehdi Karrubi contacted Jamshid Hashemi during the first week of August and asked him to arrange another meeting with Casey in Madrid. On about August 12, according to Jamshid Hashemi, the same group reassembled in Madrid, again at the Hotel Ritz.[33]

Karrubi opened the meeting by saying that Khomeini had approved Casey's proposal. The hostages would be removed from their prisoner status and would be "treated as guests." The Islamic Republic of Iran, Karrubi said, would "go through the protocol" with the Carter administration, but the hostages would only be freed as a "gesture of goodwill" to the U.S. government on the day of Reagan's inauguration.

In return, Karrubi said, the Islamic Republic of Iran expected that Casey and his colleagues, although not currently holding government office, would help the Iranians obtain certain arms and ammunition that they needed. Casey replied that he could not promise, but he said he had friends and he would try. He would give Karrubi an answer later.

Karrubi said that the Islamic Republic of Iran would prolong the hostage negotiations with Carter in order to make sure the release came after the Reagan inauguration. However, Karrubi warned, if there were no arms, there would be no hostages.

On the following day, Casey opened the meeting by saying that Cyrus Hashemi would be introduced to a gentleman who would help him receive and execute orders for military equipment. The details of the arms deliveries had yet to be worked out, but the Iranians felt they had reason to be satisfied. As Jamshid Hashemi told me many years later, "It was so rosy— the money, the military spares, everything. It was too good to refuse."

Soon after Mehdi Karrubi returned to Iran, Jamshid Hashemi met his brother at the Ritz, where Cyrus introduced him to a man Jamshid believed to be an Israeli general. This man was to be their contact for the arms deal that began not long after the Madrid meetings.

Israel certainly had its own independent sources of information about the meetings. Ari Ben-Menashe said he was shown Israeli intelligence reports on the Madrid meetings. From these reports he was later able to give me a general description. According to him, Israel knew the exact dates and locations of these meetings with Karrubi. "Casey," he said, "was in all four meetings in Spain. We were positive of that. We also believed there were another two to three people" on the U.S. side. According to the Israeli account, the Iranians promised to release the hostages to the Republicans, while the Americans promised to release Iran's assets and to pursue improved relations with Iran after Reagan and Bush took office. The Americans also promised to permit indirect arms shipments to Iran, "and this is why Israel was brought in."[34]

Ben-Menashe added one intriguing detail. It was his understanding that at the close of the Madrid meetings in August, the various parties agreed to meet again in October to review their respective performances and to finalize their agreement. If true, this arrangement would guarantee that Casey and his close associates, and not Jimmy Carter, would have an "October surprise" in their pockets—an October surprise that would keep the American hostages in Iran at least until after the elections.

In the days following the second set of Madrid meetings, Cyrus Hashemi purchased a five-thousand-ton Greek ship, which made arms deliveries from the Israeli port of Eilat to Bandar Abbas, the Iranian port at the mouth of the Persian Gulf. In four months, in defiance of the Carter administration's embargo, four shipments were made, including 155mm and 105mm ammunition, 100mm tank ammunition, and 106mm antitank guns and ammunition. Jamshid Hashemi estimated the total value of the shipments to be $150 million.

Iran paid Israel for these arms through a letter of credit, using Cyrus Hashemi as an intermediary. Cyrus received the letter of credit from an Iranian entity (not the defense ministry), then opened back-to-back letters of credit through a Swiss bank with an Israeli front company represented by a Mr. Nishri, representing the Israeli Military Industries. This arrangement was similar to a documented shipping deal Jamshid would set up in 1985, in which a letter of credit was opened by Hashemi's Tagell Company in Iran to an Israeli front company named Olitor via the Israeli Bank Hapoalim. The Israeli representative of Olitor in 1985 was Yehoshua Nishri.[35]

Jamshid Hashemi was certain that the deliveries called for in the 1980 deal were completed before Ronald Reagan's inauguration on January 20, 1981, since Cyrus had received his commission before that date. He was paid very handsomely for his services; a typical commission for an arms deal was 5 percent, which in this case would have amounted to more than $7 million.

Once the deliveries were completed, Jamshid Hashemi believed that Cyrus made a gift of the $1 million ship to Iran. It was the kind of grand gesture they both loved, and it probably did him no harm with the Iranians, who were emerging as promising long-term customers. Although the shipments were intended to be absolutely secret, they did not go unobserved for long. Within three months, a British paper reported that Israel was shipping military equipment to Iran by sea, using third-country ships. Some of the equipment, they reported, was of U.S. origin.[36]

■ ■ ■

Just after the Madrid meetings, on August 16, Iranian Foreign Minister Sadegh Ghotbzadeh wrote a letter to the Majles on the subject of the hostages. "We have information that the American Republican Party, in order to win in the upcoming election, is trying very hard to delay the resolution of the hostage question until after the American election," he claimed.[37] Ghotbzadeh continued to trumpet this theme over the next few months, but no one listened to him at the time.[38]

On August 18, Speaker Rafsanjani told a press conference that the "hostage situation was not urgent, that the Majles had other business to attend to, and that the Majles would take up the hostage problem after dealing with more pressing matters." Two days later, Ayatollah Beheshti made a similar statement in another press conference in Tehran, declaring that the American hostages are not "of primary importance" to Iran.[39] This pair of statements, by the two most influential leaders in the clerical circles around Khomeini, appeared to confirm what Mehdi Karrubi had told Casey in Madrid. Iran would be in no hurry to solve the hostage problem before the U.S. elections.

On the evening of August 20, just hours after Beheshti's press conference, Iranian President Bani-Sadr attended a meeting of the Revolutionary Command Council at the home of Ayatollah Mohammed Reza Mahdavi-Khani. At this meeting, Bani-Sadr warned of impending war with Iraq and stressed Iran's need for military spare parts. He argued that Iran's preparations for war were being hampered by the U.S.-led embargo, and he pleaded for an early solution to the hostage crisis. At this point he was interrupted by Ayatollah Beheshti, who said to him, "If we [the mullahs] solve the hostage problem, you must not criticize us!" He even asked Bani-Sadr to put such a promise in writing.[40]

Bani-Sadr found this stance peculiar, since he had been outspoken in support of a settlement and would have had no reason to criticize it. He was also in contact with the Carter administration through intermediaries, and he knew that nothing was moving on that front. So Beheshti's enigmatic comments led him to believe that a secret deal on the hostages was being worked out behind his back between certain high-level clerics and individuals in the Reagan campaign.

It is a measure of Bani-Sadr's precarious circumstances that he was forced to rely on such fragmentary comments to determine what was going on in his own government. It is nevertheless true that by mid-August 1980, the president of Iran was being excluded systematically from almost all important political decisions. He was engaged in a battle for his political life, and he was losing.

· 5 ·

IRANIAN
INTRIGUES

A s the summer of 1980 drew to a close, Iran was still without a fully
functioning government. Bani-Sadr had been elected president in
January, and the Majles had finally convened in late May after a
series of runoff elections. But that was just the beginning of the tortuous
process of assembling a Cabinet. It took nearly two months before the
Majles elected Rafsanjani as its first speaker, and three more weeks before
the new prime minister, Mohammed Ali Raja'i, was named.

Bani-Sadr bitterly opposed the choice of Raja'i, a former schoolteacher
whose only qualification for the position was a lifetime of opposition to the
shah, but to no avail. The Islamic Republic Party (IRP), which had opposed Bani-Sadr's election as president, was in full control of the Majles
and refused to accept any of his nominations for key Cabinet posts. On
August 31, Bani-Sadr vetoed the entire IRP Cabinet list, causing an almost
complete breakdown of government authority.

The political struggle that raged over the summer of 1980 involved the
crucial principle of clerical rule. Most of the candidates nominated by
President Bani-Sadr were secular and technocratic. Most of the IRP candi-

dates were closely affiliated with the clerical circles around Khomeini. Polarization of the two opposing factions became increasingly violent as IRP mobs tried to break up rallies and demonstrations on behalf of the president. Although Khomeini denounced the violence, there was no question that his sympathies lay with the clerical faction. In June, Khomeini had launched a mini–cultural revolution, ordering a purge of all remnants of the shah's rule and sharply criticizing Bani-Sadr for his failure to act more decisively against the old order. His speech led to a new wave of purges in government. The 150 purge committees throughout the country seeking to expel "monarchists" and "agents of East and West" worked overtime. By mid-September, according to an incomplete tally, four thousand civil servants had lost their jobs and perhaps as many as two thousand to four thousand officers had been dismissed from the armed forces.[1]

There were other signs of severe political rifts. In late May, the Iranian Army Joint Staff announced that it had uncovered plans for a coup attempt by army officers. Two other plots were revealed in June. On July 10, Iranian security forces intervened at the last second to foil a potential coup by royalist Iranian air force officers to bomb Khomeini's home and seize strategic military installations. This plot, probably the most serious threat to the revolutionary regime since its takeover in February 1979, was apparently organized from Paris by former Prime Minister Bakhtiar and probably received financial support from Iraq.

Bani-Sadr said he had advance warning of the coup but allowed it to develop in order to identify dissident elements within the military. More than ninety people, most of them military officers, were eventually executed for participation in the attempted overthrow.

Many Iranians in the exile community believed the plot had been betrayed by Manuchehr Ghorbanifar, a businessman and arms dealer with well-established connections to both Iranian and Israeli intelligence.[2] Ghorbanifar, who had left Iran before the revolution, was close to Bakhtiar at the time of the coup, and many suspected that he betrayed the plot as a means of establishing his credibility with the Khomeini regime. Ghorbanifar denied these charges, but suspicions revived when he emerged later as the principal contact with Tehran during the Iran-Contra Affair. He was also being recruited by U.S. intelligence during this same period, from January to September 1980, but was rejected on the grounds that he could not be trusted.[3]

On July 18, scarcely a week after the abortive coup attempt, gunmen tried to assassinate Bakhtiar in Paris. Iran officially denied responsibility, but its fingerprints were unmistakable. The leader of the hit team, Anis Naccache, was an Iranian national, and Iran's insistence on his release from prison after his conviction complicated all subsequent efforts to improve Iranian-French relations. (Efforts continued, however, to eliminate Bakhtiar, who had been sentenced to death by an Iranian religious court in May 1979. In August 1991, despite round-the-clock police protection, the former prime minister and his secretary were stabbed to death in Bakhtiar's home in a quiet suburb outside Paris.)[4]

This surge of political violence throughout the summer of 1980, together with the growing threat of war with Iraq, wholly engaged Iran's leaders and inhibited any efforts toward a settlement of the hostage crisis. In fact, from the Iranian perspective, the hostage issue by this point was more of an irritant than an imperative. The ideological fireworks had served their purpose admirably by mobilizing the population behind Khomeini's radical program of clerical rule, but they were no longer needed.

But by the first week of September, circumstances conspired to move the hostage issue back to the center of attention in Tehran. Iraq was accelerating its preparations for war, and the mounting frequency and intensity of skirmishes along the border no longer permitted the Iranian leadership to ignore the danger. As long as the hostages were being held, Iran was denied both its $12 billion or so in monetary assets frozen in U.S. banks, and the military spare parts that had been trapped in the pipeline when the crisis erupted. The U.S. embargo, although insufficient to bring Iran to its knees economically, severely complicated efforts to purchase military equipment, for Iran was forced to purchase limited quantities of relatively low-technology items through intermediaries such as North Korea, or else to pay exorbitant rates for first-line equipment on the black market.

Thus, even though the clerics and technocrats had failed to resolve the internal political disputes that had preoccupied them throughout the summer, they nonetheless agreed on a temporary truce. Prodded by Khomeini, Bani-Sadr and the IRP agreed to disagree over the selection of a Cabinet. Fourteen positions were filled and the remaining seven posts continued in a caretaker status.[5] At least technically, this satisfied Khomeini's earlier injunction that the hostage issue could only be addressed after a new government had been formed. The way was now open for the clerical forces to try a new bargaining ploy.

There is an old Persian proverb that says, "The only thing better than having a rich man who wants to buy your carpet is to have two rich men who both want to buy your carpet." With a clear understanding of the importance of the hostage issue in the American presidential campaign, the Beheshti faction of the IRP already had in hand one very attractive offer for the American hostages from Casey and the Republicans. Would the Democrats in the Carter administration come up with an even higher bid?

On September 9, one day before the Majles approved the truncated Cabinet, Iran delivered an authoritative offer to the U.S. government, the first in the ten months since the hostage crisis began. Early that morning, an Iranian emissary named Sadegh Tabatabai contacted Gerhard Ritzel, the West German ambassador in Tehran, and asked him to deliver an urgent message to Washington calling for direct negotiations to end the hostage crisis.

Tabatabai was little more than a name to the hostage negotiating group in Washington, though he would become a familiar—even notorious—participant in the secret U.S.-Iranian arms dealings of the 1980s. Only thirty-seven years old in the fall of 1980, Tabatabai was already an experienced member of the revolutionary government. He had been the deputy interior minister in the provisional government of Mehdi Bazargan immediately after the revolution. Shortly thereafter he became the official government spokesman, then deputy prime minister. After the Bazargan government fell in November 1979, Tabatabai became the director of the prime minister's office, a position of great political authority that he held until the new Cabinet was approved on September 10, 1980.

Tabatabai was unique among the new revolutionary elite of Iran as a Western-educated scientist with close family ties to Khomeini. He had lived and studied for many years in West Germany, where he earned a doctorate in biochemistry from the University of Karlsruhe. Because of this background and his fluent German, in the years after the revolution he developed good contacts with senior West German officials, including Minister of Foreign Affairs Hans-Dietrich Genscher. The marriage of Tabatabai's sister to Ahmed Khomeini, the ayatollah's only surviving son, gave him access to the innermost circles of power and protection against changes in the political wind. It also made him the ideal man to act as Khomeini's trusted emissary to the Western world. Tabatabai was an attractive and dynamic man who so relished his frequent trips outside Iran that Washington gave him the code name The Traveller. He was a born dealer, and he thrived in the furtive world of arms dealers and high stakes.[6]

The message Tabatabai asked the West Germans to relay to Washington was a classic Iranian opening gambit, skillfully blending concessions, delicately implied threats, truths, half-truths, and outrageous lies. The conditions he offered were relatively mild and in some respects resembled those outlined privately to Colonel Scott by Khamene'i on May Day in Tabriz: (1) the unfreezing of Iranian assets; (2) a binding commitment of no U.S. military or political intervention in Iranian affairs; and (3) the return of the shah's assets. Khomeini later added a fourth: cancellation of all U.S. claims against Iran.[7] As they stood, the demands were not acceptable to the United States, but they did offer a reasonable basis for negotiation.

According to Tabatabai's message of September 9, a small group of senior officials had met the night before. They were of the opinion, he said, that the hostage issue could be resolved before November 4, the first anniversary of the hostage-taking. That, of course, was also the date of the U.S. presidential election, and its mention was a not-too-subtle reminder to the Carter administration that Iran understood the political stakes and was prepared to use them as leverage if necessary. To underline the sense of urgency, Tabatabai asked for a U.S. response within forty-eight hours and announced that he would arrive in Germany to begin talks three days later.

Tabatabai said that Khomeini had approved this approach, that the message had been prepared by three individuals—himself, Ahmed Khomeini, and Rafsanjani—and that only a tiny group of individuals knew about the initiative. Although the circle was probably larger than he suggested, his statement was essentially correct. The message was unquestionably initiated by the clerical faction around Ayatollah Beheshti. Bani-Sadr did not learn about it until a month later.

Tabatabai also said that he and Ahmed Khomeini had informally canvassed two-thirds of the Majles members, who supported a resolution of the hostage issue. That statement was obviously intended to reassure Washington that Tabatabai and the young Khomeini had the votes to implement an agreement, and it may have fairly represented their own judgment that Tabatabai and his allies could push an agreement through the parliament. It was, however, a half-truth at best. No serious preparatory work had been undertaken with the Majles, and later many of its members resisted the effort at every step.

Finally, as the ultimate incentive for immediate action, Tabatabai warned that Khomeini was very ill and that he might die within a matter of hours. This was pure invention. At the time, Khomeini was approaching his seventy-eighth birthday, and there were persistent rumors that he was in poor health, especially after having been hospitalized earlier in the year for a heart condition. Khomeini may have been tired, but according to Bani-Sadr and others who dealt with him regularly, his health at this time was perfectly satisfactory, and he was actively engaged in day-to-day politics. Deputy Secretary of State Warren Christopher and his negotiating team received this claim with great skepticism and scarcely mentioned it in the hectic discussions of the following days, but the Iranians seemed to be fascinated with the ploy. They would use it again, with considerably more success, five years later in the Iran-Contra Affair.[8]

The Iranian message had two other elements, which did not appear in the written version Washington received and which have never been made public.[9] Tabatabai's original proposal included a demand for the United States to apologize to the Iranian people for its past actions in Iran. Ambassador Ritzel knew that Washington would reject such a request, and he asked Tabatabai to delete it from the list. Tabatabai said he would check. Several hours later, he called Ritzel and said that the demand for an apology would be deleted from the demands.

That was absolutely crucial. Washington's positive reaction to the Iranian message was based largely on the fact that it had omitted any request for an apology. Over the previous ten months of the hostage crisis, the Carter administration had made it clear that there would be no apology and that this condition was non-negotiable. The unilateral action of the West German ambassador, which was never reported to Washington, cleared the way for substantive talks and was instrumental in getting a quick affirmative reply from the American side. The Iranians, moreover, were not giving up much; the omission of this condition was consistent with the Iranian position as outlined by Khamene'i in his conversation with Colonel Scott four months earlier.

The second "invisible" condition in Tabatabai's message was a demand for the return of all Iranian military equipment being held by the United States. The West German Foreign Ministry was well aware of the Carter administration's reluctance to engage in a perceived trade of arms for hostages, so after some hesitation Bonn decided to delete the military condition from the message. The West German diplomats reasoned that this subject could be raised verbally in the talks, but they felt it was too sensitive to be included in the written list of Iranian demands.

In this case, the West Germans may have been unduly sensitive. When the message was received in Washington, my colleagues and I were surprised that it made no mention of Iran's frozen military assets. While such a demand would have been unwelcome to the Carter administration, it certainly would have been viewed as a legitimate negotiating point.

In fact, the absence of any mention of military equipment in Tabatabai's list of conditions may have had an adverse effect on the negotiations. The working assumption of the negotiating team in Washington, based on the written demands of the original message, was that the question of military supply was not among Iran's highest priorities. That assumption was false. As a result, when the arms issue did arise in the negotiations, Washington never accorded it the degree of urgency and importance that the Iranians probably intended.

On September 11, two days after Iran's offer was received, Washington relayed a message back to Tehran through the West Germans, accepting in principle the invitation for secret talks. Christopher and his small negotiating team continued to wonder, however, whether this was an authoritative channel or simply the views of a breakaway faction that did not have Khomeini's backing. On the following day, those doubts were removed. A radio announcer in Tehran read a rambling speech by Khomeini. Near the end, obviously spliced into the text, was a brief statement of conditions for the release of the hostages that included the points identified in Tabatabai's message three days earlier. There was no mention of an apology or of military equipment. The signal seemed to be clear, and the talks were on.[10]

Christopher quickly assembled a negotiating team and flew to West Germany. Four black Mercedes limos swept the American team from the air force base to Schloss Gymnich, a secluded old palace outside Bonn. Christopher met secretly with Sadegh Tabatabai on September 16 and 18 in the presence of Foreign Minister Genscher.[11] It soon became apparent that the question of military supply could not be avoided. The United States held a substantial amount of Iranian military equipment, including some $300 million worth of military items that Iran had paid for but that had been frozen in the delivery pipeline at the time of the revolution. The matériel consisted of an almost random assortment of military hardware, from Harpoon missiles to truck parts. Since this was undeniably Iran's property, there was never any doubt on the part of the U.S. negotiators that at some point, either it would have to be returned to Iran or else Iran would have to be compensated.[12] The only question was whether its return should be tied to the release of the hostages.

As a member of the negotiating team, I was responsible for preparing a weapons inventory. Before Warren Christopher's first meeting with Tabatabai, I had separated these items into three categories:

1. About $50 million of nonlethal and nonsensitive items: for example, tires, trucks, or routine spares.
2. Approximately $100 million worth of "gray area" items, which were not classified and not lethal in themselves, but which could be used as part of offensive weapons systems such as aircraft.
3. Another $150 million or so of bombs, missiles, or items that incorporated sensitive technology or software.[13]

Though arms were not mentioned as a condition in Tabatabai's message of September 9, the Iranians did include a suggestion that the United States might consider providing military equipment in lieu of nonmilitary Iranian assets that had been attached by U.S. courts. Tabatabai and his group evidently understood that the court attachments of Iran's assets in the United States could not easily be reversed, and they were ready to bargain. Their preferred unit of exchange was arms.

When Christopher did not mention military supplies in his initial presentation of the U.S. position on September 16, Tabatabai pointedly asked whether the United States would be willing to supply Iran with spare parts for its American weapons systems after the hostages were free. Christopher was very guarded in his response, mentioning only the $50 million order for nonlethal equipment already paid for by Iran. He suggested that the introduction of military resupply issues would complicate the negotiations. Tabatabai did not press further, and the matter was dropped.

Was that all there was to it? The Carter administration was indeed uncomfortable with the idea of sending military equipment to Iran. They had no desire to give the impression of rewarding Iran for hostage-taking, nor did they want it to appear that the United States was siding with Iran in its incipient border conflict with Iraq. Christopher was therefore relieved when Tabatabai did not insist. Once the hostage crisis had ended, however, there would be no legal basis for denying Iran the equipment it had already paid for. So the $300 million package remained on the table.

But that was not what Tabatabai had asked, and it was probably not what Iran wanted. Tabatabai's suggestion of arms deliveries to compensate Iran for dollar accounts that were under court attachment, and his inquiry whether the United States would resume military deliveries once the hostages were free, did not concern the military equipment that happened to be in the pipeline at the time of the revolution but was a first step toward initiating a new military-supply relationship. He was, in effect, offering a swap of arms for hostages. And the American negotiators made it clear by their failure to respond that this was not a welcome proposition.

If these talks had been strictly a two-sided game between Iran and the U.S. government, then the American negotiators would have been in a position to either accept or reject the Iranian suggestions, which they regarded as a preliminary feeler to see if the United States was prepared, in effect, to pay military ransom for the hostages. When the offer was pointedly ignored, Iran had the choice either to insist on military supply as a condition for the hostages' release or else to drop the idea and proceed with the discussions on other grounds. Iran did not insist, and Christopher and his team drew the reasonable conclusion that Iran was unwilling to press the military issue.

None of us were surprised at this hesitation, since a key rallying point for the revolutionaries had been total opposition to the shah's military links with the United States. We believed that the resumption of overt arms deals with the United States would have been extraordinarily controversial and divisive within Iran. Consequently, we focused on the very thorny issues of how to unfreeze Iranian financial assets and how to address the Iranians' demands concerning the shah's assets in the United States.

If, however, the negotiation was not a two-sided game, then this exchange takes on quite a different interpretation. According to Jamshid Hashemi, by the time Tabatabai met with Warren Christopher, William Casey had already promised Iran that the Republicans would reopen an arms relationship once Ronald Reagan was in office, provided the hostages were released after the inauguration. If that is true, then Tabatabai's several suggestions about arms supply may well have been solicitations for a bid from the U.S. government, which could then be compared with Casey's bid. The failure of the Carter administration to respond to Iran's suggestions of an arms-for-hostages swap did not put the issue to rest, as we believed at the time. Rather, it may have enhanced the attractiveness of Casey's offer and increased the likelihood of its being accepted.

As a result of the Republicans' political treachery, the Carter administration's principled insistence that it would not swap arms for hostages—a decision that required some considerable measure of courage at the time—is revealed to have been irrelevant and self-defeating. It was irrelevant since the Iranians were aware that an arms-for-hostages swap was available elsewhere even if Carter rejected it. It was self-defeating since it put the administration in a no-win situation in its negotiations over the hostages. By refusing to compromise for his own political advantage, Carter inadvertently helped to ensure that the hostages would not be released until the next administration took office.

Looking back, the Carter administration appears to have been far too trusting and particularly blind to the intrigue swirling around it. Occasional hints and clues were overlooked or simply ignored in the noise of events. On September 6, Sadegh Ghotbzadeh, who was still the acting foreign minister of Iran, was quoted by Agence France Presse that he had information that presidential candidate Ronald Reagan was "trying to block a solution" to the hostage crisis.[14] On September 16, Ghotbzadeh was again quoted as saying that "Reagan, supported by Kissinger and others, has no intention of resolving the problem. They will do everything in their power to block it."[15] Two friends of Ghotbzadeh who spoke to him frequently during this period said that he insisted repeatedly that the Republicans were in contact with elements in Iran to try to block a hostage release.[16] Sadegh Ghotbzadeh stands out as the only person in either Iran or the United States who was prepared to say consistently and openly in 1980 what some of us have only begun to say more than a decade later.

Moreover, insufficient attention was paid to the fact that Reagan chose to make his first and only substantive statement about the hostage negotiations in the entire campaign on September 13, the day after Khomeini's speech announcing the conditions for the release of the hostages. Reagan delivered a carefully prepared response to Khomeini's statement, saying that the United States should agree to most of Khomeini's demands. The United States "can and should" agree to free frozen Iranian assets, he said. The United States should be willing to cancel claims against Iran and pledge nonintervention in Iran's domestic affairs. The return of the former shah's assets, Reagan noted, could not be done without "due process of law." "Having agreed to these points," he said, "we must above all insist that the hostages be released immediately upon the conclusion of an agreement, that there be no delays, introduction of additional demands, or waiting for fulfillment of the agreement." Reagan emphasized that he would not make negotiations with Iran a partisan issue.[17]

President Carter issued a pro forma criticism of Reagan for injecting himself into ongoing negotiations, but the Reagan statement was regarded as odd at the time. Reagan and his campaign aides repeatedly refused to be briefed on the status of the negotiations with Iran, and Reagan's occasional public statements about the hostages were little more than insinuations about Carter's mishandling of the crisis. Since August 20 he had said nothing at all on the subject, a fact that had attracted some attention in the media. His September 13 statement, however, came only twenty-four hours after Khomeini's speech, and it outlined in some detail a recommended and considered U.S. negotiating position. That position, it deserves to be noted, was entirely consistent with the agreement that William Casey had concluded with Mehdi Karrubi in Madrid one month earlier.

Finally, Mohammed Ibrahim Asgharzadeh, who was the spokesman for the hostages' captors in 1980 (and who later became a member of the Iranian parliament), would report many years afterward that he had received a message from Ronald Reagan's campaign asking that the Republicans be allowed to visit the hostages, and that during the summer of 1980, "there were attempts through different channels to send Republican figures to Iran." Though he said this had made no impact on the students' decisions regarding the hostages, Asgharzadeh told Agence France Presse that "I don't exclude the fact that the Republicans, in the very last months, tried to delay the liberation of the hostages."[18]

It is also apparent in retrospect that the Carter administration severely underestimated Iran's anxiety about the possibility of war with Iraq. Although the U.S. intelligence community expected an escalation of border skirmishes, perhaps with heavy fighting in some sectors, there was no conclusive evidence that Iraq intended to launch a full-scale invasion. Before the month of September was out, these estimates had been shattered.

The dispersal of the hostages to sites throughout Iran had proved to be a logistical nightmare. It required twelve men, for example, to guard and care for Colonel Scott and his three companions in Tabriz. Communications and transport were also complicated and expensive. The result was that during the summer of 1980, all of the hostages were slowly and secretly brought back to Tehran. Barry Rosen and his compatriots arrived from Qom in mid-June. Chuck Scott and some of the other hostages were moved on July 12. Moorhead Kennedy, who had been held with another group of hostages at a large private estate in Isfahan, was apparently among the last to arrive in Tehran, on August 16.[19] This time, however, the hostages were installed in Komiteh Prison, on the outskirts of the city in the vicinity of the airport.

Komiteh was one of the most notorious prisons in Iran, where political prisoners had been incarcerated and tortured under the shah. Khamene'i, the regime's Friday prayer leader, had spent nearly a year inside its walls when he was arrested for antiregime political activities in the mid-1970s. The prison was closed after the revolution, but it was reopened as the new regime began to need space to incarcerate and torture its own growing number of political opponents.

The decision to move the hostages to Komiteh Prison was rich in ironies. The prison got its name under the shah, when it was controlled by the "Committee for the Coordination of Counter-Terrorist Operations." After the revolution, no change of name was required since the prison was turned over to the revolutionary "committees" or komitehs. The man responsible for supervising the activities of the komitehs, including management of Komiteh Prison, was a radical by the name of Behzad Nabavi. Nabavi, who acquired institutional responsibility for the incarceration of the hostages in the summer of 1980, would be named a few months later as the head of the Majles commission to negotiate the terms of their release.

The prison was a fortress with thick walls. Its sequential checkpoints were blocked by heavy metal doors and manned by professional security guards. The maximum-security area, where most of the hostages were held, consisted of blocks of underground cells. A rescue team attempting to penetrate these defenses would have faced a formidable military and engineering task. That had not been the case with the U.S. Embassy compound, but then again, a rescue from Komiteh was never an option, since U.S. intelligence did not know the hostages were there.

On September 22, while waiting for their usual meal of bread and soup, Colonel Scott and the other U.S. hostages were shaken by a series of explosions. From their cells in Komiteh Prison they could hear the scream of jets pulling out of dives above Mehrabad airport. Navy officer Don Sharer identified the aircraft as Soviet-made MiGs by the sound of their engines. The jailors, muttering nervously among themselves, extinguished all lights. Iraq, the hostages guessed, had launched a military attack on Iran.[20]

Although the threat had been building since April, the magnitude of the Iraqi attack, when it finally came, was startling. Some forty-five thousand Iraqi ground troops attacked on a wide front across the southern border into Iran's southwestern province of Khuzistan.[21] Taking a page from Israel's tactics in the 1967 Six-Day War, Iraqi fighter-bombers struck simultaneously and without warning at all Iranian military airfields within their range. However, unlike the Israeli strikes against Egypt and Syria thirteen years earlier, the Iraqi attack failed to cripple the Iranian air force.

Throughout the summer, Iraq had been in close contact with former Iranian Prime Minister Shahpour Bakhtiar, General Gholam Ali Oveissi, and other exiled opponents to Khomeini. These Iranians had assured Iraqi intelligence that Iran's military was in total disarray, that it would collapse in the face of a massive strike, and that the Tehran government would soon disintegrate in the face of overwhelming military defeat. Iraq was also confident that the predominantly Arab population of Khuzistan, which Iraqi maps claimed as "Arabistan," would rise up to welcome their Arab brothers from Iraq.

The Iraqis were wildly optimistic in their plans for victory, confident that their military could equal and perhaps even beat the time in which the Israelis had won the Six-Day War. The Iraqi ambassador to the United Nations, Ismet Kittani, deliberately tried to stall any action by the Security Council until after Iraq had scored a complete victory. On the third day of the war, a Western diplomat asked him, "How many days do your generals need" to complete the military operation? "Two to three days," he replied.[22] But after six days had elapsed with no clear Iraqi victory in sight, Kittani lobbied the Security Council to accept his nation's view of the conflict. To Iran's dismay, Resolution 479 referred to the conflict as a "situation" rather than a "war," thereby relieving the Security Council of any responsibility under the U.N. Charter to determine if an aggression had occurred. The words "cease-fire" were deliberately omitted, since the phrase might imply withdrawal of Iraqi forces from Iranian territory. Indeed, the resolution did not call for any withdrawal but instead called for the parties "to refrain immediately from the further use of force," a formulation that would permit Iraqi troops to remain in Iran.

The Iraqis, who had conducted a vigorous and effective lobbying campaign to dilute the language of the resolution, had the active support of the powerful Arab bloc at the United Nations as well as the tacit support of many other states that disliked or feared the new revolutionary government in Tehran. Iran, by contrast, refused to participate or even acknowledge the role of the United Nations, and virtually no government was prepared to speak on Iran's behalf, except for some quiet efforts by Pakistan.

Iran had repeatedly thumbed its nose at the United Nations and the

World Court throughout the hostage crisis, and now it was paying the price. Many world leaders privately hoped that Saddam Hussein would succeed in bringing down the Khomeini regime and were not inclined to interfere while his troops still appeared to be winning. Iran was widely and accurately perceived as a renegade state that flouted international law and denied the legitimacy of international institutions. It scarcely seemed to deserve the protection of those same institutions.

Although understandable in terms of realpolitik, Resolution 479 confirmed the Iranians' perception of the Security Council as a hostile institution and further isolated them from the world community.

A more immediate result of the Iraqi invasion was to inject a sense of urgency and uncertainty into the hostage negotiations. Tabatabai, who had already reported the results of his talks with Christopher via diplomatic channels and who had planned to return to Iran on the day of the Iraqi invasion, had to remain in Europe until Tehran's airports reopened. In the meantime, the West German Foreign Ministry had prepared a detailed summary of the Christopher-Tabatabai talks, and an agreed text was initialed by both sides.

In Iran, while Tabatabai was still in Germany, the Majles had begun discussing the formation of a commission to negotiate the release of the American hostages. Those proceedings were interrupted by the Iraqi invasion, which many senior figures in Iran believed the United States had encouraged. Four days after the attack, Grand Ayatollah Hoseyn 'Ali Montazeri, speaking in the holy city of Qom, said the war "was forced upon us by the United States. . . . [It] will definitely have an adverse effect and the issue of the hostages will not be solved so soon."[23]

The charge was untrue. At the time of the invasion, the United States had no diplomatic relations with Iraq, and contacts with Baghdad were extremely limited. On the day after the attack, President Carter announced that "our own position is one of strict neutrality and we're doing all we can through the United Nations and other means to bring a peaceful conclusion" to the war.[24] In the days that followed, the United States was among the most active of the members of the United Nations Security Council to seek international action to stop the war, including a lengthy private discussion on the matter between Secretary of State Muskie and Soviet Foreign Minister Andrei A. Gromyko in New York.[25] On September 27, the United States persuaded Oman and other Gulf states not to allow Iraq to launch air strikes against Iran from their territory.[26]

Iran's revolutionary leaders were so obviously surprised by the Iraqi attack and preparations were so inadequate that it was almost irresistible to blame the Great Satan for their embarrassing failures. Blaming the United States also fit neatly with the instinctive Iranian belief that nothing ever happens by accident and that insidious external powers are behind every event. The fact that the Iraqi attack put new pressure on Iran to end the hostage crisis was enough to persuade most Iranians that the United States must have encouraged Iraq to launch the war. The chief culprit, in many Iranians' eyes, was National Security Adviser Zbigniew Brzezinski. A myth arose that Brzezinski had met secretly with Iraqi President Saddam Hussein to plan the invasion, a myth that Bani-Sadr and other Iranians believe to this day.[27]

Was this just a case of Iranian paranoia? Yes and no. Although Iranian suspicions of a secret Brzezinski-Saddam meeting were patently untrue,[28] Brzezinski was the leading advocate within the U.S. government for exerting political, diplomatic, and military pressure on Iran to release the hostages. It is also true that during the summer of 1980 Iraq was seriously considering restoring diplomatic relations with the United States. According to Saddam Hussein, "The decision to establish relations with the U.S. was taken in 1980 during the two months prior to the war between us and Iran," but Iraq postponed the decision "when the war started . . . to avoid misinterpretation."[29] Finally, the leaders in Iran were no doubt aware that the United States was maintaining contact with a number of Iranian exiles in Europe, some of whom were independently providing advice and encouragement to Saddam Hussein to invade Iran.[30] The United States was not involved in their discussions with Iraq, but the Iranians would never believe that.

In fact, during this period most of the White House's attention was focused on the Soviet Union. Intelligence reports suggested that the U.S.S.R. might be planning a military foray into the Persian Gulf; mindful of the Soviet invasion of Afghanistan only nine months earlier, Brzezinski called a series of urgent policy meetings. The Iraqi military buildup, however, prompted no such meetings. By October 1980, even Brzezinski, despite his earlier views, was counseling President Carter to oppose the Iraqi occupation of Iran because of the danger that it would encourage Soviet penetration.[31]

The outbreak of war in the midst of the hostage negotiations had two major effects. First, it focused Iran's attention on the urgency of finding a solution to the hostage problem in order to end Tehran's diplomatic isolation and break the arms embargo.[32] Second, however, the deep suspicion and anger about possible U.S. collusion with Iraq reinforced Iran's instinctive reluctance to work with the Carter administration and enhanced the attractiveness of alternative strategies.

· 6 ·

SCRAMBLING FOR
POSITION

I n the United States and Iran, rival foreign policies were being pursued
by rival factions. The possibilities for miscalculation were immense,
and the uncertainties of each party were multiplied by the absence of a
completely reliable center to deal with in either country. Israel, for its part,
tenaciously clung to its Doctrine of the Periphery, which required it to
maintain a clandestine arms relationship with Iran while simultaneously
seeking not to offend its chief patron, the United States.

Israel was not alone among U.S. allies in benefiting directly or indirectly
from the hostage crisis. Other countries, too, had national interests of their
own to look after. Years later, a former high official in the Iranian government would tell the following story:

The British were not loyal to [the United States] during the hostage
crisis. The U.K. ambassador came to me at that time and since I was
rather naive he had to put it very clearly. He told me that the British
were prepared to sell military equipment to us despite the embargo. I

can confirm that we got items from Italy, including Beretta pistols. I even had one myself.[1]

All factions sought to obtain the services of individuals who had knowledge of the inner workings of the mysterious circle of revolutionaries around Khomeini and who might act as private conduits in communicating with Tehran. This sweep netted some curious specimens, offering a rare and revealing glimpse into the twilight zone where international politics mingles with private finance and where intelligence operations blend into the underworld.

This was Eric Ambler Land, the world of the spy novel, where marginal men pursued their precarious destinies in a haze of ambiguity, uncertain loyalties, and shifting fortunes. Commonly associated with fiction, this world was all too real. Anyone who has ever made an international flight has probably unknowingly shared an airplane cabin with an arms dealer, a courier, or someone engaged in some other dubious or perhaps dangerous enterprise. An acquaintance of mine, who was involved in investigating the December 1988 bombing of Pan Am flight 103 and who participated in checking out the identities of all 259 passengers and crew, later remarked that the experience was so sobering that he would never again feel the same about taking an international flight. An intelligence officer with years of contact with the international netherworld, he nonetheless was astonished to discover how many suspicious characters happened to find themselves—apparently quite by chance—on a single transatlantic flight.

For most of us involved in the hostage affair, the discovery of this hidden stratum below the surface of events came as a revelation. Its schemes and subterfuges swirled about us invisibly as we went about our daily business. That business was complicated by the efforts of other countries—France, for example, which sought to take advantage of the American predicament.

A number of major French companies were still operating in Iran, and the French government was concerned about the safety of its citizens working there. The easiest way to buy protection was to assist the Iranian revolutionaries quietly with their clandestine arms purchases. If the arms traffic remained within reasonable bounds, it would probably remain undetected. If discovered, the French government could always disavow the operation as an unauthorized private gunrunning scheme.

Over the summer of 1980, Ahmed Heidari and Karim Minachi of the Interparts company in Iran had been in touch with Cargo Masters, an air-charter firm in Paris that specialized in "difficult" deliveries.[2] They had hoped to arrange up to seventy flights by Boeing 707s ferrying arms for Iran's Revolutionary Guards from Portugal to Iran. But an expected $200 million Iranian letter of credit never materialized, and the operation was aborted.[3]

In August, Heidari and his associates were ready to try again. They came to France with a procurement list consisting of spare parts for F-4, F-5, and F-14 aircraft, ground radars, and technical assistance and train-ing. Heidari's principal contact in France was Roger Faulques, a man who had recruited and trained military and paramilitary forces for operations in Africa and the Middle East. Heidari and Faulques reached an agreement in principle, subject to financial and technical arrangements, but Faulques insisted that he would do nothing without at least tacit approval by French intelligence.

To that end, a representative of Faulques met with Alain Gagneron de Marolles at the latter's home near Bordeaux in early September. De Ma-rolles was the director of operations in the Service de Documentation Ex-térieur et de Contre-Espionage (SDECE), the French secret service, and a principal deputy to Count Alexandre de Marenches, SDECE's head. De Marolles gave his approval, with the understanding that SDECE would be kept fully informed and could veto any operations exceeding the agreed limits of arms and technical assistance. Heidari's proposed deal was, of course, in direct violation of the U.S. arms embargo on Iran, which France had agreed to respect.

De Marenches had an interest in following the hostage affair and the unfolding presidential campaign in the United States that was inextricably bound up with his relationship with William Casey. Both had worked with the Resistance during World War II, and both shared a deep interest in conservative issues and in the intelligence business. Perhaps most impor-tant, both had a deep disdain for Jimmy Carter.

De Marenches cultivated an aura of mystery throughout the eleven years he reigned over the Piscine, the SDECE headquarters. "I never once met the Press," he later recalled with obvious pleasure.[4] Though born to an aristocratic family, he never allowed his name to be listed in the French

Who's Who and his official biography ran only five lines, a brevity that delighted him. At six-foot-one and well over two hundred pounds, he was a presence that could not easily be ignored. The French super-spy was particularly fond of quoting the famous Chinese strategist Sun Tzu: "If you reveal the plans of the enemy, you will know which strategy will be effective and which will not." Jimmy Carter, he was sure, had no understanding of that, disbanding his covert intelligence service and thus achieving "a job which the other side could not have done, even if it had worked for decades." "Under Carter," he wrote later, "the Americans committed voluntary suicide, the consequences of which are irrevocable."[5]

During the summer of 1980 De Marenches met privately with Casey, who had flown to Europe at the instigation of Albert Jolis, a wealthy dealer in diamonds and precious metals with offices in Paris and London. Jolis had known Casey since their days together in the OSS during World War II, and they both had homes on Long Island in New York, where they saw each other from time to time. Jolis, a strong Reagan supporter, had been worried about the European media's contemptuous attitude toward Reagan. Casey and Richard Allen shared Jolis's concern, and so organized a series of meetings with major European media and political figures. Together with Jolis, they flew to London on June 30, where they met with Margaret Thatcher; then they went on to Paris for several days, and returned to the United States on July 3.[6]

The Casey–De Marenches meeting deserves at least a historical footnote since it established contact between the éminence grise of French intelligence and the man who, seven months later, would become the top intelligence official in the United States—and whose performance De Marenches would applaud, noting years later that at the CIA "things improved somewhat thanks to William Casey and the support given to him by President Reagan."[7] In late 1980, after the election, De Marenches would be invited to meet Reagan in what may have been an unprecedented meeting between a foreign intelligence chief and a President-elect. They may well have had more to talk about than their shared attitudes toward the Soviet Union and their conservative philosophies.[8]

With approval from the French intelligence service in hand, Faulques and Heidari began planning their arms network in detail. They quickly agreed that it was impossible to design a proper arms-supply channel unless they knew exactly what Iran needed. It was decided to send a technical team to Iran to develop a procurement list. In September 1980, Jacques Montanès, a stocky French pilot who worked for Cargo Masters, was asked to join a three-man team to conduct a survey of Iran's military and civil requirements. The work was dangerous, but the pay was good. Each member of the team was to be paid $180,000 for a three-month stint. They arrived in Tehran on September 14, just a week before the Iraqi blitzkrieg.[9]

On September 24 there was an important meeting of the general staff of the Iranian military, according to Ahmed Salamatian, who was present.[10] Salmatian was a member of the new Majles and a close political associate of President Bani-Sadr. The defense minister, General Javad Fakuri, made a particularly powerful presentation. The air force had launched hundreds of combat missions on the second day of the war, but Fakuri, a highly respected combat pilot, said that such a level of operations could be sustained for only a few more days unless the air force could obtain spares, especially tires for the F-4 fighter-bombers. Three possible sources were identified: Pakistan, North Korea, and Israel; in addition there was the possibility of making purchases in Europe. A more formal organization was needed to organize the "indirect"—that is, clandestine—purchases of arms, and Sadegh Tabatabai was nominated to head the operation.

On the same day, Jacques Montanès and his associates worked around the clock with their Iranian counterparts from all three military services. To keep Iran's military machine in overdrive, an extensive list of military hardware needed to be purchased, and Montanès's group outlined a tentative four-stage delivery schedule for weapons whose value totaled $128 million. In addition to aircraft tires and large quantities of munitions of all sorts, they identified shortages of Israeli radio equipment in use by the Iranian military, British radar spares, spares for French torpedo boats, and spares for Israeli Tampela mortars. There was a particularly urgent need for motors and spares for Scorpio armored cars and for Iran's sizable inventory of British and American tanks.

About ten days later, Iranian authorities issued the first letters of credit to SETI International, the firm that represented Heidari and Interparts in France. At the same time, they confiscated the passports of Montanès and one of his colleagues. The Iranians, who had already been ripped off in a number of ill-fated arms deals, had decided this time to take out some insurance: The two Frenchmen were informed that they would remain as "guests" in Iran until all the promised military equipment was satisfactorily delivered.

Montanès and his colleague were not guarded, and they continued to live at their hotel in relatively pleasant conditions. They reported to work as before, and they even became good friends of some of their Iranian counterparts. But they could not leave the country. Montanès, with a family back in France, began to pray for a short war.

Meanwhile, according to three independent sources, senior Iranians, Israeli representatives, and individuals close to the Reagan campaign met in Frankfurt and Zurich between September 20 and 30.[11] Tabatabai, who was still in Europe at this time after his talks with Warren Christopher, was probably involved in these meetings. Following the Zurich meeting, a European arms dealer who had been negotiating a sale with Iran was told by his Iranian contact, Hamid Naqashan,[12] that the deal was off, at least for the time being, since the Iranians had discovered they could "get all the arms we need" from a new source. The arms, Naqashan said, were to be provided to Iran in return for assurances that the American hostages would not be released prior to the U.S. presidential elections.

On September 28, the Israeli deputy minister of defense, Mordechai Zippori, made a peculiar public statement. Israel, he said, could help Iran with weapons if the Iranians were to change their policies toward Israel.[13] Coming in the same week as the secret arms talks between Israeli and Iranian representatives in Zurich, this statement appeared to provide official confirmation of Israel's willingness to supply arms in accordance with the agreement. This interpretation would acquire additional credibility a month later, when Zippori made an almost identical statement just prior to a well-documented Israeli delivery of military equipment to Iran, a secret delivery that was carried out without U.S. knowledge or permission.

While talking with reporters on September 29, Prime Minister Menachem Begin revealed publicly for the first time that in collaboration with the shah's government Israel had furnished weapons and training to Kurdish rebels in Iraq from 1965 to 1975.[14] This unprecedented statement, which came at the very moment when Iran was again preparing to mobilize the Iraqi Kurds for a major uprising against Saddam Hussein, was unmistakably a signal. It reminded the Iranians that Israel's help with the Kurds had been very useful in the past. More important, the nature and timing of this statement seemed to suggest that the very highest levels of the Israeli government were aware of Iran's plans in Kurdistan and were potentially prepared to cooperate. This was not just rhetoric. Although Israel had been cut off from direct contact with the Kurds since 1975, they had maintained their relationship with the Kurdish leadership, including regular short-wave radio contact. As a result, the Kurdish leaders still looked to Israel for advice and guidance. The Iranians who were active in promoting rebellion in Kurdistan at the time welcomed Begin's remarks as evidence of Israeli support for a new rebellion.[15]

On October 1, three days after Zippori's statement, former Israeli Defense Minister Moshe Dayan interrupted a private visit to Europe to hold a press conference in Vienna. Iran, he declared, could not win the war without U.S. help, specifically supplies, military spare parts, and munitions. Iran had to choose: either sue for peace or else call on Washington for help. He urged the United States to forget the past and, once the hostages were free, to help Iran keep up its defenses.[16]

One week later, Ephraim Evron, the Israeli ambassador in Washington, informed Secretary of State Muskie of Israel's concern that an Iraqi victory in the war would alter the balance of power in the Middle East. According to several high-level Israeli sources, these and other presentations were intended to encourage U.S.-Israeli cooperation in providing military equipment to Iran, and the Israelis were disappointed when they received no positive response.[17] None of the Americans involved in these exchanges remembered them as anything more than general expressions of Israeli concern about a possible Iraqi victory, with no suggestion of any joint action. There was certainly no hint that Israel was in direct contact with Iran or that it might proceed independently with an arms-supply program.

Nevertheless, Israel had become aware of Heidari's attempt to supply Iran with arms via SETI International in France. Iranian funds were transferred to SETI via Zurich on October 11. Things were not running smoothly, however. Prices changed. The promised motors could not be found, and that part of the order had to be canceled and replaced by an order for, among other things, F-4 aircraft tires.[18]

In an effort to break the logjam, SETI approached Israeli diplomatic representatives in Paris. The Israelis showed an immediate interest and offered to make available a wide variety of equipment to Iran. Their only condition was that any Iranian intermediary must be an accredited representative of the Islamic Republic of Iran.[19] Apparently this was a standard requirement. Ahmed Heidari would later observe of his dealings with Israel: "They were always insisting that in order to purchase something I had to send a telex giving my name and saying I was acting in the name of the government of Iran."[20]

An Israeli diplomat then took SETI's list of requirements and forwarded them to Israel. Heidari was also in touch with the Israelis in Paris. On the recommendation of his source in Iran, whom he believed to be associated with Israeli intelligence, Heidari was introduced to someone named "Alain" at the Israeli Embassy in Paris. He and Alain agreed verbally that Israel would set up a meeting in Paris in the near future to discuss arms sales to Iran.[21]

Israeli military cooperation with Iran also took more overt forms. On September 30, Iranian F-4 fighter-bombers attacked the Iraqi nuclear complex Tamuze 17, which included the Osirak reactor and was located twenty miles east of Baghdad. The Iraqi nuclear facility, which purportedly had been built for peaceful purposes with the support of France and scientists from a number of other countries, appeared to be moving toward the production of weapons-grade fissionable material.

The prospect of Iraqi development of a nuclear weapon was obviously of great concern to Iran and other countries, particularly Israel, whose intelligence services had conducted a campaign of assassination and sabotage in France and elsewhere to disrupt Iraqi nuclear operations.[22] Israeli concern was so well-known that many suspected, incorrectly, that the strike—which damaged a number of buildings but failed to hit the reactor—was conducted by Israel under cover of the war.

One former Iranian official with good access to military planning at the time said that Israel provided Iran with information on how to attack the nuclear facility but that the Iraqi air defense was too great for the Iranian air force.[23] On the other hand, an Iranian general who was a senior commander in Iran's air force at the time claimed that the reactor bombing was an accident, maintaining that the strike was actually directed against a nearby air base and that the reactor site was hit by mistake.[24] President Bani-Sadr agreed, though conceding that he was not privy to the contacts being conducted by the Beheshti group with Israel: "If there was contact with Israel, I am unaware of it."[25] In any event, Israel would return to finish the job on June 7, 1981.

One of the most mystifying events of the entire election year took place in late September or early October 1980. The basic facts are not in dispute. Richard Allen, together with Robert McFarlane and Laurence Silberman, met at the L'Enfant Plaza Hotel in Washington, D.C., with a Middle Easterner who offered to arrange the release of the American hostages directly to the Republicans. Beyond that rudimentary description, however, there is nothing but disagreement. Even people who admit attending the same meetings cannot agree on exact dates, times, or places.

The meeting at the L'Enfant Plaza—a short stroll away from the Mall and the Smithsonian Castle—was first revealed by Allen, who, almost alone among the Reagan-Bush campaign officials, was willing to be interviewed in depth about the 1980 "October surprise" scenario. In April 1987, Allen described this meeting to Alfonso Chardy of *The Miami Herald*,[26] and thereafter he repeated his account on dozens of occasions. His description of the meeting is straightforward and has remained consistent over time.

Allen has said that he was initially contacted by Robert McFarlane, then a senior aide to Senator John Tower of Texas. Tower was a longtime friend of vice-presidential candidate George Bush and he was at that time the ranking Republican on the Senate Armed Services Committee. McFarlane, a retired Marine Corps colonel, had been the executive assistant of the National Security Council under Henry Kissinger and Brent Scowcroft in the Nixon and Ford administrations, and he was a strong supporter of the Reagan presidential candidacy.

Allen said that McFarlane called and "implored" him[27] to meet with "an individual claiming to be Iranian."[28] Allen later said he was reluctant to participate in such a meeting but finally acquiesced in response to McFarlane's entreaties. Since the man was expected to have "some interesting information about the hostages,"[29] Allen took the precaution of bringing with him as a witness Laurence Silberman, a former U.S. ambassador to Yugoslavia and the cochairman, with Allen, of the foreign-policy advisory group in the Reagan campaign. Allen later said that he refused to meet the Iranian in his office and instead chose the lobby of the L'Enfant Plaza Hotel as an appropriate public meeting place conveniently located halfway between his office and Capitol Hill.

According to Allen, Silberman, and McFarlane, they had a relatively brief meeting in late September with a man who appeared to be of Middle Eastern origin. This man, who claimed to be in contact with representatives of the Iranian government, made a presentation in which he offered to arrange the release of the American hostages directly to the Republican campaign. This offer was rejected out of hand, according to the three American participants, and the meeting was terminated abruptly. Allen and Silberman later insisted that the man made no mention of military equipment or the possibility of an arms-for-hostages swap.

None of the American participants could recall the man's name or identity. Allen said that he wrote a memorandum for the record, but he was never able to locate it and could not recall if it had gone to anyone else in the campaign. Silberman described the man as short, dark-haired, youngish, and unimpressive, with no presence or stature. He reminded Silberman of a "second-rate investment banker." The man was a flashy dresser, wearing Gucci loafers, and his remarks seemed to associate him not with Iran but with Egypt or possibly Morocco. His idea, according to Silberman, was "to induce the Iranian government to release the hostages to the Reagan campaign quickly—before the election—in order to embarrass the Carter Administration. There was no *quid pro quo* of any kind suggested." Rather, he suggested that the Iranians "wanted to release the hostages but did not want President Carter to reap the political credit." Silberman said he told the man his offer was totally unacceptable since "We have one President at a time."[30]

All of the American participants later said that they regarded the episode as a minor aberration. The offer, they argued, was outrageous and of no significance. Allen said he had no interest in a "self-starter and crook," that it was just "one of dozens of over-the-transom offers" that inevitably appeared in the course of a campaign, and for that reason it did not deserve to be reported to the Carter administration.[31] In fact, it was not reported to the administration, and that was a sensitive point with the participants.

Hushang Lavi, a self-described international arms merchant, claimed he was the unidentified "Middle Easterner" in the meeting. His account of the meeting directly contradicts some elements of the Allen/Silberman/McFarlane version. Lavi generally fit the description given by the three Republicans. With a broad nose, almost petulant lips, and a direct, intelligent gaze, he looked much like a carving of an ancient Egyptian pharaoh come to life, and could easily have been the "youngish Egyptian" Silberman remembered. In a videotaped interview almost ten years later his manner of dress fit the less-than-approving description given by Reagan's men: The pin-stripes on his dark suit were a bit too wide; highly starched cuffs stuck out too much from jacket sleeves that were a bit too short. A startlingly red tie with a cumbersome knot didn't quite hide the fact that the top button of his shirt was too tight to fasten. Highly polished Italian loafers completed the "second-rate investment banker" look.

Lavi, an Iranian expatriate, was born into a prominent Jewish merchant family in Tehran in about 1936. He attended Sacramento State College in the mid-1950s, and in 1968 moved permanently to the United States, becoming a citizen twenty years later. Lavi acquired considerable notoriety as the agent in the controversial but immensely lucrative sale of Grumman F-14 fighter aircraft to the shah's government, which embroiled him in years of contentious litigation. When General Toufanian, the shah's chief of military procurement, later expressed his pride in having opposed the payment of agents' fees, Hushang Lavi was surely one of the cases he had in mind.

For all the millions that Lavi made as an arms merchant, he was intensely proud of his adopted country and frequently sported a small American flag pin on his lapel. He liked to think of himself as a gentleman (repeatedly peppering his speech with "sir" to underscore this) and as a patriot, and, years after the meeting at L'Enfant Plaza, Lavi claimed that he had no expectation of any financial gain in the deal: "I had nothing to gain except to bring the hostages home. . . . It was my duty as a patriotic American, I would say."[32]

According to Lavi, he was in touch with "two representatives of the Iranian government" in the United States who outlined a proposal for a swap of the American hostages in return for U.S. spare F-14 parts that had already been paid for by Iran. Lavi said that he initiated the contact with the Republican campaign by a call to James A. Baker 3rd, who had managed Bush's campaign and was now a special assistant in the Reagan organization. This call resulted in the meeting in the L'Enfant Plaza Hotel, where, Lavi said, he met for about thirty minutes with Allen, Silberman, and McFarlane and outlined the arms-for-hostages plan in which the American hostages would be released to the Republicans in return for a pledge of F-14 parts.

According to Lavi, his offer was rejected, but his recollection differed from those of the Americans. Lavi said the three Americans refused his offer on the grounds that they were "in touch with the Iranians themselves" and did not need his assistance.[33] Both Allen and Silberman later insisted adamantly in interviews that the man they met was *not* Lavi.[34]

Should Lavi's claims be taken seriously? There is one important piece of evidence that lends weight to Lavi's story. A handwritten page from his notebook for October 2, 1980, was later located. It reads as follows:

OCT 2, 80

EASTERN SHUTTLE

TO D.C.

E. PLAZA HOTEL

    RING TELECON[?] WITH J. BAKER

TO MEET SILBERMAN, ALLEN

BOB MCFAR.

    40 PAGE DOCUMENT F14

PARTS ALREADY PAID FOR

IN RTUN OF HOSTAGES

SWAP IN KARACHI. CHARTER

707.

                [INITIAL]

The origin of this document is almost as interesting as its contents. Lavi himself never referred to it and never offered it as evidence, although his brother, Parviz, verified after Hushang's death that it was written in Hushang's distinctive script.[35] The note was discovered by journalist Robert Parry in 1990 among a jumble of papers in the briefcase of Ari Ben-Menashe while Ben-Menashe was in custody in New York. Although Parry made a copy of the page, he did not recognize its significance at the time, and the notebook entry was ignored until February 1991, after Lavi's death.

One of the most striking pieces of information in the note is the mention of an apparent contact with "J. Baker." As early as April 1988, in an interview with journalist Jonathan Silvers, Lavi said that he had originally contacted James Baker to request a meeting on the hostage issue.[36] According to Lavi, that contact eventually resulted in his meeting with Allen, Silberman, and McFarlane at the L'Enfant Plaza Hotel. Lavi's account of his call to Baker preceded by two years the discovery of the notebook entry.

The reference to a "40 page document [of] F14 parts already paid for" that were to be swapped for the hostages in Karachi, Pakistan, using a chartered Boeing 707 aircraft, is also identical to the offer Lavi subsequently made to Representative John Anderson's independent presidential campaign. That offer, which will be discussed in more detail below, was immediately reported to the Carter administration and is fully documented.[37] Based on the handwriting and the close resemblance between the contents of the note and Lavi's own descriptions of events, there is good reason to believe that the note is authentic.

The existence of this page from Hushang Lavi's notebook does not, in itself, prove that he met with Allen, Silberman, and McFarlane, nor does it unequivocally establish the date of the meeting. It does suggest very strongly, however, that Lavi was aware of the meeting and had some role to play in it. The note also does not substantiate the recollections of the American participants.

Ari Ben-Menashe, who was the source for the page from Lavi's notebook, provides still another account of this episode. According to Ben-Menashe, the L'Enfant Plaza meeting was the result of an effort by Israeli intelligence to hasten the end of the hostage crisis.[38]

The Israelis, Ben-Menashe said, were becoming increasingly uncomfortable about their involvement in U.S. domestic politics resulting from the Casey-Karrubi meetings in Madrid. In particular, they were aware that President Carter was moving up in the polls, and they were less certain than before that Reagan would win the election. If they were caught working with the Republicans in an election, it could be devastating for Israel's long-term relations with the United States. So they attempted, without success, to short-circuit the entire problem by arranging a swap that would put an end to the hostage issue before the election. Lavi, he said, was working for Israel when he helped to set up the L'Enfant Plaza meeting.

Ben-Menashe said that he traveled to the United States in late September 1980 with Dr. Ahmed Omshei, a former professor at Tehran University and a consultant to General Fakuri, the Iranian minister of defense. It was Omshei, according to Ben-Menashe, who met with Allen, McFarlane, and Silberman at the L'Enfant Plaza as an unofficial representative of the Iranian government. Ben-Menashe claims that there was not one meeting but two, and that he was present at one of them. Lavi, he said, was involved in making the arrangements and was briefed on the discussions, but he did not actually participate in the meetings. Ben-Menashe agrees that the meetings did not result in any action related to the hostages, but he believes the offer was considered seriously by others in the campaign, at least for several days, before it was rejected.

These three accounts—Allen's, Lavi's, and Ben-Menashe's—agree on several key points: At least one meeting took place; it occurred at the L'Enfant Plaza Hotel at the very end of September or in the first few days of October; and it was attended by Allen, McFarlane, and Silberman. All agree that the "Iranian" or "Middle Easterner" proposed a release of the hostages to the Republicans and that his proposal was rejected.

Three important questions remain unanswered: Who was the "Middle Easterner"; whom did he represent; and what was the purpose of the meeting?

■ The American participants suggest that the man was what Richard Allen called a "free-lancer," that he represented no one except himself, that he made no mention of arms, and that everything about his identity is a mystery—except that he was emphatically not Hushang Lavi.

■ Lavi says that he was the "Middle Easterner," that he represented certain factions in the Iranian government that were ready to organize a swap of arms for hostages, and that he was in direct contact with two Iranians who were at that time in the United States.

■ Ari Ben-Menashe says that he and an Iranian from the Ministry of Defense were in the United States to propose an arms-for-hostages swap in a scheme worked out by Israeli intelligence, with the assistance of Hushang Lavi.

None of the three accounts is entirely convincing. There is, however, an internal consistency that cannot easily be dismissed between Hushang Lavi's several accounts of the L'Enfant Plaza meeting and the notebook entry, in his handwriting, that came to light only after his death. Lavi clearly was involved in this incident at some level, but it is equally clear that he was not operating entirely on his own. If Lavi did not meet with Allen, Silberman, and McFarlane, as the three Republicans insist, then who did? Was it the Iranian Ahmed Omshei whom Ben-Menashe says he escorted to the United States? Or was it perhaps Ben-Menashe himself, the Israeli who could pass as Iranian? The subsequent appearance of Lavi's diary entry in Ari Ben-Menashe's papers suggests that there was some relationship, direct or indirect, between the two of them.[39]

On the basis of the available partial and contradictory evidence, the L'Enfant Plaza gathering appears to have been an abortive attempt by Hushang Lavi and certain factions in Iran, perhaps with the assistance of Israel, to find a shortcut out of the hostage dilemma. There may, in fact, have been more than one operation under way at the same time, and they short-circuited when the wires crossed. Although Lavi was probably part of a larger enterprise, he may have been only dimly aware of its scope or objectives. Once engaged, however, he seized the notion of an arms-for-hostages swap and pursued it relentlessly, as we shall see.

Whoever the man was who met with the Americans at the L'Enfant Plaza, and regardless of the nature of his offer—whether an arms-for-hostages swap or simply a misguided attempt to intervene in the U.S.

election—it should have been reported to the administration. Here was a man who claimed to be in contact with representatives of Khomeini and who was offering to arrange a prompt release of the hostages. The very fact that such an offer was being made while negotiations were under way with Tehran was relevant to the negotiations. Perhaps his offer was a hoax. Perhaps he had his own political agenda. Perhaps his scheme had only a two percent chance of success. No matter.

The correct response to such an offer is not to declare, "We have only one President at a time," as Silberman and Allen have claimed repeatedly, and then to walk away. The correct response is, "I'm sorry but you have come to the wrong address. Let me direct you to the proper authorities." The L'Enfant Plaza Hotel is only a ten-minute taxi ride from the White House or the State Department. A telephone call in 1980 was only ten cents.

Silberman, years later, argued that "such a report could have been leaked during the campaign" to embarrass the Reagan-Bush campaign in a "reverse twist."[40] That argument may accurately reflect the suspicious state of mind that existed within the Reagan-Bush campaign. At a minimum, it suggests that concern for short-term tactical political advantage outweighed the possibility, however slight, that the man actually may have had useful contacts with the Khomeini regime, as he claimed.

Would the Carter administration have used this information in the hostage negotiations, or would the information have been used for political advantage against the Reagan campaign? We can answer that question with some assurance, for it was tested in practice only days after the L'Enfant Plaza meeting. Hushang Lavi offered his plan of an arms-for-hostages swap to the Anderson campaign. The offer was immediately reported to the Carter administration, and it resulted in no leaks and no exploitation for political purposes.

Immediately after the L'Enfant Plaza meeting failed to produce any results, Hushang Lavi approached the other opposition campaign, the third-party candidacy of John Anderson. The nature of the contact in this case was simple. Lavi merely telephoned his lawyer.

Mitchell ("Mitch") Rogovin, a well-known Washington attorney who had been special counsel to the Central Intelligence Agency during the Senate investigations of the agency in 1974 and 1975, was general counsel to the

Anderson campaign. He was also the lawyer who had represented Hushang Lavi in his lengthy court battle with Grumman. Lavi contacted Rogovin on Monday, September 29, 1980, to raise with him the possibility of an exchange of U.S. military equipment for the U.S. hostages in Tehran. Lavi told Rogovin that he was coming to the Anderson campaign after having had his proposal rejected by the Reagan campaign.[41]

Rogovin had many of the same political concerns expressed by Silberman. This was a hot political issue, the campaign was in its final stages, and it was impossible to predict how an explosive proposal such as this might play in such an overheated environment. Despite his considerable misgivings, however, Rogovin decided to inform the Carter administration. On Wednesday night, October 1, Rogovin had dinner with David Aaron, who had headed a task force for the Senate Select Committee on Intelligence and was now Zbigniew Brzezinski's deputy at the National Security Council. The two men had gone head-to-head during the Senate hearings on the CIA only a few years earlier, so it was a rather unusual meeting. Rogovin told Aaron about Lavi's proposal and said that he intended to raise the matter with the CIA.

The following morning, a CIA officer met with Lavi and Rogovin in Rogovin's law offices in Washington.[42] Lavi said that he wished to arrange for the delivery to Iran of $8 million to $10 million worth of F-14 parts, which were described in a detailed computer printout. If the United States would agree to Khomeini's demands to unfreeze Iranian assets in the United States, to drop all claims against Iran, and to pledge not to interfere in Iran's internal affairs, then Lavi said he could arrange for all the American hostages to be released upon delivery of the aircraft parts. Lavi claimed to be speaking on behalf of the government of Iran, but he specifically requested that the Israeli government be informed of the arrangement. (Lavi, as it turns out, was widely and reliably suspected of having close ties to Israeli intelligence, a relationship that the Israelis reportedly severed in 1983.)[43]

The CIA officer concluded that Lavi was "trying to get an offer from us [the U.S. government] for the 'purchase' of the hostages, which he would then broker with unnamed Iranian contacts." In its report of the conversation to David Aaron, the CIA expressed serious doubts "that this matter is worth pursuing further."[44]

I learned about this conversation on about October 3, 1980, when Aaron assembled a few NSC staff members in his office to discuss the proposal. At that meeting Aaron handed me a thick computer printout of F-14 parts and asked me to check with the Department of Defense to see if it was authentic. It was.

Rogovin was surprised when his contact at the CIA called back and expressed no interest in Lavi's proposal, so he decided to pursue it through other channels. Rogovin called Deputy Secretary of State Warren Christopher and informed him of the contact. Christopher referred him to Harold Saunders, the assistant secretary of state for the Middle East, and this led to a series of meetings between Lavi and State Department officials that continued throughout most of the month of October.

Saunders reported his first meeting with Lavi, Rogovin, and Alton Frye (the foreign-policy director of the Anderson campaign) in a memorandum on October 9.[45] Lavi outlined the same proposal he had made to the CIA official a week earlier, now stating that he was speaking for the Iranian president and that the list of F-14 parts could be checked out with Bani-Sadr. Again, Lavi said, without explanation, that the "Israelis should be involved" in the operation. Saunders questioned Lavi, without much success, on exactly how a link-up would be accomplished between the hostages and the spare parts. Lavi refused to provide specifics until he had assurances that the United States was prepared to proceed. He implied, however, that the plan might involve the forcible seizure of the hostages from the militants.

Over the following days, the plan evolved. As a gesture of good faith, and as proof of his authenticity, Lavi offered to obtain the release of Bruce Laingen, the chargé d'affaires, who was being held hostage in the Foreign Ministry in Tehran. He also offered to bring two Iranian representatives from New York to Washington for detailed discussions. In turn, Lavi presented requests for F-4 and F-5 aircraft parts, in addition to those on the original list. The White House had determined that only about 25 percent of those items were included in the frozen Iranian assets; the remainder would have to come from U.S. stores. That would change the nature of the transaction considerably.

There were also political problems. Despite Lavi's claims of direct contact with Bani-Sadr, and his offer to bring two Iranian representatives to

Washington to negotiate detailed terms, he was vague about operational details and could offer no direct evidence that his sources in Iran had any control over the hostages. Lavi claimed to speak for Bani-Sadr, and Bani-Sadr had never been able to assert control over the militants holding the hostages, though he might be able to get access to Bruce Laingen and his colleagues who were being held in the Foreign Ministry, outside the control of the "students."

There was also a great danger of crossing wires with the Tabatabai initiative. It was obvious that Lavi was unaware of the other negotiating channel, and there was no inclination to encourage two competing Iranian factions that might step on each others' toes or simply cancel each other out. There was no question about the authenticity of the Tabatabai group; their earlier message had in effect been validated by Khomeini. Lavi was another matter. Saunders had been around the Iranian question long enough to realize that it was entirely possible for two separate political factions in Tehran to be in competition—knowingly or not. But he had also had painful experience of free-lancers who promised more than they could deliver. So he pushed Lavi and Rogovin very hard for concrete details and for any tangible evidence of Lavi's bona fides.

At the same time, the State Department asked West German Ambassador Ritzel in Tehran to check discreetly with Bani-Sadr to determine if this was an authorized approach from the Iranian government. Rogovin, who had no knowledge of the Tabatabai channel, was frustrated by what he saw as Saunders's excessive caution, and over the following days he became very testy and impatient.[46]

Lavi's proposal was suspect, but it was only one of several intriguing new possibilities that emerged in those days. After the shock of the Iraqi invasion, early October showed signs of a warming trend for the Carter administration's negotiating efforts.

· 7 ·

INDIAN SUMMER

October was the last full month of the U.S. presidential campaign. On the first day of the month, the Republicans launched a full-scale drive to neutralize the political effects of any unexpected developments in the hostage situation. Ronald Reagan took the opening shot that day, saying he would not be surprised if Iran released the hostages before the election since Iran probably preferred Carter to himself as President.[1] The following day, George Bush made a similar statement to a group of journalists, warning for the first time of a possible "October surprise." Sitting with his legs casually crossed, waving his hand as if shooing away some pesky insect, he predicted a move by Carter before the elections, which could involve the release of the hostages: "One thing that's at the back of everybody's minds is 'What can Carter do that is so sensational and so flamboyant, if you will, on his side to pull off an October Surprise?' And everybody kind of speculates about it, but there's not a darn thing we can do about it, nor is there any strategy we can do except possibly have it discounted."[2] At the same time, press reports began to appear in the United States and

Europe that the United States was shipping military spare parts to Iran as part of a hostage-release deal.

On September 30, the Iranian Majles named a seven-man commission to deal with the hostage issue. The commission was headed by Behzad Nabavi, a thirty-eight-year-old leftist revolutionary whose responsibilities included overseeing Komiteh Prison, where the Americans were being held. The Nabavi commission was prohibited from any direct contacts with the United States, but its mandate was to study ways to solve the hostage issue and to report its recommendations to the Majles for approval.

A week later, on or about October 8, a crucial strategy meeting was held in Iran, at which Sadegh Tabatabai presented a report to Ayatollah Beheshti, Speaker Rafsanjani, Ahmed Khomeini, and probably Behzad Nabavi on his talks with Warren Christopher almost three weeks earlier. At least three decisions were made at this meeting. First, it was decided that Tabatabai would brief Bani-Sadr on the discussions with the United States. This was the first inkling Bani-Sadr had that a direct initiative was under way with Washington.[3]

In addition, two messages were delivered to Washington from Tabatabai through the West Germans. The first arrived on October 9—coincidentally, the same date that Harold Saunders of the State Department first met with Hushang Lavi and Mitch Rogovin. This message was very reassuring. It was addressed to Christopher and reported that his proposals in Bonn had "fallen on fertile ground." Christopher immediately called President Carter, who was in Winston-Salem on a campaign trip. Carter was encouraged, and directed Christopher to "push for some sort of understanding, no later than early next week."[4]

The second message from Iran requested an inventory of all Iranian assets that were being held by the United States. Since Iran had already been informed about the status of its frozen financial assets, Washington understood this message to be a veiled request for an accounting of the military equipment and spare parts that had been seized by the United States at the beginning of the hostage crisis.

No one in Washington was surprised that Iran would be showing renewed interest in military spare parts. Iran was under tremendous military pressure in its war with Iraq. Two weeks earlier, Iraq had invaded Khuzi-stan province and had seized a substantial amount of Iranian territory. But Iraqi President Saddam Hussein had made a fatal strategic blunder. If he had concentrated his forces on the key junction city of Dezful, which commanded all of the province's road, rail, and pipeline routes, he could have severed Khuzistan from the rest of the country and conquered it almost at will. Instead, Saddam's armies attacked across a front several hundred miles wide and slowly bogged down as they ran into stubborn, if improvised, resistance. Iran poured reinforcements into Khuzistan through the Dezful gap, and within a few weeks the front was largely stabilized. On October 10, Bani-Sadr concluded that "Iraq would not win the war," and by the thirteenth Iran was able to launch a modest counterattack.[5]

But Iran still faced the problem of rebuilding and regrouping its forces, which had been severely purged and demoralized by the revolution, and had to obtain the military supplies necessary to fight a prolonged war. The international search for arms shifted into high gear. According to a high-level Iranian source, "there was a general tasking to buy military spares whenever and however they could."[6]

Iran received pledges of support from Libya, Syria, and North Korea, each of which immediately began funneling arms into Iran: Libya provided a shipment of eighty Soviet-built T-55 tanks by the end of the year; Syria and Libya both began regular flights of arms and ammunition to Iran, overflying Turkey; and North Korea began supplying substantial quantities of arms by sea and air, overflying China. Most of this equipment, however, was of Soviet origin, and was incompatible with the Western weapons and systems that the Iranians had inherited from the shah. Iranian air force equipment, for example, was almost entirely American in origin. One source of U.S. equipment and spare parts was Vietnam, which had captured large quantities of U.S. matériel when U.S. forces withdrew five years earlier.[7]

Iran also began to experience threats from a different quarter. At the beginning of October, Iran had incited an uprising among the Kurds in northern Iraq, in an attempt to draw some of Saddam's forces away from the south and to carry the war into Iraqi territory. This stratagem was partly successful, but it backfired. Saddam Hussein responded in kind by stirring up trouble among Iran's own Kurdish minority, which was disenchanted with the government in Tehran. By the second week in October, Iran was facing its own second front in Kurdistan and was required to divert forces to the northwest to quell an incipient insurrection.

It was against that background that the Carter administration replied to Tabatabai's request for an inventory of Iranian military equipment in the United States. On October 11, a message was sent to Tabatabai via West German Ambassador Ritzel, urging him to specify the terms of a hostage release within a week. This note listed various categories of Iranian-owned military equipment, totaling some $150 million, that the United States would be prepared to return to Iran after the hostages were released. This was a substantial increase over the approximately $50 million in arms mentioned to Tabatabai in Bonn. The October 11 message, in effect, sweetened the pot by adding the "Category 2" or "gray area" items to the nonlethal items that had been offered in Bonn. This offer continued to exclude, however, the third category, consisting of another $150 million worth of military items in U.S. custody that were either highly classified or lethal, such as guided missiles and radar electronics.

Time was running out for the Carter administration in its efforts to negotiate an end to the hostage crisis. After the tragedies and disappointments of the preceding eleven months, Tabatabai's message on the ninth had generated a mood of optimism and high expectations, coupled with tension and uncertainty. Zbigniew Brzezinski later recalled:

The outbreak of the Iran-Iraq war created in Iran a need for American spare parts, and we began to hold out that option as a way of enticing the Iranians into a prompt settlement. By the middle of October, we were even discussing among ourselves the possibility of pre-positioning some of these spare parts in Germany, Algeria, or Pakistan, so that the Iranians could then promptly pick them up with their own aircraft.[8]

And the President himself noted on October 10, at his weekly Friday breakfast meeting with his foreign-policy advisers, that the Iranians were now "making sensible inquiries concerning issues which would have to be addressed . . . such as a request for an inventory of military matériel and spare parts."9

Yet despite its interest in expediting the release of the hostages, the Carter administration remained extremely reluctant to get into any bargaining of arms for hostages. The military equipment in question had already been bought and paid for by Iran, yet it was parceled out, bit by bit. President Carter's distaste for even appearing to trade arms for hostages was deep-seated, but another factor had come into play since the beginning of the Iran-Iraq war. The United States had pledged to remain entirely neutral in the conflict, and supplying arms to one side—even arms already paid for—would be an apparent violation of the administration's public assurances.

After a decade of revelations about trading arms for hostages, these considerations may seem a bit quaint. After all, the arms in question had been purchased by Iran before the hostage crisis and before the Iraqi invasion. Once the hostages were safely home, the delivery of this equipment to Iran could certainly have been justified on any grounds—legal, moral, political, or humanitarian. Perhaps it would have been better not to agonize over it and simply agree from the start to turn over all the arms as an incentive for the Iranians.

I can attest from personal experience, however, that it did not look that way at the time. I was personally responsible for clearing the October 11 message with President Carter. By that time I had been in the White House for more than four years and I had dealt with tens of thousands of highly classified documents. But I vividly recall my feeling that this was the most sensitive message I had ever handled.

President Carter was at Camp David, and I had to send the draft message to him via "LDX" (Long-Distance Xerox), the secure fax line which was still a novelty in those days. I insisted on personally delivering it to the communications rooms deep in the White House basement, rather than simply giving it to a staffer in the Situation Room. It was the only time in my White House career that I visited those rooms. I handed the message to the operator, watched while it was sent, and then retrieved the original. Shortly thereafter, President Carter sent a brief note of approval. I relayed his response to the State Department, and they delivered the message to the West German Embassy for transmission to Tehran.

This message was regarded as extraordinarily sensitive not only because it substantially increased the offer of arms to Iran but also because it was incomplete. The $150 million "inventory" of military equipment that was outlined in the message did not include the additional $150 million of the most sensitive equipment—equipment that was precisely what Iran wanted and needed most at the time. The Washington negotiators knew that Iran had no reliable inventories or records of its own, so it could not challenge these figures; and they assumed that the specialized spare parts Iran needed for its U.S.-built military equipment could not be obtained from any other source.

What was not known, or even suspected at the time, was the possibility that Iran had identified a potential alternative source of supply and anticipated that it could obtain U.S. spare parts via Israel. Washington thought it held a trump hand, while Iran may have believed it was simply shopping for the most attractive offer.

Through all these negotiations, the Carter administration had relied on the good offices of West German Ambassador Gerhard Ritzel in Tehran. However, without Washington's knowledge, Ambassador Ritzel was at that moment engaged in some creative diplomacy of his own. Ritzel was an exceptionally talented ambassador, with a flair for the unconventional. In the summer of 1980 he had made a pilgrimage to the Islamic shrine city of Mashhad, where he spent several days studying with one of Iran's grand ayatollahs. By the end of his visit, he had persuaded this religious leader to intervene with Khomeini on behalf of the Americans on the grounds that hostage-taking and the mistreatment of diplomats were contrary to Koranic injunctions. Khomeini received and acknowledged this message, but it had no practical effect on the fate of the fifty-two Americans held captive.[10]

Ritzel had also cultivated a number of key figures in the government and commercial sectors, including Tabatabai. On October 14, Ritzel handed Tabatabai a letter to Khomeini, which he had personally drafted in decidedly nonbureaucratic language intended to appeal to Khomeini's vanity, his sense of justice, and his self-interest. It read as follows:

IMAM

—You are old in years
—You have a deep wisdom
—You are rich in experience
—You are young at heart,
therefore you can learn and decide.

The American people learned. They know that they hurt the Iranian people.
Give the order to free the American hostages.
They should arrive in Frankfurt this coming Friday.

In return
—the USA will unfreeze all of Iran's assets.
—will order all banks worldwide to unfreeze Iran's assets.
—the USA will promise now and in the future not to involve itself in Iranian affairs.
—the USA will do everything to seize the fortune brought to the USA by the Shah and bring it back to Iran. (This will take time.)
—the American government will require the citizens of the USA to report the Shah's hidden money.
—Iran can immediately receive all weapons and replacement parts they ordered and paid for. (SECRET)

The government of the Federal Republic of Germany will guarantee to Iran that American obligations are fulfilled.

October 14, 1980

Gerhard Ritzel

This was a totally personal initiative on Ritzel's part.[11] Neither Washington nor Bonn knew anything about it, and it has never been published until now. As an intermediary between Iran and the United States, Ritzel was familiar with the U.S. negotiating position. His brisk and informal summary of American assurances was roughly accurate, though the lawyers on the U.S. negotiating team might have taken exception to some of the phraseology. The offer of "all weapons and replacement parts they ordered and paid for" was somewhat premature, though it later became the Carter administration's position.

The most daring part of Ritzel's message was the formal offer, in effect, of a West German performance bond for the United States. This was proposed entirely on his own initiative, without the prior approval of the West German government. Ritzel was well aware that he was running a professional risk, but if his ploy had succeeded, he would have been a hero, and no one would have been inclined to second-guess him. If it failed (as it did), probably no one would ever know. The only danger was that the Iranians might publish the letter for propaganda purposes. Ritzel was undoubtedly aware of what had happened when Hector Villalon, a sometime intermediary between the Carter administration and Iran in early 1980, had delivered an unauthorized letter to Khomeini that purported to be a communication from President Carter. Khomeini published it on March 29, creating great consternation in Washington.[12] German popularity in Iran was so high, however, that Ritzel was probably justified in expecting his message to be treated with respect and discretion.

Perhaps more than anything else, Ritzel's unconventional initiative reflected the mood of those strange days. There was a feeling that the only thing standing in the way of a solution was some strange cultural quirk or a communication lapse. Iran, it was clear, wanted to be rid of the hostages, and the U.S. position was reasonable—so what was wrong? If only the ayatollah could be made to see the futility of warehousing the hostages; if only the message could be phrased in the right way; if only, if only.

The fact was that Khomeini was no fool. He had benefited immensely from the hostage crisis at the beginning. It had sustained the revolution and silenced his critics. Now the strain was beginning to tell, especially after the Iraqi invasion; but he was determined to hold out for the best possible price. In the first instance, that meant no concessions to the hated Jimmy Carter; and in the second, it meant soliciting the highest possible return on what had become an immensely expensive investment.

■ ■ ■

But to the competing factions in Washington, securing the release of the hostages was more than simply a commercial transaction. On October 9, Richard Secord and other top officials responsible for the second rescue mission assembled in their windowless quarters deep in the bowels of the Pentagon for a special intelligence briefing by the CIA liaison officer.

The rescue team had completed its training and had been declared combat-ready more than a month earlier, but no action could be taken so long as the hostages were dispersed throughout Iran. In fact, by this date most of the hostages had been reassembled in Komiteh Prison just outside Tehran, but the mission planners were unaware of this and continued to believe that many were still being held in remote locations.

It had been a frustrating time for those associated with the rescue mission. They were poised for deployment at a moment's notice, operating on the assumption that the order to launch would come quickly once the administration had reliable information about the location of the hostages. What they heard in the intelligence briefing on October 9 gave them reason to believe that perhaps their long-awaited moment had arrived.

The hostages, they were told, had now been reassembled back at the U.S. Embassy in Tehran. Years later, those who were present at the briefing would remember the shock of that moment. It appeared that the final piece had fallen into place. From their perspective, this was nothing less than a green light to launch the rescue mission that they had been planning since April. The mission planners would later refer to this dramatic piece of news as the "Eureka" briefing.[13]

The original source of the news about the hostages was never disclosed, but on October 5, 1980, only a few days before the CIA briefing, Iranian expatriate journalist Amir Taheri had written an article in the *Sunday Times* of London that claimed that all fifty-two U.S. hostages had been moved back to Tehran.[14] Obviously, rumors of hostage movement were circulating at the time within the Iranian exile community.

But the commanders of the rescue mission were skeptical. An elaborate intelligence operation had been mounted to locate and track the locations of the hostages, and these sources had not reported any movement back to the embassy. The mission planners also had painful memories of the attempted rescue of POWs in Vietnam in the 1970s. That operation was perfectly executed from a military point of view, but the prison camp was empty when the rescue team arrived. Before taking any action on the "Eureka" briefing, they decided to double-check their own sources. A premature launch of the massive strike they had planned could be disastrous.

Not long after, once they had reviewed all the available intelligence, the commanders of the rescue operation concluded that the evidence was insufficient to justify an attack. As we now know, they were correct; the hostages were never transferred back to the embassy after their dispersal in April. The rescue operation was again put on hold.

Although this was an exceptionally tense moment for the commanders of the rescue mission, in fact there was almost no chance that President Carter would have authorized the mission even if the contents of the "Eureka" briefing had been true. On October 10, at his regular Friday breakfast meeting with his foreign-policy advisers—including Zbigniew Brzezinski, the godfather of the second rescue mission—there was no discussion of a rescue, though Carter did note with some satisfaction that "we received word that all the hostages were back in the embassy compound, in good condition."[15] Instead, as discussed earlier, all attention was focused on the encouraging nature of the two messages from Tabatabai and the nature of the U.S. response that would be sent the following day.[16]

Carter was fully aware that a rescue mission had been prepared, but in his view it was an instrument to be used only in extremis, if the lives of the hostages appeared to be in imminent danger. It was important and proper that the mission commanders should be poised and leaning forward, ready to respond at a moment's notice if required. That was their military responsibility. But the political reality was different.

During the last two months before the election, the President and his top advisers focused on the negotiating track and never seriously considered launching a rescue mission. A military rescue would have been enormously risky—for the hostages, for the attacking force, and for the future of U.S. relations with Iran and the region. Given what appeared to be encouraging progress in direct talks with Iran, the only possible justification for launching an attack would be the very reason the Republican campaign feared: to create an artificial crisis that could upset the election. That was never considered as an option.

The Republicans' fears of an "October surprise," however, were aggravated by the constant flow of insider information generated by their elaborate intelligence network. Much of the information passed along by their sources within the U.S. government seemed to be alarming. It stoked the paranoia that was already omnipresent in the campaign and encouraged risk-taking and radical measures of self-defense that were wholly unnecessary.

The way the network functioned also raises questions about how classified security information was handled during the 1980 presidential campaign. Richard Allen, who later became Ronald Reagan's national security adviser, was certainly aware of these concerns. In 1984, in his sworn affidavit to the House committee investigating the disappearance of Carter's briefing book, Allen stated: "To the best of my knowledge, I did not receive, at any time during the 1980 campaign, Federal Government information or documents that were classified or not duly authorized for public release."[17] What follows are some fully documented examples of information that flowed to Allen from the Reagan-Bush intelligence penetration operation over a period of only a few days in October 1980.

On October 10, Seymour Weiss, a conservative who was a former under secretary of state and U.S. ambassador to the Bahamas, passed to Richard Allen information concerning plans for a second hostage-rescue attempt.[18]

On October 13, Richard Allen made the following notation in his telephone log:

> 1151 Angelo Codevilla—938-9702. DIA—Hostages—all back in compound, last week. Admin embargoed intelligence. Confirmed[19]

Angelo Codevilla, a former intelligence officer and a committed Reagan supporter, was on the staff of the Senate Select Committee on Intelligence in 1980. The note says that the Defense Intelligence Agency had information that the hostages were all back in the embassy and that the Carter administration had restricted dissemination of this information.[20]

The "Eureka" briefing was one of the most sensitive intelligence items in the U.S. government at the time. Apart from the mission commanders, no one but a tiny handful of the highest officials in the government had any knowledge of its contents. Yet Richard Allen, the foreign-policy director of the Republican campaign, had it on his desk only four days after it was reported to the President, an achievement that would have been the envy of the KGB.

Allen, of course, was already aware of the rescue plan, so the significance of the "Eureka" briefing was unlikely to have escaped him. He would have had every reason to believe, as the mission commanders believed, that the location of the hostages was the necessary trigger to start the rescue operation. If the information was true, as asserted by this telephone message, then the Carter administration was in a position to launch a dramatic rescue mission at any moment.

Of course, by the time Allen received this disturbing bit of news, it had already proved to be false. There is no evidence, however, that Allen was ever informed that the report was untrue. As frequently happens, the second report probably never caught up with the first.

There were other bits of intelligence data. On October 10, Richard Allen entered a note in his telephone log that said, "F.C.I.—partial release of hostages for parts."[21] The initials F.C.I. stood for Fred C. Ikle. Ikle was a Reagan loyalist and one of the inner circle of foreign-policy advisers in the campaign. Months later, during the transition period after the election, Ikle was designated as the only person on the Reagan team authorized to be briefed on the Iranian situation.[22]

The Ikle message is particularly interesting. Rafsanjani, in a private meeting in Iran at about this time, apparently raised the possibility of a four-stage release of the hostages. Iran would demand a demonstration of U.S. good faith at each stage, such as the release of some military spare parts. Four of the hostages, those most suspected of espionage, would be held until the very end.

This information was picked up by Hushang Lavi in the course of his frequent telephone calls to Iran, but it was not reported to the Carter administration until October 14, when it caused quite a stir. When President Carter learned of it, he instructed Warren Christopher to object strongly and to work urgently through the Germans to leave no doubt that such an arrangement would be unacceptable.[23]

The timing of the Ikle report, almost four days before it came to the U.S. government, suggests either that the Reagan-Bush intelligence operation had direct contact with Lavi or that it had its own lines into Iran. (Another possible source for this information was Cyrus Hashemi, who was also in regular telephone contact with individuals in Rafsanjani's office.)

The Reagan-Bush campaign apparently did not just sit on this information. On October 15, WLS-TV in Chicago, which seemed to be the favored Republican outlet for hostage information (or disinformation), carried a story that "the American hostages have been returned to the U.S. Embassy in Tehran in preparation for a trip home for all but four of them as part of an arms deal with Iran."[24] This report seemed to be a composite of the two items of intelligence information that were reported to Richard Allen on October 10 and 13 by Ikle and Codevilla.

On October 15, Allen received another startling item of information. John Wallach, a journalist and columnist with the Hearst Corporation, contacted Allen and briefed him on an interview he had just completed with Secretary of State Muskie. Reflecting the upbeat mood of those days, Muskie expressed optimism that the hostages could be released in late October.

Allen immediately wrote a memorandum marked "Sensitive and Confidential" to Ronald Reagan, Edwin Meese, and William Casey reporting that an "unimpeachable source" had alerted him to the possibility of an impending hostage settlement. "The last week of October," the memo said, "is the likely time for the hostages to be released. . . . This could come 'at any moment, as a bolt out of the blue.'" In this memorandum, Allen gave the code name "ABC XYZ" to Muskie, so the note came to be dubbed the ABC XYZ memorandum.[25]

Unlike the other items of intelligence listed above, the ABC XYZ memorandum did not include any classified or sensitive information. Secretary of State Muskie offered his views in an interview with a reporter, and Wallach reported them in his columns in the days that followed. In some respects, however, this may have been the most important of all the leaks pouring across Allen's desk, for it seemed to confirm, from a high-level administration official, what Allen had been hearing from his other sources.

Allen had been told that talks were under way for at least a partial release of the hostages in return for spare parts. He knew that a second rescue mission was primed and ready to go as soon as the hostages were located. He now had reason to believe that the hostages were back in the embassy. And at this point, he learned that the secretary of state expected the hostages to be released soon, perhaps in the last week of October, possibly as a "bolt out of the blue." The worst fears of the Reagan-Bush campaign, that an "October surprise" would materialize at the last minute to upset their election plans, seemed about to come true.

Time was running out. The intelligence information available to the Republican campaign overwhelmingly pointed to a move by the Carter administration to end the hostage crisis, probably between October 24 and October 31. It was now October 15. If something was going to be done, it had to be within the next week.

·8·

CLOSING THE DEAL

As September turned to October, the Kuwaiti newspaper *Al-Anba*, which was frequently a source of inside information about regional developments, reported that elements within the United States had contacted Israel about acting as middleman to transfer arms and equipment to Iran.[1] Indeed, the Israelis had made a fateful decision. Their natural instinct had been to reconstruct their relationship with Iran, taking advantage of Tehran's isolation during the hostage crisis and its separation from its traditional sources of military supply as a result of the American arms embargo. Many in Israel believed that a new clandestine relationship could be resurrected from the debris of the revolution. After all, Iran was now a pariah state, and Israel, out of necessity, had mastered the discreet art of forging alliances of mutual benefit with such states.

President Carter's explicit demand that Israel sell Iran no military equipment of any kind until after the hostages had been released came as a blow to the old Iran hands in Israel who saw a golden opportunity slipping away, and it hardened the already disparaging opinion of Jimmy Carter that had emerged during the tough negotiations over the Camp David Accords.

Nevertheless, the embargo was observed from April through August, when William Casey struck exactly the kind of unsentimental bargain with the Iranian clerics that the Iran lobby in Israel had been looking for. According to Ari Ben-Menashe, Israel was approached in August not only by Casey but also by officials within the CIA who encouraged Israel to cooperate with the Republican initiative as a means of freeing the hostages.[2]

The Israelis chose to interpret these entreaties as a green light from the United States and not to look too hard for confirmation from Washington. If their actions were revealed, they could say they were led to believe that Casey's opening to Iran was part of a covert plan and that, because of its unorthodox nature, they assumed the White House wanted to remain at arm's length in order to maintain plausible denial. In any event, a firm decision was taken in Israel to cooperate with Casey's plan which had been hammered out in Madrid and was to be ratified in October in Paris.

In preparation for this second round of meetings, Israel began an intensive series of briefings. Six members of the intelligence community were chosen to represent Israel in Paris, including Ben-Menashe, who was brought in primarily because of his Persian-language ability. The briefing process was intensive and concentrated, rather like studying for a set of important final exams. At these briefings, Ben-Menashe became acquainted with much of the past history of the issues, and got to know the other members of the team, some of whom had extensive experience in arms transfers.

Much of the briefing was about politics. Israel, Ben-Menashe was told, was concerned about a possible U.S. agreement with the Arabs, largely as a result of Egyptian President Anwar Sadat's increasing popularity with the American public. Israel felt particularly vulnerable to a U.S. entente with the Arabs since it had lost its principal regional counterweight to Arab power when the shah of Iran was overthrown. The Carter White House was portrayed as paralyzed and incapable of thinking of anything but the hostages in Iran. The Iran-Iraq war, though it served Israel's interests in the short run while the two antagonists were at each others' throats, was dangerous to Israel in the long run, especially if Iraq emerged as the victor. In that case, Iraq would become the dominant power in the Persian Gulf, and Israel had no assurance that it could depend on the United States to maintain the balance of power. President Carter, according to the briefers, was "bad news" and did not inspire confidence.

By contrast, the Republican camp appeared to understand how the world really worked. Israel's intelligence indicated that the Reagan-Bush campaign wanted to come to terms with Iran. Reagan believed in military strength to confront the Soviets and was sympathetic to Israel. His running mate, George Bush, was the former director of Central Intelligence, and the briefers believed that he "understood" Israel's strategic concerns. Moreover, Reagan was extremely popular with the American public, and there seemed no way Jimmy Carter could win the election.

Still, dealing with the party out of power rather than the legitimate government was a serious and dangerous step. It was well understood that Israel could not afford to get caught. This point was explicitly covered in the briefings and explains why Israel decided not to send a Cabinet minister or any senior political figure to the Paris meetings.

Specific reference was made to "the Watergate precedent," which, according to the briefers, was that "illegal things get done in the United States, but if they are exposed the roof falls in." So, while Israel might identify with the objectives of the Reagan-Bush campaign, it had to be careful to avoid any direct connection. Ben-Menashe recalls being asked in the briefing, "Do you know what would happen if Israel's dealing with the hostages were revealed?" The answer reportedly was that it could risk the termination of U.S. aid to Israel.

Ben-Menashe and his five colleagues arrived at Orly airport outside Paris on a regularly scheduled El Al flight on Tuesday afternoon, October 14. Once in Paris, they split up into three teams of two, with each team staying in a different hotel, trying to look like tourists. Ben-Menashe and another team member stayed at the Hilton near the Eiffel Tower. They were told to avoid contact with Israeli officials in Paris, though they were given the telephone number of a security official in the Israeli Embassy in case of emergency.

The Israeli team had been told in the briefings that the French regarded these meetings as a fact-finding effort intended to explore possibilities for resolving the hostage affair. The French did not participate in the conversations, though everyone assumed they were listening. In fact, upon arrival at the airport, the Israeli team spotted men with cameras, who, they assumed, were French security.

Ben-Menashe's instructions were primarily to listen. He had no authority to negotiate or make deals on behalf of Israel, and so far as he knew, the other members of the team were under the same restriction. His specific job was modest. He was told to develop a "telephone book" on the Iranians: name, title, telephone number, address, what group or faction they belonged to, and how they could be contacted.

Some members of the Iranian delegation were staying at the Hotel Montaigne. Ben-Menashe met them at about noon on the following day, and he spent much of the next few days getting acquainted with his Iranian counterparts. They wandered around Paris together, not unlike a group of tourists. That evening they went together to Pigalle, the nightclub and red-light district of Paris, where the Iranians had a few beers and stared openmouthed at the streetwalkers. After the straitlaced Islamic environment of postrevolutionary Tehran, the fleshpots of Paris were a revelation.

Ben-Menashe was quite proud of the fact that he succeeded rather quickly in eliciting the necessary information about the approximately sixteen members of the Iranian delegation, but he was also aware that his Iranian counterparts were doing exactly the same thing. Both sides were interested in developing reliable contacts, and the mutual process of developing telephone books was accomplished largely through socializing, discreetly though not surreptitiously.

Ben-Menashe did not participate in any formal policy meetings in Paris, and most of his time was spent in free-floating encounters in various hotel lobbies, cafés, and restaurants. Most of the activity centered around three hotels: the Ritz, the Waldorf Florida, and the Raphael. He focused primarily on the Iranian delegation, since that was his assignment, though he did meet some of the Americans.

The Iranians and the Israelis got along well and were relaxed together, but Ben-Menashe said everyone was "strung out" when the Americans arrived. This was a "personality thing," according to Ben-Menashe. The Iranians "simply didn't like them," and Ben-Menashe admitted that he felt much the same way. He recalled that once when he was talking with some Iranians, an American approached the group. One of the Iranians whispered in his ear in Persian, "One of the sons-of-bitches is coming." It was a peculiarity that the Iranians were able to "cozy up" to the Israelis, but not to the Americans. The Iranians and Israelis were chummy. They worked with the Americans but hated them.

Ben-Menashe understood that the meetings were intended to reach a final agreement on the terms for the timing of the hostages' release. His Iranian contacts indicated that they were prepared to release the hostages rather quickly, while the Americans took the position that it would require about three months to arrange for the release of the money and to make the banking arrangements. The U.S. side did not say directly to delay the release until the inauguration in January, but simply said that it would take that long to make the necessary arrangements. The Iranians professed to be puzzled, but Ben-Menashe said they understood perfectly well what was going on. One of the Iranians commented to him sarcastically, "Why not put off the release until March, so all the release negotiations could be done by Reagan?"

Ben-Menashe completed his assignment by Friday night, October 17. He went to synagogue on Saturday and left Paris on Sunday. According to Ben-Menashe, the most important American participants, including William Casey, did not show up until about Friday, and the most important meetings occurred over the weekend. Ben-Menashe also insisted that during the same general period there was an additional meeting in the south of France, which he refused to describe further.

On Saturday, October 18, Israeli Deputy Defense Minister Zippori issued a public statement that Israel would consider selling weapons to Iran if Iran changed its anti-Israel policy. He noted that Iran's armed forces were already equipped in part with Israeli weapons.[3] It will be recalled that Zippori had made an almost identical statement on September 28, at a time when meetings were reportedly in progress in Zurich between Israelis and Iranians concerning arms. This statement, like the earlier one, had the appearance of a prearranged signal from Israel, authenticating the discussions that were under way or were about to be completed.

Ben-Menashe's account of the Paris meetings is similar to many other accounts that have come to light. It is possible to make several general observations about the structure of the meetings:

■ The Paris meetings were organized to put the final touches on an agreement that had been worked out earlier. The essence of that agreement was that Iran would release the hostages to the Reagan-Bush forces after the election, in return for military equipment to be delivered through Israel.

■ The key participants in the Paris meetings were Americans, Israelis, and Iranians. The French were aware of the meetings and were widely suspected to have eavesdropped, but their role, at most, was that of facilitators, not players in their own right. On the fringes, a few European arms dealers stood at the ready.

■ The preliminary meetings began on or about October 15, while the main policy meetings were concentrated on the weekend of October 17–19.

■ There was not a single meeting, but rather a series of meetings—most of which were quite informal encounters in hotel lobbies and the like. The key meetings, however, where principals met to make decisions, were held in hotel rooms that had been swept for listening devices.

■ The delegations were surprisingly large, in view of the demands for secrecy. According to Ben-Menashe, there were six Israelis, sixteen Iranians, and twelve Americans. Ben-Menashe said, "A lot of people knew about this. The only concern was that the U.S. government be kept in the dark." Large delegations were reported in almost all accounts, even though intuition would suggest the opposite.

■ The level of staffing suggested that, far from being improvised on the spur of the moment, these meetings had been carefully prepared over time and had perhaps suffered a bit from bureaucratic bloat. If so, that may have been the fatal flaw in the operation, for it is only through the testimony of these incidental participants that these meetings have come to light at all. None of the principals involved have ever spoken publicly about what happened, and there will never be a full account of the discussions until that happens.

While Ari Ben-Menashe was arriving in Paris, Hushang Lavi received a telephone call from Cyrus Hashemi, urgently asking him to fly to Europe. Lavi was not personally acquainted with Hashemi, but he knew him by reputation as a fellow Iranian expatriate and as a prosperous international banker. Lavi flew immediately to London, where he met Hashemi. The two of them then flew on to Paris, where they went to the Hotel Raphael. Lavi said he remained in Paris for three or four days.[4]

Three members of the Lavi family, who prefer not to be identified by name, said that Lavi traveled to Europe during this period. He often spoke of the trip and the Paris meetings to other family members. He told them that the meeting was "arranged by the CIA," and that he had contacts with George Bush during that time.[5]

Lavi never made any claim to knowledge about the actual deliberations of the Paris meetings except what he was told by Hashemi. Lavi said he was brought in because of his reputation as an arms dealer with extensive Iranian contacts, and Hashemi told him he was to be there in the event "things started rolling." While Lavi was in Paris he met with Colonel K. Dehqan of the Iranian army and some Israelis. Two other sources have independently identified Colonel Dehqan as being present at the meetings.[6] Dehqan, one of Ahmed Heidari's partners in Interparts and a senior logistics and arms-procurement officer for the Iranian military, was alleged to have close ties to Israel.

According to Lavi, Hashemi said that he was meeting with William Casey to get the hostages free in return for a supply of U.S. arms to Iran. Lavi was told the same thing by Colonel Dehqan. Hashemi was extremely confident that this objective would be achieved. Lavi's understanding at the time was that the hostage release would be delayed until after the November 4 elections, in order to prevent President Carter from getting any credit for it. Lavi said that he was surprised when the release did not come until January, and he never understood the reason for the delay. Lavi also identified the contact man between Hashemi and Casey as "a gentleman by the name of Shaheen. . . . There were a bunch of Americans; I don't know who exactly, but I do know that he [Cyrus] was talking to Shaheen, because I remember I heard that name when I was in Paris with him, and a number of Israelis."[7]

Lavi's recollection helps to establish that John Shaheen, Hashemi's sometime business partner, served as the contact point between the Iranian expatriate banker and the Republican campaign chairman. It may have been Shaheen who put Casey in touch with the Hashemi brothers in early 1980. Shaheen had dinner with Cyrus Hashemi at several key moments in this story: on August 1, immediately after the first Casey-Karrubi meetings in Madrid, and on October 22, shortly after the Paris meetings.[8]

Cyrus Hashemi's role in Paris was far less central than it had been in Madrid, where he and his brother had been responsible for bringing Mehdi Karrubi to Spain, locating and renting the meeting sites and handling all of the organizational work. They also personally participated in all the meetings and apparently did most of the translation. In Paris, Jamshid Hashemi was absent and Cyrus appeared to have been relegated to a secondary role. He was still very much part of the operation, but he was no longer indispensable now that the principals were in direct contact with each other. That would be even more the case after the Paris meetings, when each of the delegations would have its own "telephone book" and personal contacts.

With Hashemi's role as the political "fixer" diminished, he reverted to a role as a businessman with his own interests at stake. His motivation from the beginning, it appeared, had been to get in on the ground floor of a potentially lucrative business relationship with Iran, by brokering the deal of the century—the potential restoration of political and commercial ties between the Islamic Republic of Iran and the prospective Republican administration of the United States of America.

Another account of the Paris meetings came from Richard Brenneke, an Oregon businessman who claimed to have been a contract agent for the CIA for many years. It was Brenneke, in fact, who first publicly described the Paris meetings and generated a burst of interest in the subject in 1988. Brenneke always claimed that he was present at the meetings, and he placed himself in some of the key meetings at the Hotel Waldorf Florida. Many journalists and congressional investigators who dealt with Brenneke at the time eventually concluded that he was unreliable. His story changed over time, growing ever more elaborate and Byzantine, and his sources and allegations—including his own claims to have worked for the CIA—simply did not check out. Subsequent research appears to confirm that their suspicions were fully justified. Examination of Brenneke's signed credit-card receipts for the summer and fall of 1980 shows that he was seldom far from the Portland, Oregon, area, even on the key dates of the Paris meetings.[9]

Nevertheless, Brenneke often had surprising access to insider information, which he would then use for self-promotion. I once spent an entire evening listening to Brenneke spin out an elaborate tale relating to the Madrid meetings. His version was a bit baroque, but it incorporated some information that my colleagues and I had earlier discovered to be true. Only later did I discover that Brenneke had managed to acquire that same information through a circuitous leak and was feeding it back to us with frills and flourishes that he improvised on the spot, apparently enjoying the process immensely.[10]

The bottom line on Brenneke was that he had access on occasion to information that was extremely sensitive and known only to a few individuals. When he spoke publicly about any of these issues, however, he exaggerated his own role and tried to place himself at the center of the action. The basic information was often true, but the flourishes and claims of firsthand knowledge were often false.

Reduced to its essentials, Brenneke's account is very simple. There was a series of meetings in Paris extending over several days; the most important was probably on Sunday, October 19, 1980. The meetings, some of which were held in the Hotel Waldorf Florida, involved Americans, Iranians, and Israelis. The leader of the U.S. delegation was William Casey. According to Brenneke, Donald Gregg was also present, a charge Gregg has categorically denied.[11] The meetings appeared to be intended to put the final touches on an agreement that had been concluded at some earlier date. A substantial sum of money, perhaps $40 million, was made available to the Iranians by the U.S. side, either to buy arms or to go into their personal bank accounts. The purpose of the meeting, Brenneke said, was to secure the release of the U.S. hostages in Tehran. The Iranians were amenable and seemed indifferent about the timing, but the U.S. participants let it be known that they wanted the release to be delayed.

Another man who claimed to have participated in the Paris meetings was Oswald LeWinter, an intelligence operative who would have felt at home in any spy novel.[12] LeWinter was a brilliant, erratic man whose friends and family regarded him as "a genius." He was a graduate of the University of California at Berkeley and had a master's degree in English literature from San Francisco State. Born in Vienna to Jewish parents, he spoke German and English, but he had also acquired a working knowledge of Hebrew, Persian, and French, and some Urdu. His abiding interests were literature and poetry. He published a book on Shakespeare[13] and was

a friend of the American novelist Saul Bellow.[14] LeWinter had served with
U.S. forces in Vietnam and also claimed long experience with various U.S.
and Israeli intelligence agencies. In October 1980, LeWinter was attached
to U.S. military intelligence in West Germany, where, according to German
intelligence sources, he sometimes operated in the uniform of a brigadier
general.[15]

According to LeWinter, he was instructed by intelligence authorities to
go to Paris on the weekend of October 19, to assist with security for
meetings that were to take place at the Hotel Raphael and the Hotel
Waldorf Florida. He did not take part in any of the meetings. His only
responsibility was to collect hotel registrations or any other documentation
or evidence that might indicate that the meetings had taken place. He was,
as he put it, part of the "clean-up team."[16]

Because of his participation in the security team covering the October
meetings, LeWinter said, he acquired some information about the nature of
the meetings and their participants. LeWinter said that he and other members of the team were told to stay away from the Raphael and the Waldorf
Florida while the actual meetings were in progress, and they were told that
William Casey was moving back and forth between the two hotels.

It was his understanding at the time that the subject of the discussions
was to provide arms to Iran, that the participants included Iranians and
Israelis, and that the arms supply was intended to get the American hostages out of Iran. Only years later did he hear that the real reason for the
meetings was to delay the release of the hostages until after the U.S.
elections.

Two men with ties to French intelligence claimed to have knowledge of the
Paris meetings through their own access to French internal information.
One of these men, a former senior deputy to Alexandre de Marenches who
was personally acquainted with William Casey, said that he had read an
internal French intelligence report dated October 28, 1980, that described
the Paris meetings and listed the names of at least some of the participants.[17] According to this report, there was a series of meetings in Paris on
the weekend of October 19 at several hotels, including the Hilton, the
Raphael, and the Waldorf Florida. The main parties involved in the dis-

Ayatollah Ruhollah Khomeini led the revolution that overthrew the Iranian monarchy in February 1979.

UPI/Bettmann

UPI/Bettmann

Ronald Reagan and George Bush at the Republican National Convention. Their campaign was accused of secret dealings with individuals close to Khomeini.

Anti-Americanism in
revolutionary Iran.

AP/Wide World Photos

Above: Iranian crowds at the gate of the U.S. embassy the day after the hostages were taken.

Below: American television brought the hostages into American living rooms.

AP/Wide World Photos

The hostage crisis dominated the American landscape for more than a year.

Israeli Prime Minister Menachem Begin raised with President Jimmy Carter his interest in arms sales to Iran during their Oval Office meeting in April 1980. Carter rejected the idea.

Above: The U.S. rescue mission in April 1980 ended in disaster at the landing site dubbed Desert One.
Below: Sadegh Khalkhali, Iran's hanging judge, surveys the bodies and wreckage of the failed rescue attempt.

Iran's President Abol Hassan Bani-Sadr sought arms for Iran as war loomed with Iraq.

Ayatollah Mohammed Hussein Beheshti directed Iran's politics from behind the scenes and engineered the impeachment of Bani-Sadr.

Hojjat ol-Eslam Ali Akbar Hashemi Rafsanjani, the speaker of the Iranian Majles in 1980.

Reagan confers with his campaign manager, William Casey.

Hojjat ol-Eslam Mehdi Karrubi reportedly met secretly with Casey to arrange a swap of the hostages for arms and political favors.

Casey (*second from left*) at a conference of military historians in London in July 1980. He evidently shuttled from London to Madrid to meet Karrubi.

Cyrus Hashemi, the Iranian financier and "double agent" who worked for the Carter administration while secretly serving as Casey's principal intermediary with Iran. He died mysteriously in 1986.

Jamshid Hashemi, Cyrus' older brother, participated in the Madrid meetings between Casey and Karrubi.

Businessman John Shaheen may have introduced the Hashemi brothers to his close friend William Casey.

Peter Bregg/CANAPRESS Photo Service

Donald Gregg served on the National Security Council staff in the Carter administration. His responsibility was intelligence coordination.

Richard Brenneke's often contradictory descriptions of events in 1980 first brought this story to public attention. He was aquitted in 1990 of charges that he had lied about the "October surprise" allegations.

UPI/Bettmann

Ari Ben-Menashe, an Israeli military intelligence official, detailed Israel's role in the "October surprise."

Phil Linsalata/St. Louis Post Dispatch

Maj. Gen. Richard Secord helped plan a second rescue mission. It was never launched, but knowledge of the operation aroused Republican concern.

Opposite page, top photo: Edwin Meese III, chief of staff in the Reagan-Bush campaign, reportedly met with Cyrus Hashemi in December 1980, during the transition between the Carter and Reagan administrations.
Opposite page, bottom photo: Richard V. Allen, the foreign policy adviser in the Reagan-Bush campaign, formed an "October surprise" committee.

UPI/Bettmann

Gary Sick briefing President Carter in the Oval Office on Inauguration Day 1981, waiting for Iran to release the hostages.

Opposite page, top photo: The hostages were released only minutes after Ronald Reagan was sworn in as president of the United States.
Opposite page, bottom photo: Jimmy Carter and freed hostage L. Bruce Laingen in Germany on the day after the inauguration.

President Reagan greets the hostages at the White House.

cussions were Americans, Iranians, and Israelis. The main participant on the U.S. side was William Casey. Cyrus Hashemi was a participant. The broad outlines of a deal involving arms, money, and the U.S. hostages in Iran had been worked out in advance, and the weekend meetings were carried out in a series of compartmentalized sessions with those responsible for implementation at each stage. The identities of the participants changed from one meeting to the next, except for Casey, who was clearly in charge.

The second man, Nicholas Ignatiew, was a graduate of the prestigious Ecole des Sciences Politiques in Paris, a reserve officer in the French cavalry, and a man who moved in conservative French political circles. He was also an acknowledged arms dealer, who worked closely with French intelligence. Ignatiew said that he had learned of the October 1980 Paris meetings many years afterward. He was curious about the story and attempted to confirm it with his own sources in the French government. He was told that it did happen and that a report was prepared for Alexandre de Marenches and later provided to the Reagan people in the United States.[18]

According to his information, some "very important meetings" took place roughly between October 19 and 22, 1980. One meeting was in the Hotel Raphael in Paris, and there were possibly two meetings in the Hotel Waldorf Florida. William Casey was a key player on the American side. It was Ignatiew's understanding that the objective of the meetings was to obtain the earliest possible release for the U.S. hostages in Iran. In his view, the operation was partly a success, partly not. It succeeded in getting the hostages out of Iran, but it took a much longer time than had been anticipated.

A third French source, who had no connection with intelligence, was François Cheron, a lawyer in Paris who had developed close and trusting relations with Sadegh Ghotbzadeh, the foreign minister of Iran during much of the hostage crisis. Cheron had been associated with some secret negotiations regarding the hostages that the Carter administration had conducted with the Iranians in early 1980,[19] and he maintained an active interest in the hostage issue throughout the crisis. Cheron said he learned from Iranian sources in 1980 that the Republicans were attempting to make a deal with Iran and discussed this fact with Ghotbzadeh at the time.

According to Cheron, Casey's meetings in Paris were at the Crillon and the Raphael. It was his understanding that, because of the Paris meetings, some Frenchmen were held under house arrest at the Intercontinental Hotel in Tehran. Apart from Jacques Montanès himself, who was then under detention in Iran, Cheron was the only source, to my knowledge, who was aware of the Frenchmen being held in Tehran.

For the international fraternity of men who make their living selling arms, the deal that resulted from the Paris meetings was a major event. It opened up lucrative opportunities for arms brokers to ply their trade, and it eventually touched the lives of many dealers. After the story began to emerge publicly, many of these individuals were willing to say on the record what they had been saying only to each other for years.

Arif Durrani was born in Pakistan and came to the United States in 1973 where he founded the Merex company in California, which manufactured weapons components and other hardware for the United States military and for export to other countries.[20] He had good contacts with officials of the Iranian Revolutionary Guards Corps and with the government of Pakistan, which was attempting to broker a release of the U.S. hostages. During 1980 he traveled to Iran on several occasions to discuss a possible arms-for-hostages swap through Pakistan. During these visits, he was informed by Iranian officials that a hostage deal with members of the Reagan campaign was in the works. His principal sources in Iran were: Mohsen Rafiqdust, the political leader of the Revolutionary Guards; Mohsen Rezai'e, the military commander of the Revolutionary Guards; and Hamid Naqashan, the chief arms-procurement officer for the Guards Corps. According to these sources, the initial contacts occurred during the summer of 1980 between William Casey and Mehdi Karrubi in Spain, culminating in a series of meetings in Paris in October. Cyrus Hashemi, according to Durrani, was a key figure in establishing these contacts. Durrani said that the contact between Casey and Hashemi was established through John Shaheen and that it was Hashemi who arranged for Karrubi to meet with Casey in Europe.

Durrani said he was not personally involved in any of these meetings.

He did, however, participate in some of the arms deals that flowed from these agreements after the Reagan administration came to office in 1981.[21]

A German arms dealer, who insists on anonymity, said that he was engaged in a prospective arms deal with Hamid Naqashan of Iran's Revolutionary Guards Corps in the fall of 1980. Through Naqashan, he learned that Iran had instead arranged to buy substantial quantities of arms from the United States via Israel. As a result of these agreements, the German arms dealer lost what could have been a sizable arms contract of his own. He also said that his Iranian contacts had provided him with firsthand accounts of the various meetings in Europe during September and October 1980. He was confident that the key final meeting in Paris—among members of the Reagan-Bush campaign, Iranians, and Israelis—took place on October 19. He was told that the purpose of these meetings was to reach an agreement whereby the Americans and Israelis would provide arms to Iran and that the Iranians in turn would delay the release of the U.S. hostages until after the election but before Reagan's inauguration. The key participant on the U.S. side was William Casey.[22]

William Herrmann was an American citizen who in 1964 started his own freight-forwarding company operating out of John F. Kennedy International Airport in New York. His company did occasional contract work for the CIA, arranging air shipments to various parts of the world. Herrmann then began to do more contract work for the CIA and other U.S. intelligence services, starting in the late 1960s and 1970s. In the early 1970s Herrmann formed his own company in Frankfurt, which specialized in international arms sales.

He had no business dealings with Iran before the revolution, but he became familiar with the family of a man who had been a Cabinet minister under the shah. When this man fled Iran at the time of the revolution, he and some of his friends worked with Herrmann to reestablish a network of contacts in the new Islamic Republic. After the Iraqi invasion in September 1980, Hamid Naqashan approached Herrmann in Europe, seeking to buy arms for the Revolutionary Guards.

According to Herrmann, his relationship with Naqashan was "strictly business" for the first few months. Then, in December 1980, Herrmann and Naqashan traveled together to Brazil to arrange for the purchase of military equipment for Iran. The combination of the trip and the success of the Brazilian venture created an enduring sense of friendship and confidence between the two men.

Herrmann went to Iran on January 17, 1981, just prior to the Reagan inauguration and the release of the hostages, for a series of meetings with high-level political and military officials to discuss arms purchases. He was in Tehran on the day the hostages were released. On the following evening, Herrmann had dinner with Naqashan, who told him that the hostage release deal had been prenegotiated even before Reagan was elected, with the understanding that the hostages would not be released until Reagan was sworn in. Naqashan said that he had attended some meetings in Paris, in mid- to late October 1980, in which the deal was made final. The key negotiator on the U.S. side was William Casey.[23]

Finally, there are two important sources who have confirmed their personal knowledge about the meetings in Paris and the hostage deal between the Reagan-Bush campaign and Iran. Both of these men hold high-level positions in their respective governments. One of them, an Israeli, had firsthand knowledge of the 1980 operations. The other is a diplomat from an Arab country. Neither is an arms dealer. Neither has ever been accused of a crime. Both are highly respected officials. Regrettably, for those very reasons, neither of these men can be cited by name. The Arab diplomat was in Paris in October 1980 and had access to reliable intelligence reports at the time that meetings were being held between Americans and Iranians regarding the hostages. He said he paid no attention to the reports at the time, since he assumed that this was a secret channel to Iran being pursued by the Carter administration. There were, of course, no secret negotiations with the Iranians in Paris by the Carter administration during October 1980. The Israeli official, speaking in complete confidence to a close friend, simply confirmed that a deal had been done and that the political implications for both Reagan and Bush would be severe if it ever became known.

When all the preceding accounts are checked against one another, one fundamental question looms above all others: Did William Casey, without the knowledge of the U.S. government, travel to Paris during the period of October 15–20, 1980, and there meet with Iranian and Israeli representatives to arrange the release of the U.S. hostages to the Reagan-Bush forces in return for promises of military equipment? The answer, it appears, is yes. Everything else is of secondary importance.

· 9 ·

REVERSAL OF
FORTUNE

T here was a peculiar silence on the hostage issue in the White House
from October 15 to 20. The days and weeks prior to the fifteenth had
been marked by almost daily reports from Tehran through a variety of
sources, describing new political developments and various plans that were
being floated for a settlement. This flurry had generated a mood of cautious
optimism within the Carter administration that its latest offer was being
taken seriously and that Iran was moving toward an early resolution of the
crisis. For five days in mid-October, however, everything seemed to stop.
Hushang Lavi and Cyrus Hashemi, both of whom had been calling in
reports through intermediaries about their contacts in Tehran, suddenly
went silent. European diplomatic channels also dried up. There were no
new pronouncements, public or private, from the leadership in Tehran.

However, in the week that would follow the conclusion of the meetings
in Paris, everything would change. The Carter administration's negotiations
with Iran, which had appeared so promising, would collapse. The Iranian
leadership, which had previously signaled its interest in an early resolution
of the hostage issue and had shown great interest in obtaining military

equipment frozen in the United States, would reject any deal with the Carter administration. Iran would declare that it was uninterested in the arms even though it was engaged in a bitter war with Iraq.

On the surface, nothing had happened that would seem to justify this reversal. The terms of the U.S. offer, which had been received with interest in Iran in late September and early October, had gradually become more, not less generous. Iran's strategic position had stabilized but had not significantly improved, and the port city of Khorramshahr had fallen to the Iraqis over the course of that week. Moreover, the Iranian leaders, who understood the bargaining leverage of a political deadline, were fully aware of the Carter administration's eagerness to end the hostage crisis before the election. That had not changed, and the prospect that Iran would get a better deal from the Carter administration after November 4—regardless of the outcome of the election—was remote in the extreme.

Yet everything had changed. On October 21, Iran apparently concluded that its interests would best be served by delaying the release of the hostages until after the U.S. presidential election. One explanation, which many analysts inside and outside the Carter administration accepted at the time, was that Khomeini's unconcealed and unremitting hatred of Jimmy Carter had led him to place his personal feelings above the interests of Iran and even the survival of the revolution at a moment of great national peril. Another explanation, unsuspected at the time, was that Khomeini and the Iranian leadership had what they considered to be a more attractive offer if they were willing to wait. The ayatollah's sense of personal vindictiveness may indeed have made his decision easier, but the question was whether the Iranians could get substantially more than what the administration had offered by waiting, particularly the supply of military equipment. Jimmy Carter had been extremely uncooperative in Israel's efforts to restore an arms relationship with Iran whereas the Reagan-Bush campaign held out the prospect of improved relations, at least at the covert level, and a steady supply of military equipment through Israel. Unlike Carter, who had his own reasons for being harsh with Iran and who had shown no penchant for dealing under the table, Iran might anticipate a more tolerant policy from an administration that owed it a huge favor, that had demonstrated a willingness to cut covert deals, and that was committed in advance to a clandestine Israel-Iran arms relationship. That prospect, plus the opportunity to cripple Carter's reelection chances, provided a reasonable, indeed compelling, justification for Iran's decision to postpone a hostage settlement.

This pivotal week began with the visit of Iranian Prime Minister Mohammed Ali Raja'i to the United Nations on Friday, October 17, to address the Security Council. Iran had refused to recognize the Council's authority after it had criticized Tehran over the hostage crisis, but in the wake of the Iraqi invasion the Iranians began to realize that their absence from New York had left an open field for the Iraqis. The Raja'i visit to New York was widely viewed as a tacit acknowledgment by Iran that the posture of defiance and international isolation it had adopted after the hostage-taking could no longer be sustained without severe damage to the nation's broader interests. Iran's renewed desire to repair its international image presented an unexpected opportunity for some direct diplomacy, and that was the focus of the Carter administration's policy while the secret meetings were going on in Paris.

President Carter announced on October 16 that he would be willing to meet directly with Raja'i during his visit, and Warren Christopher made an unannounced trip to New York to see if direct contact could be established through the U.N. or possibly through the good offices of the Algerians. But Raja'i and Dr. Ali Shams Ardekani, the Iranian ambassador to the U.N., refused to meet with any American official, either publicly or privately.

Raja'i, however, had agreed to meet secretly with Katherine Keough, the wife of William Keough, Jr. Mr. Keough was the director of the American School in Islamabad, Pakistan; by monumental bad fortune he had been visiting the Tehran embassy on business when it was seized, and he was taken hostage. Katherine Keough was the president of the hostage families' organization, and she had requested a private meeting with Raja'i. She was at the Iranian ambassador's residence when Raja'i returned from his meeting with the Security Council. He apologized profusely for keeping her waiting for two hours. The reception room in the residence was crowded, so Raja'i ushered her and an interpreter to his bedroom on the top floor, where he sat down on the bed, took off his shoes and jacket, and motioned for her to sit beside him.[1]

They sat side by side on the edge of the bed and talked for forty minutes.

Raja'i asked about her husband. She said that he was a teacher, and so was she. Raja'i, who was himself a former secondary-school teacher, responded warmly. "These are remarkable times for teachers," he said. Raja'i was on the verge of exhaustion; he seemed to be overwhelmed by his new prominence and responsibilities, and at the same time exhilarated by the experience. He said that these were major life events for him, as they were for her. He said he understood her problem and seemed to want to make her understand his. Keough said it was almost like talking to her brother or another family member about a personal problem. He took her hand, looked directly into her eyes, and promised her that nothing would happen to her husband. If she wanted, he said, he could arrange for her husband to be released immediately, as early as the next week.

What about the others? she asked. No, he said, they would have to remain for several more weeks.

Keough said that her husband could not come home without the others. How could he hold up his head as a man, if he had been given special treatment as a result of a personal favor? And how could she, as the leader of the hostage families, face the other members of the organization if she accepted a personal favor to have her husband released? All had to come home. Raja'i seemed to be impressed. "Within two to three weeks," he said, "you will no longer have to speak to me on this subject, certainly within a month." She said she took that as a very significant statement and would tell the families that the release would be soon.

Keough was convinced that Raja'i was telling the truth, at least what he believed to be the truth. Raja'i had just come from Iran, and his statement probably reflected the thinking in Tehran just before the meetings in Paris. His indication that Iran was planning to release the hostages in the relatively near future, perhaps just after the November 4 elections, was perfectly consistent with what Ari Ben-Menashe, Hushang Lavi, and others said was the Iranian position going into the Paris meetings.

On Sunday, October 19, Raja'i flew to Algiers, where he had discussions with Algerian officials. He left Algiers for Tehran the following day, stopping briefly in Libya. As Raja'i was on his way back to Tehran, President Carter announced that if the hostages were released, "I will unfreeze the assets in banks here and in Europe, drop the embargo against trade and work toward resumption of normal commerce with Iran in the future."[2]

Also on October 20, Secretary of State Muskie said that the United States was "opposed to the dismemberment" of Iran. "The cohesion and stability of Iran is in the interest of the stability of the region as a whole," he said, adding that "the integrity of Iran is today threatened by the new Iraqi invasion."[3] This was the first time that a senior U.S. official had publicly characterized the Iraqi attack as an "invasion." Muskie called for an end to the Iran-Iraq war, and the State Department officially called on Iraq to withdraw from Iranian territory. Muskie's formulation would be repeated by the U.S. ambassador to the U.N., Donald McHenry, at a meeting of the Security Council on October 23, along with a call for Iraq to withdraw from Iranian territory. These statements were intended to inject life into the negotiations with Iran, which had languished since the U.S. message of October 11. In Tehran, however, no one was listening.

On Monday, October 20, the participants in the Paris meetings began to resurface. William Casey called Richard Allen in Washington. It was seven-thirty in the morning. In his telephone log Allen jotted down: "Casey re attack."[4] Allen later said that he could not recall what was meant by "attack," although on another occasion he said the phone call was on a "very specific" subject.[5] One possible explanation is that Casey was relaying information or instructions for the men who called themselves the "Attack Group." They were a small group of key campaign aides who met at six-thirty every morning in pollster Richard Wirthlin's apartment in suburban Virginia to go over the latest information concerning the hostages and to plan strategies for a Reagan-Bush response. (After the campaign each member would receive a paperweight inscribed with the legend "Attack Group.")[6]

Later on the same day, Cyrus Hashemi was back in his New York office. Almost immediately he called one of his contacts about stepping up efforts to purchase arms for Iran.[7]

On the following day, Tuesday, October 21, the Iranian government transferred $250,000 to the Israeli purchasing mission in Paris, followed by another $80,000 on the twenty-third to cover the cost of a planeload of F-4 tires and spare parts for Tampela mortars.[8] The two telexes involved in this transaction read as follows:

> October 21, 1980: Telex #240955-001/$U/15/5 (Zurich): Transfer $250,000 to Bank Hapoalim (Swiss) AG, Bahnhofstr. 20, 8022 Zurich for acct 1301812 of Israeli Govt Purchasing Mission.[9]

> October 23, 1980: Telex #240955-001/$U/15/5 (Zurich): Transfer $80,000 to Bank Hapoalim (Swiss) AG, 8022 Zurich for acct 1301812 of Israeli Govt Purchasing Mission.[10]

Hushang Lavi also reappeared on October 21. He contacted Mitch Rogovin by telephone, and Rogovin made the following entry about the conversation in his diary:

> Foreign agent in Paris sold documents endangering U.S. and Israel. Involved in war with Iraq. 48 hours Iranian agent coming —no release of anyone before election—want to talk to Bush.[11]

Neither Rogovin nor Lavi was later able or willing to explain this notation.[12] The foreign agent and the documents are not identified, but the note does tend to associate Lavi with Paris, where Lavi said he had been just days before. It also seems to suggest that an Iranian was coming in the next forty-eight hours, that there would be no release of U.S. hostages before the election, and that the Iranian wanted to talk to George Bush.

Later that day, Rogovin spoke to Harold Saunders at the State Department. Saunders had a message of his own. Ambassador Ritzel in Tehran had made contact with Bani-Sadr and had determined that Hushang Lavi had no authority to speak on the Iranian president's behalf. As a result, Lavi's proposed swap of F-14 spare parts for the hostages was no longer under active consideration. Rogovin, in turn, said he had heard that "the Iranians were not going to make a negotiation with the Carter administration." Saunders replied that he had "not heard that."[13]

Meanwhile, in his New York office, Cyrus Hashemi convened a meeting to discuss how to organize new arms sales to Iran.[14] According to his intermediary with the Carter administration, Hashemi also spoke to Rafsanjani or to someone in the speaker's office on two different occasions on this date. Hashemi claimed that Rafsanjani and Raja'i had gone together to see Khomeini to discuss the timing of the hostage release. Khomeini reportedly told them that he was "not disposed to release the hostages before November 4."[15] Indeed, that same day, Raja'i declared that he and the ayatollah had agreed that Iran would not negotiate the release of the hostages with the Carter administration, even if the United States "might offer to provide spare parts" in exchange for the hostages. "The hostages," he said, "are not really a problem for us; we are in the process of resolving [the crisis]. The nature of the hostage taking was important for us. We got the results long ago."[16]

This stunning renunciation of the entire negotiating process with the Carter administration brought to a crashing end the optimism that had blossomed in the White House only a few days earlier. It was also a reversal of the assurances that Raja'i had personally given to Katherine Keough only four days earlier. The implication was clear: When Raja'i left for New York on the sixteenth, it was assumed in Iran that the hostage episode would end shortly after the U.S. presidential elections; by the time Raja'i returned on the twenty-first, the entire concept of a negotiation with the Carter administration was no longer acceptable, and the likelihood of an early hostage release had receded. Something had happened while Raja'i was gone.

While campaigning in Kentucky, Ronald Reagan chose this day to address the hostage issue, the first time he had done so in weeks. He said the hostage crisis had been "a humiliation and a disgrace for this country." When asked what could be done, Reagan replied: "I've had some ideas, but you don't talk about them."[17] Reagan refused, then or later, to expand on what commentators dubbed his "secret plan."

On the campaign trail in Beaufort, Texas, Carter responded that Reagan's "secret plan" reminded him of Richard Nixon's promises in the 1968 presidential campaign to end the Vietnam War.[18] The analogy, it turned out, was apt. Twelve years earlier, representatives of Richard Nixon's cam-

paign intervened with the North Vietnamese government to spike a negotiating process by the Johnson administration, already under way in Paris,
holding out the promise of a better deal once the Republicans came to
power.

George Bush also raised the hostage issue on October 21. Noting that
the Carter administration might try to pull an "October surprise" with the
hostages in the last days of the campaign, Bush said, "Frankly, we've been
concerned about it."[19]

The Iranians were also concerned. They probably suspected that the
Carter administration had the capacity to launch a second rescue mission.
They may well have feared that if Carter was convinced that the negotiating
track was truly dead, he might be tempted to implement a military solution.
There is some evidence that this was a genuine concern. On Wednesday,
October 22, the day after Raja'i announced that Iran would not negotiate
the release of the hostages, Iran took defensive measures. In the middle of
the night, Chuck Scott and Don Sharer were roused from their cell in
Komiteh Prison, blindfolded, shoved into a vehicle and moved to Evin
Prison. In the dark, barefoot, and with a blanket tossed over his head,
Colonel Scott heard the guards talking among themselves about a U.S.
military attack. Scott and Sharer were tossed into a tiny cell with no heat,
no blankets, and no mattresses. It was snowing outside, and the cell was as
cold as a freezer.

Evin Prison was the largest and most sinister political prison in Iran. It
was the site of torture and political executions under the shah, and the
revolutionaries continued the same tradition, with televised mass machine-
gunnings of opponents of the new regime. Scott's cell bore the grisly marks
of its doomed predecessors and was empty except for puddles of what
appeared to be bodily fluids. Scott knew Evin's reputation, and he assumed
that he and a select group of his colleagues had been singled out for
punishment or death. It was his lowest psychological moment of the entire
ordeal.[20]

Most of the hostages had been assembled in Komiteh Prison during the
summer and had remained there despite the outbreak of the war and the
publication of the Jack Anderson columns warning of a possible U.S. military strike. However, on October 22, having struck a deal with the Republicans in Paris and rejected all overtures by the Carter administration, the

Iranian leaders were concerned about the possibility of just such a rescue attempt.

What is indisputable is that within days of the reported end of the Paris meetings, Colonel Scott and about a dozen other hostages were abruptly ousted from Komiteh and moved to Evin Prison, where they remained in appalling conditions for another sixty days.

At the same time, the Iranian leadership began on October 22 to back away from the absolute rejection of negotiations, apparently in hopes of forestalling any precipitous action by the Carter administration which would jeopardize the deal struck in Paris with Casey. In public statements in Tehran and in messages relayed through Cyrus Hashemi, the new line was that the decision was up to the Majles. In an interview with Agence France Presse that day, Prime Minister Raja'i said he was certain that the United States was ready to meet the conditions announced by Khomeini in September but that the decision to negotiate or not to negotiate with the United States was up to the Majles. He seemed to be fully aware of the implications for U.S. politics, since he added that the Majles would debate the hostage question "even if the debate lasts until the elections."[21]

Hojjat ol-Eslam Mohammed Asqar Musavi Kho'eniha, one of the members of the seven-man commission established by the Majles to define the conditions for the release of the hostages, also said on October 22 that the Majles might make a decision as early as October 26. If the United States accepted the Majles's conditions, he said, the hostages could be set free the following day.[22] The Carter administration viewed this statement as particularly significant since Kho'eniha was one of the ultra-radicals in Iran's revolutionary hierarchy. He was routinely described in the Iranian media as the "spiritual leader" of the militants holding the U.S. hostages, and he had been intimately involved in planning the original attack on the embassy.

Meanwhile, Cyrus Hashemi reported to the Carter administration that morning that there had been another meeting in Tehran with Khomeini, who seemed much calmer than he had been the day before. According to Hashemi, the clerical leadership had concluded that Khomeini was less adamant about the possibility of negotiations with the Carter administration. Khomeini had not rejected the idea under all circumstances, and if the Majles acted promptly there might still be negotiations, perhaps in time to arrange a release before the election. Hashemi, however, was playing a double game. He was reporting to the U.S. government information he claimed to have obtained through his telephone contacts with Rafsanjani's office, but he was also closely associated with those who had apparently just concluded a separate deal. Especially in the period after the Paris meetings, Hashemi had the potential to put a spin on the information out of Tehran and thereby lull or mislead the negotiators in the Carter administration.

In the end, the Iranian posturing was nothing but a charade. The evidence overwhelmingly suggests that Khomeini's pronouncement on October 21 was final and that there was no inclination on the part of Iran to negotiate a release prior to the U.S. elections. Ahmed Salamatian was an influential member of the Majles during this period, and he served as informal liaison between the Majles and President Bani-Sadr. He was responsible for tracking the actions of the hostage commission, and he later vividly recalled the experience:

> In mid-October, I started going to the Majles every day, asking them for the results of their consultations. Tabatabai had already presented a paper approved by Khomeini outlining the terms for the release of the hostages, so there really was nothing to discuss. Yet day after day nothing happened. When I talked to the members of the commission, they looked at me with disdain, as if I did not understand what was really going on. Later I understood why. They were stalling.[23]

One last piece of information reached the Carter administration on October 22. That afternoon, through CIA channels, the government of Israel reported that it had been in touch with the Iranians concerning a possible exchange of "hostages for spares," specifically Israeli-made F-4 aircraft tires and possibly some other matériel.[24] This part of the drama would play itself out on the following day.

Before dawn on the morning of Thursday, October 23, a cargo aircraft of the French company Aerotour took off from Paris. The plane touched down briefly in Bastia, an out-of-the-way airport on the northern tip of the French island of Corsica in the Mediterranean, and then flew on to Tel Aviv. This flight was the culmination of the arms deal that Ahmed Heidari had been preparing for several months. It was eagerly awaited in Tehran not only by Heidari but especially by Jacques Montanès, who hoped that the successful completion of this mission would end his status as an involuntary guest of the Iranian government.

Shortly after the plane touched down in Tel Aviv, President Carter was told of the proposed shipment of arms to Iran. Carter immediately fired off an urgent message to Prime Minister Begin. Carter's tone was extremely angry; he implied that Begin had double-crossed him by again selling arms to Iran.

Within hours, a delegation from the American Embassy met with Begin to deliver Carter's message. Begin listened and indicated some surprise at its pungent nature. He observed laconically that one delivery had already left Israel, but he would now see what could be done about halting any further deliveries. He said it was his duty to take seriously the U.S. point of view, and Israel would hold off for the time being on any further arms deliveries, particularly in view of the current rumors of the imminent release of the hostages.

As this conversation was taking place, the French Aerotour aircraft may indeed have already left Tel Aviv, but not by much.[25] The plane had arrived in Israel only hours before, and the loading took some time. In fact, the loading of the aircraft may have been cut short to make sure the plane took off before Begin met with the Americans so that the prime minister could truthfully inform them that one delivery had already departed. Originally, the plane was to have been loaded with 250 F-4 tires and spare parts for the Israeli-made Tampela mortar. When the aircraft returned that night to France, the F-4 tires were in the cargo bay but the mortar spares were not. Israel offered no explanation to Heidari and his partners for the failure to deliver the mortar parts.

Late on the night of the twenty-third, the Aerotour plane arrived in Nîmes, France, where it was met by a DC-8 rented from the Cargolux Company. The 250 F-4 tires were transferred to the DC-8, together with spare parts for M-60 tanks, several thousand PRC 77 batteries from Spain, and a J60 motor for a Scorpio armored car. An M-60 tank motor that was supposed to be included had been delayed at the Spanish border and failed to get on the flight. Iran Air, the Iranian commercial airline, arranged for this aircraft to use the call sign of Iran Air flight 999 for the flight to Tehran on the twenty-fourth.

The invoice for Iran Air flight 999 from Nîmes to Tehran shows a delivery from SETI International consigned to the "Presidency, Republic of Iran, Tehran." The cargo, slightly disguised, was listed as: 366 packages, 15,066 kilograms, consisting of 1 Caterpillar motor; 1 truck motor; 250 tires; 100 telephone units; 4 batteries; and 10 heavy spare parts for motors. The invoice, dated October 24, 1980, bears the stamp: "All the cargo received by 707-747—terminal Shams."

Despite a solemn promise to the President of the United States and despite the fact that U.S. negotiations with Iran were in a particularly delicate phase, Israel had succeeded in fulfilling what it apparently regarded as an overriding commitment to deliver military equipment to Iran. The shipment had been planned for weeks, but the final arrangements were carried out only after the meetings in Paris. Israel's notification to the United States of the prospective shipment seemed to be timed so the shipment would be gone before the United States could react.

Judging from the surreptitious and deceptive manner in which this arms sale was organized and carried out, as well as Prime Minister Begin's almost casual revocation of his own orders not to send Iran any equipment, "not even shoelaces" (which had been circulated in writing to the Israeli security establishment six months earlier), it is difficult to avoid a troubling conclusion. The Israeli leadership, at the very highest level, had deliberately, almost contemptuously, turned its back on Jimmy Carter's administration.

For any Israeli government, there are few decisions more grave than to risk its relations with its principal political, military, and financial backer. That risk would scarcely be justified by mere impatience to reopen a channel to the Iranian military. It might be justified, however, if Israel had already decided that its future lay not with the Carter administration but with its likely successor.

On Friday, October 24, at President Carter's weekly breakfast meeting with his top national security advisers, the participants focused on the positive statements emanating from Tehran since Wednesday. Carter decided that if there was a favorable reply from Iran over the weekend, he would return from Camp David and go on television to explain to the

American people what had happened in the negotiations and the terms he had accepted. The President and his advisers reviewed the Israeli delivery of spare parts and considered a follow-up message to Begin, and there was a brief discussion of contingency plans for how to handle the hostages once they were released. There was no discussion of a rescue mission.[26]

While this meeting was going on, the Reagan-Bush campaign was preparing for any eventuality. Despite the deal in Paris, Casey could not be entirely sure that the Iranians might not double-cross him by concluding negotiations with Carter before Election Day. Edwin Meese III, the campaign's chief of staff, wrote a pair of memorandums on October 24 to all of the key Reagan campaign deputies notifying them that Bob Garrick, the reserve admiral who had set up the surveillance of military air bases, would assume "special responsibility for coordinating Campaign Headquarters activities relating to our response to the hostage situation."[27]

Although the memo was from Meese, Garrick believed that Casey was primarily responsible. In his opinion, Casey "had information that something tangible was happening," and wanted to make sure it was closely watched. Garrick interpreted his duties as keeping track of anything the Carter administration did with respect to the hostages.[28]

Some of the mood of apprehension within the campaign was reflected by a Reagan-Bush campaign adviser who said in Atlanta that day that it would be better "for the Republic as a whole" if the hostages were released after the elections were over.[29] Another campaign aide said, "It would be curtains" for the Reagan-Bush campaign if the hostages were released,[30] and a "worried" Reagan campaign aide commented that "It would be a great injustice if the hostages got the president off the hook," but that is what could happen if they were released before the election.[31] And Richard Allen was convinced that Carter was capable of pulling off some desperate last-minute stunt.[32]

Not every Republican was focused on the immediate prospects of a hostage release. Former Secretary of State Henry Kissinger told the press that day that there was no reason a Reagan administration could not work with Iran once the hostages were freed. Iran, he said, was a strategic country and the hostility need not be permanent.[33] That, of course, was precisely the nature of the bargain proposed by Casey to the Iranians.

The news from Tehran suggested that the Republicans had little to worry about. Khomeini, speaking in the Friday prayers at Tehran University, said that the rumors of a deal with the Carter administration were nothing but the product of the foreign media. Iran, he said, had not asked the United States for assistance or spare parts in exchange for the hostages.[34] As usual, in the welter of information and rumors, Khomeini's voice was consistent. He had reportedly rejected a deal with the Carter administration on October 21, and this statement provided no hint that he had altered his position in any way. And on Saturday the twenty-fifth, Kho'eniha now insisted, "We are not in a hurry to release the hostages. We have no intention of helping Jimmy Carter in his presidential campaign." The Majles debate, he added, might be "long and tough."[35] Indeed it was. One session after another failed to produce an agreed set of negotiating terms. One session at the end of the month had to be canceled for lack of a quorum. Action was successively postponed until the final days before the election in November.

The Carter administration settled into gloom and frustration as the Majles repeatedly failed to act. Brzezinski later described the mood:

Our hopes for a positive resolution of the hostage issue were dashed in late October. On the twenty-seventh, at 10:30 a.m., just prior to Carter's departure for Cleveland, where he was to make a campaign speech, Muskie, Christopher and I met with him to tell him that the Iranians had postponed any decision and that all we had were some hints that the Iranians might release a portion of the hostages and then wait to see whether we were implementing our part of the bargain. This would be clearly unsatisfactory. The President listened, instructed us to keep him informed, gave us a wave, and abruptly terminated the meeting.[36]

At this time, the Reagan-Bush campaign asked for and received its first and only briefing from the administration on the hostage situation. William Casey, Edwin Meese, Richard Allen, and Representative Dean Birch came to the State Department at six-fifteen P.M. on Monday, October 27, and met with Harold Saunders for a review of the negotiations with Iran. They listened carefully to his description of the situation and left without comment.[37]

■ ■ ■

What is usually forgotten about the 1980 election is just how close it appeared going into the final days of the campaign. The comfortable lead Reagan had enjoyed over Carter in July and August had dwindled, and the two contenders appeared to be in a dead heat. A survey conducted on October 14 by Richard Wirthlin, Reagan's chief pollster and strategist, actually showed Carter ahead, 41 percent to 39 percent. It was the first time the Georgian had been the front runner in the Republican polls in months.[38] By the third week in October, Robert Teeter, who worked with Wirthlin, told Elizabeth Drew of *The New Yorker* that the race was quite close in most of the important states, with both candidates having somewhere between 36 percent and 41 percent of the votes. The voters who were naturally attracted to one or the other had already made their choices. What was left now was for the two politicians "to do something a little different to get the last 1 or 8 percent," Teeter said, and then added, "In the Detroit vernacular, 'You've sold everyone a Chevrolet who's going to buy one.' "[39]

Teeter was referring to the debate between the candidates to be held on Tuesday, October 28, when he spoke of "something a little different," but in fact, release of the hostages would have been "a little different" as well. According to Reagan's own polls, there would be a 10 percent boost for Carter if he brought the hostages home between October 18 and 25. That 10 percent might easily have kept Carter in the White House for four more years.[40]

When the candidates showed up in Cleveland for the debate—their only face-to-face encounter of the campaign—all the major polls showed them in a neck-and-neck race. The election was just one week away and the media had built up enormous expectations: "It has become the world heavyweight championship and the Super Bowl combined," wrote Elizabeth Drew. "The only thing missing is Howard Cosell."[41]

In fact, the only thing missing was a copy of Carter's foreign-policy and national-defense briefing book, which had been assembled only days before. That the briefing book fell into the Republicans' hands so soon after having been compiled is further evidence of the Reagan-Bush campaign's successful intelligence penetration of the Carter White House. The Republican operatives had earlier obtained copies of foreign-policy and national-defense briefing papers prepared for the use of President Carter and Vice President Mondale, and the campaign apparently had acquired a version of Carter's domestic-policy briefing book as well.

During the ninety-minute debate, the hostage issue was very much on the candidates' minds. Reagan spoke of the national humiliation that the United States had experienced as a result of the prolonged holding of American hostages. Once they were safely home, he said, a congressional investigation should be undertaken to look into the diplomatic handling of the situation. (Reagan was President when the hostages were released. He did not call for an investigation of any kind.)

Carter reiterated previous administration statements about U.S. neutrality in the Iran-Iraq war. On the question of arms, he said, "We have no plans to sell additional material or goods to Iran that might be of a warlike nature." But, he added, if the hostages were released safely, then the United States would complete delivery of items that had been bought and paid for by Iran and were in the supply pipeline when the hostages were taken. The frozen Iranian assets would also be released, Carter said. "That's been a consistent policy—one I intend to carry out."

Reagan asserted it was "high time that the civilized countries of the world made it plain that there is no room worldwide for terrorism." "There will be no negotiation with terrorists of any kind," he declared. Asked about his campaign suggestion that he had ideas on what to do about the hostage crisis, Reagan said, yes, he had ideas on the subject just as other people probably had. But they were just ideas, he said, and he would be fearful of injecting them at this point and maybe endangering the hostages.

The debate was not primarily about hostages, but in retrospect, it is clear that it introduced some important new elements. Carter, for the first time, unequivocally and publicly announced that he would return all of Iran's impounded military equipment if the hostages were returned safely. It is doubtful that this offer to return all the Iranian weaponry had any significant effect in Tehran, where all the major leaders had already stated that Iran was no longer interested in arms as a component of the hostage negotiations. The offer was, quite simply, too little too late. But the statement is interesting in retrospect, if only as evidence of how long it took for Jimmy Carter to reconcile himself to anything that appeared to be a swap of arms for hostages. Despite the pressures of the election and his own commitment to free the hostages, he was unwilling to offer the entire package of arms—already owned and long since paid for by Iran—until literally the last days of the campaign, when it seemed he had no other realistic choice. Then, characteristically, once he had decided that it could not be avoided, he announced his decision directly to the American public.

The second new element was Ronald Reagan's assertion in the debate that "there will be no negotiation with terrorists of any kind," which certainly included the Iranians. Yet just about a week before, his campaign manager had returned from Paris, where he had negotiated—for at least the third time—with Iranians over the nature and timing of the release of the hostages in return for promises of political and military favors from the United States. And it will be recalled that on September 13, Reagan himself had issued a statement that spelled out in some detail a negotiating position with Iran, responding positively to each of the four conditions imposed by Khomeini for the release of the hostages.

In the final days of October, there was another flurry of contradictory reports out of Tehran. Hushang Lavi reported through Mitch Rogovin on the twenty-eighth that Tehran would send a team to the United States to wrap up the hostage negotiations sometime between the fifth and the tenth of November.[42] Lavi's information proved surprisingly accurate. The Iranians would soon nominate the Algerians to represent them, and the final negotiating phase would begin in earnest immediately after the November 4 election. Lavi asked that these talks be initiated through him to Tehran. When contacted, Harold Saunders of the State Department refused.

Cyrus Hashemi, back in London, reported on October 30 that he had been in contact with Rafsanjani, who said Iran had all the necessary answers from the United States and the rest was up to the Iranians. He indicated that all the hostages might be released except for those most strongly suspected of spying, who would be put on trial. The next day, Hashemi reported that Khomeini had reversed himself and decided on the immediate release of the hostages. This was utter nonsense, and in retrospect it strengthens the view that Hashemi was by this time deliberately attempting to mislead the Carter administration into false optimism to ensure no drastic action would be taken to rescue the hostages.

The Republican disinformation campaign was also back in high gear as the election approached. There were detailed reports from WLS-TV in Chicago and from several pro-Reagan columnists that U.S. military aircraft were already en route to Iran and that the swap of arms for hostages would take place over the weekend, just before the election.[43] As before, the reports were wholly imaginary.

On the eve of the election, William Casey could take heart from the fact that he had been able to prevent his candidate from falling victim to an "October surprise." Indeed, as he well knew, it was Carter's campaign that was most vulnerable to events that were now beyond its control. The Iranians, it appeared, had honored the terms of their Paris bargain. (Casey had no way to know, however, that contrary to Karrubi's assurance, the treatment of the hostages had not improved. And, in some cases, had actually worsened.) The hostages would not be released before November 4. And Israel, for its part, had sent a first shipment of military matériel in defiance of Carter's embargo. The administration was increasingly constrained, its policies enfeebled, its authority under siege. Casey's elaborate plot against the democratically elected government of the United States was almost complete. All that was left was for the American people to elect Ronald Reagan as their President.

· 10 ·

CARTER UNDONE

On Sunday morning, November 2, Jimmy Carter was awakened with the news that the Majles had issued an important declaration on the hostages. Carter, who was in Chicago campaigning, immediately returned to Washington. When the President's helicopter touched down on the South Lawn of the White House at precisely eight o'clock, National Security Adviser Zbigniew Brzezinski met him at the foot of the steps. While the rotor blades were still turning, he handed Carter the full translation of the Majles declaration. Without a word, the President took the text and read it as he walked to the Oval Office. Its contents would determine not only the fate of the hostages but his own as well. As Hamilton Jordan, Carter's campaign manager, would write in his memoirs: "If something dramatic happened Monday—like the release of the hostages—it would probably allow us to nose Reagan out; a bad signal from the Iranian Parliament Sunday would probably mean Reagan's election."[1]

When Carter emerged from the Oval Office, he had concluded that while the declaration provided a useful basis for negotiations, it did not provide adequate grounds for the United States to take immediate action. The hostages were not going to be released before the election, and probably not for some time thereafter.

It must have been a moment of profound disappointment for Carter. He had devoted most of the past year to securing freedom for the hostages. Beginning in September, his strategy of patient exploration had seemed to be paying off: Messages were exchanged with Tehran and a negotiating structure appeared to be emerging. Moreover, the Iranians' need to resolve the hostage crisis and remove the U.S.-imposed arms embargo had increased with the Iraqi invasion. Iran, Carter believed, had everything to gain by negotiating a settlement under the pressure of the November 4 deadline, and everything to lose by delaying. The Iranians' best chance with Carter would be before the American election. Afterward, they risked facing a hostile Carter or, it seemed, the more belligerent Reagan. Carter believed that he held a strong hand. If the Iranians wanted to rid themselves of the albatross that the hostage situation had become, they had to deal with him, and he was not inclined to be unduly generous. He had adopted what he regarded as a dignified negotiating posture consistent with American interests, principles, and honor. He was not willing to deal under the table or to pay ransom, but he was prepared to restore the status quo ante.

The Iranians, however, had refused to follow the script. Unaccountably, everything had stopped in mid-October, and there had been nothing but frustration and conflicting signals ever since. While revolutionary Iran operated according to its own peculiar set of rules, neither Carter nor any of his advisers could tease the thread of logic out of Iran's recent baffling behavior. It would never have occurred to them that a group of private citizens might have entered into diplomatic negotiations with a hostile foreign power to undercut their own government in a ruthless quest for political power.

Carter betrayed none of his emotions. "There are several things in the list of conditions that we cannot do," he said. "They've got some words like 'confiscate the shah's property,' and they demand that the U.S. government remove all private claims against Iranian assets. These are things we cannot do under our law, and they're not right anyway."

Carter decided to adopt a two-track response. He sent a private message to Iran through the West Germans, identifying the areas of agreement and those that required further negotiation. He drafted a second brief statement that he would deliver to the American people on television that evening. When he went on the air, he described the action by the Majles as constructive and as providing the basis for resolving U.S.-Iran differences. He said his response would not be affected by the calendar and that the other presidential candidates and the bipartisan leadership of the Congress were being kept informed. He wanted to see the hostages released, he said, but only if the honor and integrity of the United States were maintained in the process.

The statement was honest and responsible, but it was a political disaster. Carter's gloomy report reminded viewers of all the year's other dashed hopes. This was underscored the following day, when virtually every newspaper, radio station, and television station in the country featured retrospectives on the year-long hostage ordeal.

The effect was dramatic. Until then, the election had not appeared to be entirely beyond Carter's reach. But on November 3, Pat Caddell, the pollster for the Carter campaign, detected a shift of stunning proportions. Normally, the "undecideds" in the polls split approximately along the lines of those who have already made up their minds. But Caddell found the "undecideds" stampeding away from Carter, and by two A.M. on Election Day, he called Hamilton Jordan with the news. "It's all over," he said, "—it's gone."[2] In the end, it was indeed a rout; Reagan won by a margin of nine million popular votes, swamping Carter in the Electoral College, 489 votes to 49.

Early in the morning of November 5, Chuck Scott and his cellmate in Evin Prison waited to hear the election returns. A few days earlier, one guard, Akbar, who had consistently displayed some measure of human sympathy for Scott and his fellow prisoners, had sneaked a tiny radio into the cell so the prisoners could hear the news after the Majles had sent its list of demands to Washington. This was an unprecedented breach of security, but Akbar clearly believed that this was an exceptional day. He sat with his ear glued to the radio and said there was "good news coming." "We have information from someone in Washington confirming Carter's willingness to agree," Akbar had told Scott. But no agreement was made and Akbar left, saying, "This was supposed to be a great day for all of us. I wonder what happened."[3]

The next day Akbar had been reprimanded. So it was another young guard who brought tea and news of the American elections. Carter, he told them, had lost. "We have changed your President."

Before the Paris meetings, there had seemed to be an almost universal belief among those Iranians associated with the hostage issue that the hostages would be released shortly after the U.S. elections. The prison guards were at the lowest end of the information chain, and they still seemed to be operating on the basis of those earlier rumors or reports. However, on November 24, Hojjat ol-Eslam Sadegh Khalkhali was quoted by Tehran radio as saying that the American hostages would not be released before Ronald Reagan's inaugural.[4] Khalkhali had a reputation for saying aloud what others were only thinking. In this case he was exactly right.

While the Iranians had agreed in Paris to delay the release of the hostages in exchange for the promise of future arms shipments via Israel, they had not made any arrangements or reached any understanding regarding the financial and military assets that were frozen in the United States. As Casey had reminded them, Ronald Reagan would not take office until January 20, and the Republicans were powerless to release these assets before that date. The Iranians would have to work out the exact terms of the release with the lame-duck Carter administration.

Since Behzad Nabavi's commission, which the Majles had appointed on September 30 to negotiate the end of the hostage problem, was not authorized to have any direct contact with the United States, the Iranians chose to deliver the official text of the Majles's declaration to the State Department on November 3 through the Algerian ambassador in Washington, Redha Malek. Iran had apparently decided that the West Germans were too close to the United States to continue to serve as intermediaries, so they proposed that the Algerians assume this role. The United States agreed, and one week later Warren Christopher arrived in Algiers for an extended preparatory session. A detailed U.S. reply to the Majles's declaration was given to the Algerians on November 11, and a team of Algerian diplomats began a series of periodic shuttles between Tehran, Algiers, and Washington.[5]

On November 21, the Iranian negotiators responded haughtily to the U.S. note. They could not, they said, deviate in any way from the conditions laid down by the Majles, and they rejected the U.S. counterproposals as "unrelated" to the issue. What they needed, according to the Algerian intermediaries, was a simple "yes or no" answer or else a request for clarification.

The Iranian negotiators had seemingly painted themselves into a corner. They could not talk to the United States, nor could they afford to be perceived as deviating in any way from the terms spelled out by the Majles. The United States, in turn, could not accept the Majles's conditions as they stood. It is also possible that that the unstated purpose behind the negotiators' tactics may have been to drag out the process deliberately, since they had no intention of setting the hostages free before January 20.

Christopher and his negotiating team, after intensive consultations with the Algerians, squared the circle with some creative drafting. A brief letter of the "yes, but" variety was prepared. Each of the Iranian conditions was answered in the positive, but in each case the reader was referred to a separate document that spelled out the conditions of the U.S. acceptance. Christopher made it clear that the U.S. position on the key legal issues was not going to change and that the Iranians could expect no cooperation on identifying their assets in the United States unless they provided a similar accounting of the location and condition of each of the hostages.

The final text of the U.S. reply, which the Algerians carried back to Tehran on December 3, had two important new additions. First, it raised the possibility of a claims settlement procedure, which would permit the myriad private claims and counterclaims between the United States and Iran to be resolved through international arbitration. This provision would help resolve one of the key differences between Iran and the United States, by prescribing a method for freeing Iranian assets in the United States that were under attachment by U.S. companies claiming commercial losses because of the revolution. However, it was fundamentally contrary to Iran's interests.

If U.S. claims against Iran were pursued only in U.S. courts, Iran could claim sovereign immunity and there was no realistic prospect that any American claimant could win a judgment, or if a claimant did win, he could not expect to collect. If the cases were handled by a mutually accepted arbitration court, however, American claimants could both win and collect damages. The fact that Iran was now willing to consider such a solution was the first real sign that its position was eroding and that it might accept unfavorable terms if necessary to bring the hostage problem to a close.

The second element of the U.S. note on December 3 was a clear message to Iran that time was running out, that Iran would have to accept some financial loss in any settlement, just as the U.S. hostages had suffered great personal loss, and that there was no assurance about what would happen if the hostage situation went on into the next administration. During this period, White House counsel Lloyd Cutler asked Casey and other members of the Reagan team to assist in the negotiations by stating that they would offer no better terms than those negotiated by Carter. Casey and the Reagan team refused to make such a commitment or to help in any way, so the Carter negotiating team made a virtue of necessity by warning Iran that there was no certainty about what the new Reagan administration would do.[6]

While they had no ironclad guarantees that the Republicans would live up to their end of the Paris agreement, the Iranians could find encouragement in the fact that the Israelis had begun laying the groundwork for a new arms and intelligence relationship with Iran.

On November 13, Israeli Prime Minister Begin visited Washington and met for the last time with President Carter. Begin reiterated Israel's interest in selling military equipment to Iran. Without referring to the shipment of F-4 tires that Israel had made despite U.S. objections some three weeks earlier, Begin noted that the Iranians had asked Israel for help and that his government would like to oblige. Israel was interested in developing a long-term relationship with Iran, and this was an attractive opportunity. It would also give Israel an opening to encourage the release of the hostages.

Carter's reply was sharp and unequivocal. He said that arms sales to Iran would be a violation of the embargo that the United States had imposed on Iran and would be harmful to U.S. interests. Carter strongly urged Begin to refuse any further trade with Iran until after the hostages were released.[7]

Begin promised to comply, but he was not seriously deterred. Just two weeks later, a special Israeli task force was formed to coordinate and manage Israel's covert policies toward Iran, including arms sales. The members of this group, who referred to themselves simply as "the Committee," were drawn from various parts of the Israeli intelligence community, and its founding members were the six Israelis who had represented their country in the Paris meetings in mid-October.[8] They were responsible for coordinating Israel's intelligence dealings with Iran, and they reported through their "chief" directly to the office of the prime minister. Since the committee was not established as a separate bureaucratic entity, all of its participants continued to perform their existing jobs within Israeli intelligence. They were all given secrecy oaths to sign and were told that even the mention of the group's existence was prohibited. However, Ari Ben-Menashe has reported that he was inducted into the group on November 28, 1980. The existence of a joint working group on Iran drawn from various agencies was subsequently confirmed by General Yehoshua Saguy, who had been the director of Israeli military intelligence from 1979 to 1983.[9]

Cyrus Hashemi also launched into action immediately after the Paris meetings, spearheading a major effort to purchase military equipment for Iran.[10] He and his brother Reza were regularly in contact with a number of American arms manufacturers and brokers, along with several influential Iranians, including Cyrus Davari and Djarfar Karimi, both of whom were naval officers attached to the Iranian military-procurement office in London. The items that Cyrus and Reza attempted to buy and ship to Iran were numerous and varied. They included voltage regulators for military aircraft, crankshafts for Scorpion armored cars, night-vision devices, large quantities of military field-communications wire, spare parts for Cobra helicopters, tires, air-to-ground missiles, inflatable rafts conforming to military specifications, underwater television cameras, machine guns, and so on.

In late November, while talking to an American who had offered to sell them military equipment, Reza Hashemi said that if they wanted to make money on the deal, "it is important that the money be made now . . . because when the hostages are released, Iran will no longer request the spare parts."[11] Reza, who was clearly uncomfortable with his role, repeated this same statement to other potential clients at other times, noting with some anticipation that this was "a short temporary business" and that he hoped to be out of it before long.

Reza firmly believed that as soon as the hostages were released, Iran would have a reliable source of military supplies, and he saw his illegal actions as simply a temporary and lucrative expedient to fill the gap. That is consistent with the description of Casey's agreement in Paris: The hostages would be released upon the inauguration of Ronald Reagan, and the new Reagan administration, once in office, would permit the flow of military supplies to Iran through Israel.

So much is known of the Hashemi brothers' activities during this period because they were under intense surveillance by the FBI. In August 1980, the FBI sought permission to install an elaborate surveillance system in the offices of Cyrus Hashemi's First Gulf Bank & Trust Company in New York. The original application was for national-security reasons and was apparently requested by the CIA or other elements of the Carter administration on the grounds that Cyrus Hashemi was suspected of being an agent of a foreign country, presumably Iran. The timing of this request, the text of which remains sealed to this day, suggested that it was intended as a check on the bona fides of Cyrus Hashemi at a time when he was providing regular information to the Carter administration on political developments in Iran. The special agent of the FBI assigned to the case was a supervisor in the New York office responsible for investigations of foreign counter-intelligence matters relating to the Middle East. The request was approved on August 29, but the actual installation, which involved breaking into Hashemi's offices, was not completed until about October 14, just before the Paris meetings began.

The surveillance of the Hashemis had been instituted by the Carter administration for national-security purposes, but it quickly turned into a criminal investigation as evidence mounted of illegal arms activities by Cyrus and Reza. The White House first learned of this in mid-November when Lloyd Cutler was contacted by U.S. Customs officials, who reported on the evidence of illegal behavior by the Hashemis and asked if the administration had any objection to proceeding with a criminal investigation.

This was startling to Cutler, for he had met Cyrus Hashemi only days before, on November 15, to discuss the status of the private negotiations between key U.S. banks and Iran, the so-called "banking channel" in the hostage negotiations. He knew that Hashemi was in contact with several agencies of the U.S. government and had provided information during the tumultuous final weeks before the election. After checking with other agencies, Cutler informed Customs that the Carter administration had no objection to proceeding with the criminal investigation. On November 23, the surveillance of Cyrus Hashemi's offices was extended for another ninety days, until February 23, 1981.[12]

Everything seemed to be proceeding according to plan. The Republicans had won the election, the Israelis were setting up shop, and the Hashemi brothers were lining up potential arms suppliers. But on December 19, the Carter administration received a message from the Iranians that seemed to demolish all chance of working out an agreement before Reagan took office. Iran now proposed that the United States adhere to an extraordinary set of guarantees under any hostage agreement. The Iranian scheme had several elements:

- The United States should deposit $9.6 billion in Iranian assets, plus interest, and the gold on deposit with the Federal Reserve Bank, with the Central Bank of Algeria prior to the hostage release. These funds were to be available to Iran immediately upon release.
- The United States should also deposit $4 billion with Algeria as security for eventual repayment to Iran of Iranian funds held under attachment in the United States.
- The United States should accept liability for any claims against Iran for damages associated with the takeover of the embassy and incarceration of the hostages.
- The United States should provide an immediate accounting of the shah's assets in the United States and deposit $10 billion as security against their eventual return to Iran.
- If this was done, Iran would agree to bring current all outstanding payments on its loans from U.S. banks and would authorize the Central Bank of Algeria to hold $1 billion as a guarantee of future Iranian payments against the loans.

- Finally, Iran agreed to accept some form of claims-settlement procedure and would set aside another $1 billion to cover payment of claims. This fund would be replenished as necessary to ensure that it did not drop below $500 million until the settlement process was completed.

The outrageous effrontery of this proposal inspired shock and disbelief in Washington, where it was dubbed the "$24 billion misunderstanding." The United States could not and would not provide financial guarantees of future performance, and it seemed that the entire negotiating process had collapsed. Every American who read the text had the same initial reaction: The Iranians were not serious, and there was no possibility of continuing the negotiations.

As if to confirm this interpretation, Iran published a summary of its demands on December 21. This was the first break in confidentiality in the negotiations, and the United States responded by publishing the text of its own messages to Iran. This public exchange further dimmed whatever measure of trust or confidence may have existed between the two parties and seemed to mark the end of the process.

The breakdown in the talks also got the attention of the Reagan camp, where it apparently stirred fears that the Carter administration might not resolve the hostage situation before the inauguration, as they had hoped and expected. In that case, they would inherit the entire mess. It began to look as if the first foreign-policy crisis of the Reagan administration would be the same unrewarding predicament that had bedeviled Jimmy Carter. Reagan would perhaps have an opportunity after all to try his own "ideas" about a solution.

On about December 21, Edwin Meese, Reagan's trusted chief of staff, who was in charge of the presidential transition, paid an evening visit to Cyrus Hashemi, according to Robert McQueen, an agent with the U.S. Immigration and Naturalization Service. McQueen spent several days in December at the Hashemi home as part of an investigation, with which Cyrus's wife was cooperating, into a ring that was illegally selling "green cards" to wealthy Iranians. As McQueen was leaving late one afternoon, Mrs. Hashemi remarked to him that Meese was coming to their home for dinner that evening. McQueen, who later became a private investigator in

Washington, was startled by this news and reported it to his supervisor, who later verified McQueen's recollection of the incident. Their notes indicated that the date was probably December 21.[13]

At the time of that meeting, Cyrus Hashemi was involved in two major activities. He was still attempting to assist the hostage negotiations through the "banking channel," and was maintaining his contacts with various individuals in Iran. His contacts with the U.S. government, however, had become quite infrequent since knowledge of his illegal arms dealing had come to light. Only a few days earlier, on December 10, Hashemi had convened a small group in his New York office to discuss the military-equipment requests he had received from Captain Davari in London and how such transactions could be carried out without revealing the true identity of the goods and their destination. The group decided to consign the goods to a Swiss company in the Netherlands Antilles to avoid attracting attention.[14]

At the time of his dinner meeting with Hashemi, Meese was deeply involved in managing the transition and organizing the new administration. The Reagan transition team had steadfastly refused all offers by the Carter administration for a briefing on the hostage negotiations. Yet just as the hostage talks appeared to be breaking down, Edwin Meese found time in his schedule to drive to Wilton, Connecticut, to spend an evening with Cyrus Hashemi. Many years later, as evidence began to accumulate about the activities of the 1980 Reagan-Bush campaign with regard to the hostages, Meese would assert that "At no time did anyone in the campaign, connected with the campaign, associated with the campaign meet or negotiate or agree or conspire with anyone to delay the release of the hostages."[15] The December 21 dinner meeting illustrates just how much that carefully worded statement did *not* include. The campaign was over by that date, and the interest was presumably not to delay the hostage release but to insure that the release occurred by the date of Reagan's inauguration.

A few days after Meese's meeting with Hashemi, Ronald Reagan addressed the hostage question. In a Christmas Eve message to the nation, Reagan asserted that "the captors today are still making demands on us for their return, when their captors are nothing better than criminals and kidnappers who have violated international law totally in taking these innocent people and holding them this long." Four days later, he returned to the same topic. Criticizing Iran's new demands for billions of dollars, he said he opposed such a "down payment" on the grounds that one doesn't "pay ransom for people that have been kidnapped by barbarians." Reagan said he did not mean for his statements to be interpreted as a message to Tehran. "But if they got a message out of it they shouldn't wait for me," he added, "I'd be very happy."[16]

Only a few weeks earlier, Casey and the Reagan forces had refused the Carter administration's request for a strong statement from the Reagan transition team to help build a fire under Iran and thus speed the release of the hostages. Now, as the shoe began to pinch, they were pulling out all the stops.

In the meantime, Warren Christopher and his negotiating team had been taking a hard second look at the explosive Iranian proposal of December 19. The request for billions of dollars of indemnities was totally unacceptable, but there were two new elements in the Iranian message that attracted Washington's attention once the initial shock had subsided. Iran had accepted the principle of a claims-settlement procedure, which was very favorable to U.S. claimants. They had also accepted an escrow arrangement through the Bank of Algeria, which would be an essential element in any financial settlement. And, most surprisingly, they had agreed to pay U.S. banks all overdue installments on loans made under the shah. They had not insisted on a detailed accounting, which the United States note of December 3 had refused to provide, and they had indirectly acknowledged that the shah's assets in the United States could only be pursued through the U.S. judicial system. Shorn of its insulting language, the Iranian response contained substantial concessions. But even this more positive reading left a huge gap between what Iran was willing to offer and what the United States would be willing to accept. The question was whether to go back to the negotiating table, with only limited prospects of success in the few weeks remaining, or whether simply to present the problem to the incoming Reagan administration.

Carter's deep commitment to the hostages won out over political pragmatism. He ordered Christopher to make one final attempt, a decision made easier by the news from Tehran that on Christmas Eve the hostages had been moved from their prison sites to more comfortable quarters. The Algerian ambassador visited them on Christmas Day and positively identified all fifty-two, the first time in 420 days that all of the hostages had been confirmed to be alive.

The Algerian team arrived in Washington on December 29 for an intensive round of consultations. On New Year's Eve they departed for Tehran with a new U.S. proposal that incorporated the positive elements of the last Iranian message and simply ignored the parts that were unrealistic or offensive. The new proposal was written in the form of a "declaration" by the government of Algeria incorporating the points of agreement between the two parties. By this device, Iran and the United States would each make promises to Algeria, not to each other, thus removing one of the most serious sticking points for the Iranians.

The United States agreed to place $7.3 billion into an escrow account with the Central Bank of Algeria. These funds, representing the estimated value of Iran's frozen assets that could be immediately freed, plus unspecified interest, would be turned over to Iran when Algeria certified the safe release of all the hostages. Another $2.2 billion was under attachment by U.S. courts and was not included. The Carter administration accepted the Iranian proposal of a claims-settlement procedure with binding arbitration backed by an Iranian escrow account that would never fall below $500 million until all claims were resolved. With regard to the shah's assets, the United States reiterated its willingness to freeze existing assets, to direct collection of information about remaining assets, and to facilitate Iranian access to U.S. courts.

The proposal, which the Algerian team presented to Nabavi on January 3, established January 16 as the deadline for an agreement. Beyond that date, the Carter administration probably could not complete the necessary drafting and implementation before the inauguration on January 20. If there was no agreement by the sixteenth, the United States was authorized to withdraw from any obligations it had previously assumed. This was not a negotiating ploy. It was simply a realistic estimate in view of the impending change of administration in the United States, and it would assume increasing importance in the days that followed.

Iran's response to the latest U.S. proposal was businesslike. The members of Nabavi's commission made no further reference to the "$24 billion misunderstanding," and they began to flood the Algerians with requests for clarifications. These queries were transmitted in French from Tehran to Algiers, which forwarded them to Washington, where they were translated; Washington then sent the answer back to Algiers, whence it was relayed to Tehran. On January 7, Warren Christopher and a small group of aides moved to Algiers to speed up the response process.

The Iranian concerns were now focused almost entirely on money. They had publicly demanded the return of $9.6 billion in frozen assets, while the United States said only $7.3 billion was immediately available. The settlement of Iran's loans from U.S. banks was also a major issue. The Iranians had agreed to bring these loans current, that is, to make all overdue payments that had been allowed to lapse after the revolution and the hostage crisis; but the banks were suspicious and demanded some sort of fund that would guarantee future payments as well. For nearly two weeks, there was no real progress on either of these fundamental issues, but on January 15, the day before the U.S. deadline, Iran did a dramatic about-face. In a new memorandum, Nabavi and his commission offered not only to bring the loans current but to pay them off entirely, thus eliminating the issue. This possibility had never been seriously explored by either side in the negotiations, for it was immensely costly and wasteful for Iran. In effect, the Iranians were now agreeing to transfer large sums of hard currency to the Western banks in order to buy themselves out of the hostage impasse. It was an extraordinary concession, and in Iran it caused a sensation. Bani-Sadr later described the moment:

On January 15, Nabavi suddenly threw the engines into reverse. Not only did he renounce the $24 billion, he agreed to pay all of Iran's external debts in cash. The mere fact of paying in cash gave the Americans $500 million. What a windfall! . . . With only six days remaining until Reagan's inauguration, everyone aware of the secret agreement with the future president clearly understood this maneuver. Nabavi was making last-minute sacrifices to guarantee the success of the agreement and the release of the hostages as a gift to Ronald Reagan on the day of his inauguration.[17]

Ali Nobari, the head of Iran's Central Bank and a supporter of Bani-Sadr, had not been included in the decisions of the Nabavi commission. He was, however, responsible for Iran's finances and vividly recalled this sudden reversal.[18] According to Nobari, his deputy attended a meeting in mid-January, at which Nabavi announced without explanation that "it has been decided to give the money back to the U.S. banks." Nobari had long been opposed to the hostage-taking as harmful to Iran's national interests, and he had openly favored their release, but he saw this last-minute maneuver as harmful and wholly unnecessary.

As soon as he learned of the decision, Nobari was outraged. He prepared a fifteen-page letter to all 270 members of the Majles arguing that it was wrong and even contrary to Khomeini's conditions. Nobari recalled that he ran the copy machine in his office all night to get this letter into the hands of the Majles members before they voted, but it had no effect. The Majles was asked to approve the principle of the claims-settlement procedure and the nationalization of the shah's assets, but it was not presented with the text of the Algiers Accords, and the debate was pro forma.

Nobari also wrote to Khomeini about the decision, but he said his letter was "just tossed aside." Several months later Nobari met personally with Khomeini and used the occasion to argue forcefully that they should not have agreed to give the money back. Khomeini indicated that he had known about the decision and he was fully aware of its economic implications, but he simply dismissed Nobari's arguments.

According to Christian Bourguet, a French lawyer who was close to Ghotbzadeh and who was following events in Tehran very closely at the time, the group of radical mullahs around Khomeini brought heavy pressure on Nabavi to resolve the crisis before January 20. This pressure resulted in Iran's dramatic turnabout on the fifteenth.[19]

Jamshid Hashemi reported that this pressure had its source in the United States. He recalled that his brother Cyrus organized a meeting at the Sherry Netherland Hotel in New York in mid-January between members of the Reagan transition team, Iranian representatives, and at least one Israeli. In this meeting, the Iranians were told that "the deal was off" unless the hostages were out by January 20.[20] Jamshid Hashemi said he believed that Richard Allen was the person who delivered the message for the Republicans. (Allen later testified that he could recall no trip to New

York during the time in question and that to the best of his knowledge he was in Washington for the entire period just before the inauguration.)[21] A senior U.S. Customs agent who worked closely with Cyrus Hashemi in the mid-1980s has also stated that it was his understanding that there were contacts between the Republicans and the Iranians during this period and that a very tough message was delivered to end the hostage crisis before the inauguration or face severe consequences.[22]

This account is consistent with the known facts. The Republicans were deeply concerned that they would inherit the hostage problem. Reagan himself had made two statements castigating Iran for their delaying tactics, and he had publicly informed the Iranians that if they ended the crisis before he took office he would be "very happy." Casey and Meese were by now reliably reported to have personal relationships with Cyrus Hashemi, who had arranged the New York meeting, and Hashemi was in contact with Iran on a regular basis. There was, in short, a motive, an opportunity, and a "corpse"—Iran's sudden, embarrassing, and costly policy reversal.

Back in Tehran, on January 17, Bani-Sadr wrote to Khomeini, "This declaration is a shameful declaration, a capitulation, and it will be remembered as such in history. You must act quickly to prevent its signature."[23] There was no answer from Khomeini. Twelve days later, Bani-Sadr chided the Algerian ambassador for his government's endorsement of an agreement so harmful to Iran. According to Bani-Sadr, the ambassador replied: "On the contrary, we explained to Nabavi that this agreement was not good for Iran, but he told us he would sign it anyway. We were intermediaries in the agreement with Carter, but not the other one, the one Beheshti and Rafsanjani concluded with Reagan."[24]

Iran's concessions on January 15 broke the logjam, but required that almost every piece of paper associated with the negotiations had to be redrafted in a furious effort in the last four days of Carter's term. Iran took a beating. At the beginning of the hostage crisis, some $12 billion of Iranian assets was frozen by the United States, but because of attachments and other limitations only about $8 billion could in fact be transferred to the escrow account before the hostage release. Once the hostages were freed, these funds were distributed as follows:

- $3.67 billion to pay off U.S. bank loans to Iran.
- $1.42 billion to remain in escrow as security against payment on disputed claims between U.S. banks and Iran.
- $2.88 billion to be paid directly to Iran.

In addition, some $2.2 billion would be freed of attachment and the claims referred to an international tribunal for arbitration. Of those funds, Iran agreed to place $1 billion in an escrow account to secure payment of claims by U.S. citizens and companies against Iran as decided by the tribunal.

In the end, Iran received approximately $4 billion, or roughly one-third of the total it had originally lost as a result of the hostage-taking. The cash loss to the Iranian treasury amounted to about $150 million for each of the hostages, more than $300,000 per day per hostage.

Perhaps even more important than the cash was the military equipment. Through September and October, President Carter had proposed returning various categories of Iran's military assets upon the release of the hostages, but after Khomeini's declaration on October 21 Iran turned its back on those offers. The question of arms was not raised even in passing during the negotiations from November 4 to January 20, even though Carter had pledged in the October 28 debate to unfreeze all of Iran's military assets and Iran was at the time engaged in a fight with Iraq for its national survival. There was no reference to this matériel in the Algiers Accords, and as of 1991, it was still in storage in the United States and Iran had received not a penny of compensation.[25]

By delaying the release of the hostages until January 20, the Iranians got significantly less than they could have expected had they acted before the election. That outcome was entirely predictable and it was well understood in some circles in Tehran at the time. Nonetheless, Iran had evidently decided in October to waive its maximum bargaining leverage in the hope of getting much more in January.

The revolutionary leadership in Tehran has been accused of many things, but never of being indifferent or inept bargainers. Simply put, they were probably gambling on a bigger payoff from Reagan than they could hope to get from Carter. They had reason to believe that the favor they had done for Reagan would not only be remembered by Casey and by other influential Republicans, but would be rewarded with a new arms relationship with the incoming administration and with Israel. But this was high-risk poker. Reagan's bellicose public statements after the election had provided the Iranians with no assurance that he would respect the Paris agreement. They began to perceive that prolonging the negotiations past the inauguration might well be regarded by the Republicans as an abrogation of the secret understandings reached in October. And then all bets would be off. Perhaps, the Iranians must have reasoned, it would be better to settle with Carter, for despite Casey's promises in Madrid and Paris, they had begun to fear that Reagan, once in power, might not honor the terms of the deal that had been struck on his behalf.

·11·

QUID PRO QUO

When President Jimmy Carter greeted President-elect Ronald Reagan on the portico of the White House on the morning of Tuesday, January 20, 1981, he had not been to bed for two nights. The Oval Office had been turned into a twenty-four-hour command center during the final roller coaster of the hostage negotiations, and he had managed with occasional naps on the couch.

Despite the last-minute nature of the Iranian reversal, the U.S.-Iranian agreement was completed and signed by both sides on January 19. At that point the transfer of funds into the various escrow accounts began and it appeared that the hostages would be released in time for Carter to greet them while he was still President. Then Iran threw one last monkey wrench into the works by taking exception to a routine clause in a technical supplement to the escrow agreement. The wrangling over this minor point occupied most of a day, putting all the arrangements on hold. This maneuver appears to have been a deliberate effort by Iran to interrupt the process and ensure that the release would not take place on Carter's watch.

Finally, at 8:04 on the morning of January 20, the banking transactions were completed and the government of Algeria transmitted its certification to Iran. Again, everything seemed to be in place for the release, but for four hours there was total silence from Tehran. Iran did not acknowledge the Algerian message until 12:05, just minutes after Ronald Reagan had taken the oath of office on the steps of the Capitol. Thirty minutes later, the Algerian planes that had been waiting for a day at Mehrabad airport took off with all the hostages on board. As the planes safely passed out of Iranian airspace, President Reagan, who was attending a luncheon at the Capitol, made the first official announcement of his presidency, reporting that the hostages were now free.

There is no doubt that the Iranians timed the hostage release to coincide with Reagan's inauguration. The timing was too perfect to be mere coincidence. During the tense final hours on January 20, observers in Tehran reported that Revolutionary Guards were standing around looking at their watches, waiting for the appropriate moment to proceed with the release.[1]

Iran's deliberate delay was widely perceived as a final gesture of defiance intended to rub salt in Jimmy Carter's wounds. Few suspected that it was the dénouement of an elaborate plot that had been hatched months before by William Casey. After the celebrations were over, the Reagan administration faced a serious decision: whether or not to fulfill its own part of the bargain with Iran. Although Casey had reportedly made political and military promises to Iran if the hostage release was timed to benefit Reagan, there is no reason to believe that there was ever any admiration or mutual respect between the two parties. Both sides were driven by narrow self-interest, and neither could count on the goodwill of the other. There was always the possibility of a double-cross by either side.

Once the election was over and Reagan had won, Iran lost much of its bargaining power. Its leverage declined even further once the hostages were back in the United States and Reagan had derived maximum political benefit from the national outpouring of relief and joy. Reagan had denounced the Iranians at the end of December as "barbarians," and he had declared that terrorism was going to be at the top of his administration's foreign-policy agenda. Many of Reagan's own advisers claimed that the Algiers agreement, despite its substantial benefits for the United States, was a shameful example of negotiating with terrorists and was little better than paying ransom. They were intent on showing that Reagan could be tougher than Carter, perhaps by renouncing the remaining U.S. commitments to Iran. They argued that since Iran had obtained Carter's consent by coercion, Reagan was not obliged to respect the terms of the Algiers Accords. They chose to ignore the fact that the Accords represented a freely undertaken set of pledges to a third party, that they were fully consistent with the negotiating positions outlined by Reagan in his speech on September 13 (and reiterated by Meese in a statement on November 2), and that they included some important benefits for U.S. claimants against Iran. What was more important was the symbolic act of refusing to do business with terrorists.

Ronald Reagan had been swept into office partly on the widespread perception that he would be strong where Carter had been weak. Reagan and his supporters often and loudly proclaimed that, once in power, they would teach hostage-takers a lesson. They would know how to be tough with terrorists and with nations that sponsored them. From the earliest days, administration representatives attacked international terrorism in the harshest words they could find.

One week after taking office, President Reagan welcomed the freed American hostages at an elaborate ceremony on the South Lawn of the White House. He used that occasion to issue what would become a celebrated warning: "Let terrorists be aware that when the rules of international behavior are violated, our policy will be one of swift and effective retribution."[2] At the same time, however, the administration resisted publicly labeling Iran a practitioner of international terrorism and would privately tolerate or even encourage cooperative ventures with Iran. When Reagan held his first press conference two days after the South Lawn ceremony, he was asked about his policy toward Iran. He replied that he was "certainly not thinking of revenge. . . . I think that any country would want to help another if they really showed an intent to have a government that would abide by international law. . . . But until such a thing appears apparent [in Iran], I don't know that there's anything we can do."[3]

The "no negotiation" slogan became a cardinal principle of policy under the Reagan administration. It was formally enshrined in the report of a "Task Force on Combatting Terrorism" headed by Vice President George Bush.[4] That report was issued with some fanfare in February 1986, just as five hundred U.S. TOW missiles were being covertly delivered to Iran in an attempt to barter the release of U.S. hostages in Lebanon and just three months before Robert McFarlane, Oliver North, and others flew off to Tehran with a cake in the expectation of meeting Rafsanjani. The no-negotiation-with-terrorists edict was a deception of the worst kind. It never deceived terrorists, or arms dealers, or hostile governments. It deceived only the American people, who were too far from the center of power to notice that the order was delivered with a wink and a nod.

With the release of the hostages, Iran had only one weapon it could use against the new administration in Washington, and blackmail was a most ambiguous weapon. If Iran chose to leak details of its secret deal with the Reagan campaign, the effects might be almost as devastating in Tehran as they would be in Washington. The Iranian leadership would have to think twice before revealing that direct talks had been conducted with the Great Satan, contrary to the explicit orders of the Majles, and that these meetings were also attended by representatives from Israel. Once the story broke, it might also reveal that the Iranian representatives came away from the table with their personal bank accounts considerably fatter than when they arrived. Further, if it became known that the Algiers Accords, which were regarded in Iran as unreasonably costly and harmful, had been accepted to avoid scuttling the secret deal and in the hope of future good behavior by the Reagan administration, the Iranian negotiators might have faced a revolt of their own. President Bani-Sadr, for example, believed that Nabavi was so concerned about the reaction to the Algiers Accords that he literally feared for his life.[5]

In considering its policies toward Iran, the Reagan administration probably assigned greater weight to strategic concerns than to any risk of blackmail. Iran was not only the largest and most populous of the oil-rich states in the Persian Gulf region, but it also stood directly in the path of the Soviet Union's purported expansionist drive to warm-water ports. Moreover, any decision by Washington to renege on its promises to Iran would immediately have created an unwelcome crisis in its relations with Israel. The Israelis had reason to believe, as a result of their contacts with the Reagan campaign, that the new U.S. administration would be sympathetic to their strategic concerns and would cooperate with Israel's arms sales to Iran, as the Carter administration had not. It was no secret that the Israelis felt so strongly about the need for a powerful Iran to divert Arab attention that they had shown themselves willing to ship arms to Iran in the face of a U.S. embargo.

Some of the earliest foreign-policy decisions of the Reagan administration concerned the hostages, Iran, and Israel. Those decisions—some public, others known only to a few policy officials—contained many elements of ambiguity and contradiction.

Shortly after the inauguration, the new foreign-policy team became aware that several Americans continued to be held in Iranian jails. One of these was an American free-lance writer, Cynthia B. Dwyer, who had been arrested on May 5, 1980, shortly after the failed rescue mission. Dwyer, it turned out, was married to Richard Allen's college roommate. Allen had just become national security adviser, and he discussed this issue on January 23 with President Reagan, who told him that "the deal is off" unless Dwyer was freed.[6]

This message was relayed to Iran and had a dramatic effect. Not only was Dwyer released on February 10, but an Iranian-American employee of Rockwell International and three British missionaries, all of whom had been accused of spying, were also set free within a month. One week after Dwyer was released, the Reagan administration announced that it would fulfill all the terms of the Algiers Accords.[7] Thus, the first official communication and transaction between the Reagan administration and Iran involved a successful use of pressure to release American hostages.

Richard Allen later claimed that the "deal" to which Reagan referred in this instance involved nothing more than the implementation of the remaining provisions of the Algiers Accords. Perhaps so. The message, however, was apparently not transmitted through normal diplomatic channels. I was the Middle East desk officer on the National Security Council at the time, and I never saw such a message. The key officials at the State Department at the time, who would have been responsible for transmitting such a message through the Swiss, the Germans, the Algerians, or other possible channels, have no recollection of any such communication with Tehran.[8]

This was not a message that would have been overlooked or regarded as routine. It was the first substantive communication between the Reagan administration and Iran at a time of heated debate within the administration over carrying out the Algiers Accords. The wording of such a message and the choice of which diplomatic or informal channel to use would have been important considerations at the time, with potentially major implications for future contacts.

This raises a number of questions. If the message was simply to put Iran on notice that the Reagan administration would not accept responsibility for the Algiers Accords unless Cynthia Dwyer was released, it seems odd that it was not sent through one or more of the same channels that had been used to negotiate the Accords only a few days earlier. What channels of communications to Iran were available to the Reagan administration in its first days in office that would not have been known to or observed by the National Security Council and the State Department?

Communications with Tehran were difficult. More than a year had been spent developing an array of secure and reliable means to deliver messages. It is at least curious that the new Reagan administration was able to deliver a message of this importance, apparently without going through any of the established channels. It suggests that the administration had its own means of communicating with Iran—means that may have been developed during the campaign.

The Reagan administration knew that there were many ways of communicating with Iran. Signals could be sent through a variety of channels, both private and public. In his first press conference on January 28, Secretary of State Alexander M. Haig, Jr., was asked about terrorism, Iran, and arms sales. He was basically accommodating toward Iran, saying only that future policy would be determined by Iran's behavior and choosing not to emphasize Iran's role in international terrorism. Instead, he placed responsibility for such terrorism directly on the Soviets, who "foster, support and expand this activity." International terrorism, he said, would "take the place of human rights" in the Reagan administration "because it is the ultimate of abuse of human rights." With regard to arms sales, he was unequivocal: "Let me state categorically today, there will be no military equipment provided to the Government of Iran, either under earlier obligations and contractual arrangements or as yet unstated requests."[9]

When Haig made that statement, Israel had already resumed military shipments to Iran. In fact, some small shipments had begun virtually within hours after the inauguration and the release of the hostages. Samuel Lewis, the U.S. ambassador to Israel, had learned of new Israeli arms shipments to Iran almost immediately after the inauguration, and he had raised the subject with Begin. The Israeli prime minister insisted that he was being pressured by his own military to ship arms to Iran and, moreover, that his promise to Carter was no longer applicable since the hostages were now free.

Lewis duly reported this exchange to Washington, where he received conflicting signals. He was told through regular State Department channels to protest Israeli weapons shipments to Iran. At the same time, his contacts in Israel had informed him that the arms shipments were in fact being carried out with U.S. approval.[10]

Over the following months, knowledgeable individuals in the State Department and elsewhere came to regard the apparent U.S. acquiescence in Israeli arms shipments to Iran as an open secret. Haig and the Israelis discussed the issue privately during the secretary of state's two trips to the Middle East in 1981. Although officially the United States continued to oppose the Israeli arms program, in fact Haig never intervened to stop it. On the contrary, Israel soon initiated a major weapons-transfer program, including matériel of U.S. origin. The Israelis consulted on this program with Haig and provided detailed lists of their shipments to senior individuals in the Reagan administration.

A former high-level official in the Reagan White House said that Haig had approved Israeli shipments of arms to Iran in 1981 after discussions between Robert McFarlane, then a member of Haig's staff, and David Kimche, deputy director of the Mossad.[11] A former high-level State Department official who participated in the initial decisions on the arms program said that Kimche met secretly on three occasions with McFarlane in Geneva, Washington, and Jerusalem during December 1980 to secure prior approval for arms sales to Iran. McFarlane, according to this source, later persuaded Haig to go along with these shipments. When asked about this report, McFarlane said he was "generally" aware of the 1981 Israeli arms sales to Iran but denied that he had approved them.[12]

David Satterfield, a Foreign Service officer who was on the Israel desk at the State Department at the time, testified years later that "Haig told Israel that 'in principle' [shipping arms to Iran] was okay, but only for F-4 spare parts. . . . Haig also insisted that the United States had to approve in advance specific lists of parts to be sold by Israel to Iran."[13]

A senior Defense Department official recalled that he was approached shortly after the inauguration by a newly appointed member of the Pentagon's legal-affairs office, who questioned him at length about the legal implications of Israeli sales of U.S.-origin military items to Iran, specifically parts for F-4 fighter-bombers and C-130 transport aircraft. This official, who had extensive experience with U.S. foreign military sales, believed that the initiative came from Haig's office and that the shipments were substantial. Despite his official responsibility for such matters, he was not consulted further, and he was never informed about the final decision.[14]

Major General Avraham Tamir, a former senior official in the Israeli Ministry of Defense, remembered the transactions somewhat differently. Tamir was directly involved in the shipments and had personal knowledge of the arrangements. According to Tamir, Haig explicitly approved Israel's arms-sales program with Iran after speaking to Israeli Minister of Defense Ariel Sharon in 1981. Much of the matériel was of Israeli origin, especially the ammunition that made up the bulk of the shipments. Israel also provided Washington with detailed lists of U.S.-origin equipment being shipped to Iran, including aircraft spares and antitank weapons.[15]

The covert arms dealings among the United States, Israel, and Iran were confirmed in 1982 by Moshe Arens, the Israeli ambassador to the United States. Arens told the *Boston Globe* that not only did the United States know of this program in advance, but Israel coordinated its arms sales to Iran "at almost the highest of levels" in the U.S. government. The State Department objected strongly to his remarks, saying the program "was purely an Israeli decision." But Ambassador Arens, a cautious and responsible professional diplomat, refused to retract or alter his remarks.[16]

Haig, for his part, denied that he had ever given explicit permission for these arms sales. "On every occasion," he said, "I was very adamant in refusing permission." He did not deny, however, that arms were shipped, admitting that "some equipment may have actually been shipped that was U.S. supplied to Israel and then trans-shipped to Iran." But he maintained that the program was not conducted at his direction or even with his approval. Instead, he pointed the finger at his old nemesis, the White House staff. "If that happened," Haig said, "it happened through the good offices of somebody in the White House staff, and I don't discount that. That could have happened."[17]

It is not surprising that no one was willing to take credit for this policy, for it was illegal. If any country that is a recipient of U.S. military aid or sales wishes to sell that equipment to a third country, it must first obtain the formal consent of the U.S. government. The rule is that such third-country transfers will be approved only when it is formally determined that the United States would itself have been prepared to sell the same equipment to the third party. In the case of Iran, such arms transfers were prohibited by U.S. policy. It was precisely for that reason that the deliveries had to be made surreptitiously through Israel. Permitting a flow of arms to Iran through Israel was probably the first illegal act committed by members of the Reagan administration, and it happened within days of the inauguration.

According to a senior U.S. intelligence official, Israel sent about $300 million in military equipment to Iran in the period immediately after the release of the hostages. These shipments were tracked by intelligence sources, and many in the CIA were puzzled that the United States did not intervene to stop them.[18] A senior Israeli intelligence official reported that the U.S. equipment that Israel sent to Iran included spares for F-4 aircraft, M-48 tanks, and M-113 armored personnel carriers, a total value of $246 million.[19] William Northrop, an Israeli intelligence operative, said under oath that Israel agreed in early 1981 to supply Iran with $200 million worth of military equipment. According to Northrop, Ambassador Samuel Lewis was informed of the deal, and Israel was told that it would be able to replenish its supplies from U.S. stores.[20]

Northrop's report is probably a reference to the approximately $200 million arms transaction that was contracted in an umbrella deal coordinated by the "Arms Sales Committee" of the Israeli Ministry of Defense. The agents representing Israel in one part of this transaction were Andreas

Jenni, a Swiss, and Ian Smalley, a British national, according to Northrop. On the Iranian side was Ahmed Heidari.[21]

Heidari had brokered the air shipment of F-4 tires in October, immediately after the meetings in Paris. This deal was a continuation of that arrangement and called for the delivery of twelve planeloads of equipment. A chartered Argentine CL-44 turboprop was to make twelve successive round trips from Tel Aviv to Tehran via Larnaca, Cyprus. The first flight left on July 11, 1981, and other flights followed on July 14 and July 18.

The third time was not a charm in this case. On its way back from Tehran, the Argentine aircraft strayed over the Soviet border and crashed under mysterious circumstances.[22] As information leaked out about the incident, it created a brief flurry of news reports. Some weeks later, a senior State Department official presented Haig with a draft press statement that carefully avoided any comment about U.S. knowledge or approval of Israeli arms sales to Iran. Haig, however, personally penciled in changes that shifted the burden of responsibility to Israel. The Israeli-Iran arms connection, including allegations of the shipment of U.S.-origin equipment, had by that time been reported in U.S. diplomatic cables. In this official's view, the Haig formulation misrepresented the extent of U.S. awareness of and acquiescence in the Israeli program.[23] The Israeli and Iranian foreign ministries also dismissed reports that the plane had carried Israeli-supplied spare parts to Iran, denying unequivocally that there was any arms relationship. But once the press furor began to die away, the charter flights resumed and all twelve deliveries were eventually completed.[24]

Colonel Dehqan of the Iranian army was also instrumental in facilitating Israeli arms sales to Iran in the months following Reagan's inauguration. In July 1981 Dehqan signed a contract with an Israeli, Ya'acov Nimrodi (a multi-millionaire arms dealer who would later emerge as a prominent figure in the Iran-Contra scandal in 1986), for the purchase of $135 million in arms on behalf of the deputy minister of logistics of the Iranian Ministry of Defense.[25]

Iranian President Bani-Sadr asserted that Iran's major purchases of military equipment from Israel began in March 1981, a timetable corroborated by other participants. In fact, he published the invoices from some of these transactions in a French newspaper in March 1984.[26] One invoice, dated March 9, 1981, listed more than $2.5 million of new and overhauled aircraft parts for the Iranian air force, among other items. (The broker on that deal was Jamshid Hashemi, whose business card identified him as M.A. Hashemi-Balanian,[27] president of R.R.C. Import-Export Co. in Stamford, Connecticut.) Other invoices dated March 28 totaled nearly $18 million and involved air-to-air missiles and other equipment.[28] Once the flow of arms from Israel to Iran began, Jacques Montanès, the luckless French pilot, was finally permitted to leave Iran on June 1. His colleague had been released in late 1980, as a favor to Ahmed Heidari.[29]

The evidence is also substantial that the Israelis were not the only arms suppliers who took advantage of the Reagan administration's tacit green light to sell arms to Iran. Free-lancers with access to U.S. and NATO stores found a ready market for their imaginative and often brazen illegal deals. William Herrmann, the American shipping expert and arms dealer, was in Tehran at the time of Reagan's inauguration, when he met with Hamid Naqashan, the military-procurement officer for the Revolutionary Guards. Over dinner, Naqashan told Herrmann that the release of the hostages had been decided in October 1980 in Paris and that the payoff for Iran was to be a supply of military equipment. When they met over the following years, Naqashan confirmed that Iran had received "a lot of materials from the United States." Herrmann said that through his own sources he became aware that NATO supplies had been shipped to Iran, principally from Belgium and Holland, including F-4 aircraft spare parts and tank parts and engines. Hawk missile parts, according to Herrmann, had come from Israel. "The actual shipments started six to eight weeks after Mr. Reagan became President," he reported.[30]

Arif Durrani, the Pakistan-born manufacturer of U.S. military equipment and sometime arms salesman, recalled a similar sequence of events.[31] He claimed that documents existed in Belgium that indicated a substantial flow of arms from NATO stocks to Iran. According to Durrani, the United States later replenished these stocks. Durrani said that he visited NATO warehouses in Portugal, where he inspected military equipment and parts and then reported his findings to representatives of the Iranian Revolutionary Guards, who were waiting for him outside the NATO base. If they liked what they heard, a transaction would be set in motion.

Durrani recalled that orders began to show up at his company and elsewhere for certain aircraft parts unique to the Iranian F-4s that had been purchased by the shah. These tell-tale parts were initially ordered by Israel, but later orders were received from Turkey as well. Durrani also recalled that on one occasion thirteen Cobra helicopters were sold to Iran from a U.S. base in Germany and were shipped to Iran via Zaire for cover. Other sources also claimed that Zaire was used as a transit point to launder arms shipments that went directly from U.S. sources to Iran without passing through Israel.[32]

Hushang Lavi had a similar memory:

LAVI: Anything that they could not supply from Israel, they would supply from Belgium. The Iranians would come there, they would be taken to NATO bases, particularly the bases in the border in between Belgium and Germany, and they would pick whatever they want, and . . . the Belgians would ship it to Iran.

QUESTION: Like a shopping expedition?

LAVI: That's correct.

QUESTION: Well, would they just say, "We want that electron tube over here?"

LAVI: Yes, sir, believe you me, sir, I swear to God, I've seen this with my own eyes![33]

When asked years later about the possibility of Iranian representatives visiting NATO bases and selecting certain types of military equipment, Secretary of State Haig, the former Supreme Allied Commander in Europe, replied: "Well . . . it wouldn't be preposterous. If a nation—Germany for example—decided to let some of their NATO stockpiles be diverted to Iran, they'd have total control over such a decision. It would surprise me very much if American controlled equipment were trans-shipped from Europe to Iran. I would be very surprised."[34]

However, it comes as no surprise that the Hashemi brothers also got a piece of the action. According to a 1984 federal indictment against Cyrus Hashemi for arms trafficking, on February 4, 1981, Reza Hashemi contacted a military-supply business based in Englewood, New Jersey, with a request for flight-direction indicators and radar equipment. They also discussed walkie-talkies, surface-to-air missiles, RPG-7 rocket launchers, 81mm and 60mm mortars, 85mm howitzers, and automatic weapons including the M-16 and AK-47, as well as Browning rifles. Some of these items were shipped to a fake address in Switzerland in mid-February.[35] In June, according to the indictment, Reza and Jamshid Hashemi cooperated to purchase a Klystron tube, a key radar component, which they successfully shipped from the United States to Iran.[36] A month later, according to a federal search warrant application, the same New Jersey company attempted to ship an entire C-130 aircraft engine to Iran, but it was discovered in the cargo area of the London airport, and the shipment was halted. Two additional shipments of the same nature had been planned but were never completed.[37]

Even though the Hashemi brothers were increasingly involved in arms sales to Iran, the FBI surveillance of Cyrus Hashemi's New York office was abruptly terminated on February 13, ten days before the court order authorizing that surveillance was due to expire. (The Carter administration had extended the coverage in November specifically to investigate the accumulating evidence of criminal activity on the part of at least Cyrus and his brother, Reza.) Mid-February was the time when a request for an extension of authorization for surveillance would have been routinely submitted to the White House for approval; the submission would have alerted the Reagan administration, which had been in office less than one month, to the fact that Cyrus Hashemi was under close surveillance. It would be interesting to know what reasons were given by the Reagan administration for halting surveillance in a case that was producing a wealth of information about illegal arms purchases and deliveries to Iran. Until the court papers are unsealed, the suspicion must exist that the Reagan administration decided to cut off any further surveillance when they suddenly discovered that one of their principal intermediaries with Iran, a man who had had dinner with Ed Meese less than two months earlier, was under intensive surveillance by the FBI as "an alleged Agent of a foreign power," and was also under investigation by the U.S. Customs Service for organizing illegal arms sales to Iran.

It was Cyrus Hashemi who had made the initial contacts between William Casey and Iran. It was he who had set up the series of meetings in Madrid in July and August that produced the first agreements concerning the swap of U.S. arms in return for release of the hostages at a moment favorable to the Reagan campaign. It was Cyrus Hashemi who reportedly set up the first deliveries of Israeli arms by ship from Israel to Iran in late 1980, and it was Cyrus Hashemi who attended the Paris meetings, who brought in Hushang Lavi, and who returned to New York immediately afterward to launch a new round of arms deliveries to Iran.

It was Cyrus Hashemi who had dinner with Ed Meese at a crucial moment in the hostage negotiations. It was Cyrus Hashemi who was responsible for setting up a meeting in mid-January, in which Iran was persuaded to reverse itself and accept an unfavorable outcome in order to ensure that the hostages were released on January 20. Cyrus Hashemi may even have been the channel through which the new Reagan administration relayed its threatening message to Iran that resulted in the release of Cynthia Dwyer and four other Westerners still in custody.

By all accounts, Hashemi was extremely important to the Reagan administration, and any knowledge of their association was a matter of supreme sensitivity. The fact that he was under FBI surveillance must have come as a shock. The quickest way to try to kill the case would be to stop the surveillance. It stopped.

As the Reagan administration was tying up loose ends, events in Iran were spinning out of control. The factional disputes that had been carried on behind the scenes during the hostage crisis and the early months of the Iran-Iraq war now burst into the open. Intellectuals and former political leaders began writing open letters and hosting public rallies to protest repression and the widespread abuse of human rights. The "liberals," as members of the nascent opposition movement were called by the hard-liners, gravitated toward President Bani-Sadr as the only public figure who was even modestly sympathetic to their views. The embattled president, who had been roundly criticized for having recently launched a disastrous military offensive, did not discourage this rare display of popular support, but it was fatal. In postrevolutionary Iran, the one constituent that no political leader could afford to offend was Khomeini, and his sentiments in favor of clerical rule and against the burgeoning opposition movement were never in doubt.

Thugs from the *hezbollah,* or "Party of God," infiltrated and disrupted opposition rallies, including those where the president was speaking. One rally at Tehran University in early March collapsed into pitched battles, leading Sadegh Khalkhali, the radical prosecutor of the revolution and a sworn enemy of Bani-Sadr, to call for the president's resignation on grounds of "treason." In May, one of Bani-Sadr's aides and a Foreign Ministry official were arrested for removing classified information from the ministry, as part of a running battle between Bani-Sadr and the prime minister over control of foreign policy. Shortly thereafter Khomeini made a speech labeling critics of the Islamic government "infidels" and telling them to "go back to Europe, to the United States or wherever else you want." Most observers believed that the barb was aimed at Bani-Sadr.

On June 10, Khomeini dismissed the president as commander-in-chief of the armed forces, and on June 16 the Majles began impeachment proceedings against him. On June 21 he was formally declared incompetent and his arrest was ordered. By this time Bani-Sadr was in hiding, and he issued a broadside charging that Iran was in the grip of a "climate of a reign of terror" and calling for resistance against despotism. The controversy sparked bloody fighting between his supporters and opponents and led to a new wave of executions.

On June 27 an attempt was made on the life of Mohammed Ali Khamene'i, and on the following day a massive bomb destroyed the headquarters of the Islamic Republican Party, killing more than seventy high officials, many of them clergy, including Ayatollah Beheshti. Iran erupted into near civil war. One month later, Bani-Sadr was granted political asylum in France after having arrived on board an Iranian military aircraft that had secretly flown him out of the country.

In his subsequent public statements and writings, Bani-Sadr went to great lengths to avoid any suggestion that he dealt with Israel during his presidency. But Bani-Sadr, like Jimmy Carter, was one of the losers in the hostage deal, and the new order was rapidly taking shape. The restoration of covert arms and intelligence links between Iran and Israel went forward, unimpeded by Iran's internal turmoil. Mutual interests not only led to transfers of military equipment but may have also given rise to strategic coordination of the most sensitive nature.

In the months following the Reagan inaugural, the two nations turned their attention to the potential nuclear threat posed by Iraqi President Saddam Hussein. The Iranians had tried without success to destroy the Osirak nuclear reactor near Baghdad on September 30, and Israel now sought to finish the job. Although the Iranians could not openly aid Israel in attacking a Muslim country—even one with which they were at war— they were keenly aware that the first target of any Iraqi nuclear weapon was more likely to be Iran than Israel. Toward the end of destroying the Osirak installation, some have claimed, the Israelis obtained aerial photographs of the reactor site from Iranian intelligence,[38] and according to Ari Ben-Menashe, in about mid-May a senior Israeli official met in the south of France with a high-level Iranian official well known to President Bani-Sadr to discuss the Osirak raid. The officials reportedly agreed that in the event of an emergency, Israeli aircraft would be permitted to land at the Iranian airfield in Tabriz.[39]

Israeli warplanes bombed and destroyed the Osirak reactor on June 7, only days before Menachem Begin faced reelection—providing the prime minister with an "October surprise" of his own. In the United States, admiration for the technical perfection of the Israeli raid was mixed with concern for U.S. relations with the Arab states, and the delivery of several F-16 fighter aircraft to Israel was temporarily delayed as an official gesture of disapproval. Insiders, however, reported that Secretary of State Haig had been informed of the Israeli raid during a recent visit to Israel and that his equivocal reaction at the time was interpreted by the Begin government as a green light.[40]

Bani-Sadr condemned the Israeli attack against the nuclear reactor, and in later years he characteristically denied any collusion with Israel in advance of the June 7 raid.[41] The Israelis, for their part, have consistently maintained that they carried out the raid solely to safeguard their own national interests. However, Israel and Iran had also routinely and vigorously denied other dealings with each other that were later confirmed, and in view of their burgeoning arms relationship, together with their mutual interest in weakening Saddam Hussein's offensive power, it is quite credible that these contacts extended to the nuclear concerns that were of supreme importance to both countries.

The full truth may never be known.

CONCLUSION

I do not regard myself as a political partisan. I spent more than twenty years as a naval officer in nonpolitical posts as an analyst of military and political affairs. While in the navy, I served in political and military jobs in the Mediterranean and the Middle East and earned a doctorate in political science from Columbia University. I held a policy position in the Pentagon during the Nixon administration; I came to the White House under the Republican presidency of Gerald Ford, having been hired by his national security adviser, Brent Scowcroft; I remained there throughout the Carter administration; and then I stayed on at the National Security Council staff during the early months of the Reagan administration. Although I was a Democrat, I had served nearly half of my career under Republican Presidents, beginning with Eisenhower, and my only participation in partisan politics was to vote in national elections.

In 1988, when George Bush was running for President against Michael Dukakis, allegations of secret dealings by the Reagan-Bush campaign with Iran in 1980 began to surface. As Election Day approached, the drumbeat of these charges reached a crescendo. Skepticism and doubt about the nature of the Reagan administration's dealings with Iran had been fueled by the revelations of the Iran-Contra Affair in 1986. In the wake of that scandal, reports circulated that there had been a series of secret meetings in Paris concerning the hostages in October 1980. The participants allegedly included William Casey, Reagan's campaign manager, and Donald Gregg, who at that time was a colleague of mine on the National Security Council staff of the Carter administration. The most sensational allegation was that George Bush, the Republican vice-presidential candidate in 1980 and the presidential candidate in 1988, had attended the Paris meetings. Because of my past involvement with the hostage issue, I was approached repeatedly during the campaign to comment on these charges. In the absence of hard evidence I was unwilling to endorse the allegations as true.

At the time, I was planning to write a book about the Reagan administration's involvement with Iran, particularly the Iran-Contra Affair, but I found myself spending more and more time thinking about the 1980 election. I felt that I could not write about the Iran-Contra Affair without first answering the question about a possible prior deal. If there had been such a deal, then Iran-Contra had to be seen not as a onetime policy aberration but as a rerun of the earlier hostage deal with Iran. I gradually became so engrossed that I began to concentrate on the 1980 events almost full time.

A year later, in the fall of 1989, I had the opportunity to talk to a number of reporters who had worked on this story during the 1988 election campaign and had subsequently dropped it. I was puzzled by this development, and I wondered why they had developed such an aversion to the story. I was told that several major newspapers and television networks had publicized sensational allegations by Richard Brenneke that high officials in the Reagan administration and the CIA had been involved in the traffic of guns and drugs in Central America. In the process of investigating these stories, they had concluded that Brenneke was a thoroughly unreliable source. Many of his claims about his own background did not check out, and his self-professed firsthand knowledge of events and individuals often did not stand up upon close inspection. An impressive string of journalists vowed never to have anything to do with him again. Since Brenneke was so closely associated with the story of the 1980 elections, when they walked away from Brenneke they also walked away from the story of the alleged secret deal.

In one respect the journalists were right. Richard Brenneke as a source was particularly exasperating. While he was familiar with names, places, and events associated with covert operations, his own role and direct involvement with those operations were unclear. His self-proclaimed association with the Central Intelligence Agency was dubious, and he was not above using doctored papers to make his association appear more formal than perhaps it was. While he was willing to talk about some of his experiences, he often resorted to hints and suggestions rather than a straightforward recitation of facts. He routinely exaggerated his own importance and changed his story over time, apparently taking perverse pleasure in muddying the waters or sending his interviewers off on a wild-goose chase.

Nonetheless, Brenneke occasionally demonstrated access to unique insider information before it became available from any other source. One example was his statement to a Defense Intelligence Agency official on January 3, 1986, that "Admiral [John] Poindexter had given permission to sell 10,000 missiles to Iran." On that date, a draft presidential "finding" was being prepared, based on conversations with Israeli counterterrorism adviser Amiram Nir, that provided for the sale of TOW missiles to Iran. President Reagan signed the "finding" on January 6.[1] This fact, which became a front-page story when it was discovered many months later, was known only to a tiny handful of people in the U.S. government at the time Brenneke learned about it. There is no question at all that he had exceptional access to sensitive information at various times, for reasons that are not entirely clear.

Brenneke stuck by his story of a secret deal between Republicans and Iranians, to the extent of risking a jail sentence. On September 23, 1988, he testified in a hearing before a judge who was to sentence Heinrich Rupp, a friend and former colleague of Brenneke's, who had been convicted of fraud related to the collapse of the Aurora Bank in Denver, Colorado. In this hearing, Brenneke declared under oath that he had attended one of a series of meetings in Paris in late October 1980 where William Casey, Donald Gregg, and other American, Iranian, and French individuals had convened to discuss the release of the U.S. hostages in Iran. He said Rupp had told him that George Bush was also present in Paris. The *Rocky Mountain News* obtained a transcript of Brenneke's testimony and published it in early October, just before the Bush-Dukakis election, thereby adding to the media interest in the so-called October surprise.[2]

Seven months later, on May 12, 1989, Assistant U.S. Attorney Thomas O'Rourke brought an indictment against Brenneke for making false declarations to a federal judge.[3] The indictment was returned on the very day that the Senate began confirmation hearings on Gregg, whom Bush had appointed as U.S. ambassador to South Korea. According to Brenneke's lawyer, Michael Scott, once Gregg had been confirmed the government offered Brenneke a plea bargain: If Brenneke would admit that he had lied about the October surprise, he would be released without a prison term or fine. Brenneke refused.

The trial began on April 24, 1990, in Portland, Oregon.[4] O'Rourke presented two Secret Service officers to testify that George Bush had not been out of the country in the several weeks before the 1980 election. The two agents, however, were unable to specify when they had been on duty, and no records were produced to clarify their testimony. Two of William Casey's secretaries were called to testify about his whereabouts, but they contradicted each other and left open the possibility that he might have made brief trips abroad without their knowledge.

Ambassador Gregg, who flew to Portland from his new post in South Korea, testified that he had spent the weekend of October 18–19, 1980, at Bethany Beach, Delaware, with his wife and daughter. He further testified that he was in his office at the National Security Council on Monday, October 20. In support of his claim, he produced a photograph of himself and his daughter in swimming attire, which he said had been taken that weekend. The defense produced a meteorologist who testified that it was unlikely that the photograph was taken on that weekend since the weather was chilly and cloudy.

Although the trial took nine days, it took the jury only five hours to find Richard Brenneke not guilty on all counts. It was a stunning outcome. The jury's verdict, of course, did not mean that Bush, Casey, or Gregg was in Paris in October 1980. It did mean that the U.S. government was unable to prove to the satisfaction of twelve Americans that they were not. The U.S. Attorney, to everyone's surprise, chose not to introduce into evidence any documentary records about the whereabouts of Bush, Casey, and Gregg on the dates in question. His decision remains a mystery, since he has subsequently refused to comment on the case.

More than two years later, a journalist discovered and published new evidence that seemed to demonstrate conclusively that Brenneke himself was not in Paris, but in Portland, Oregon, on the weekend of October 19, 1980.[5] That, however, was not an issue in the trial. Brenneke had been accused of falsely stating that William Casey, Donald Gregg, and possibly George Bush were in Paris on that particular weekend, and that he was employed by the CIA at that time. Neither the prosecution nor the defense made any attempt to establish Brenneke's whereabouts on the dates in question, and the issue was never raised in the testimony.

Although this case received virtually no attention in the national media, it marked the only time that the U.S. government had systematically and authoritatively attempted to refute the allegations of an October surprise. All of those accused had an unparalleled opportunity to rebut the charges, and they had all the resources of the U.S. government at their command to research and document their case. To my surprise, and to the surprise of nearly everyone who followed the trial closely, they failed.

Until the trial, I had found it utterly incredible that Donald Gregg, one of my colleagues on the National Security Council staff in 1980 and a man whose professionalism I respected, would have collaborated with the Reagan-Bush campaign to delay the release of the hostages, with the intent of bringing down the government of which he was a part.

After reviewing the trial transcript, I no longer knew what to think. One credit-card receipt from the restaurant where he said they had a seafood dinner was all that was required to prove his story. Or the record of a telephone call from the beach house to the White House Situation Room, a normal activity for any NSC staff member. Or the testimony of the neighbor who loaned them the beach house. Or even the supporting testimony of his wife and daughter. But there was nothing except Gregg's word and a photograph with a processing date stamped on it.

Gregg firmly denied the charges under oath, and his lawyers later made available diaries and NSC correspondence logs showing that he was not overseas on the dates in question.[6] During the period of the July meetings in Madrid, the diary pages indicate social events and a trip to a CIA facility in Virginia. During the time of the August Madrid meetings, there are some notations indicating tennis matches. In October, the diaries of both Gregg and his wife have entries referring to a visit to Bethany Beach on Saturday and Sunday, October 18 and 19, returning to Washington Sunday night. Correspondence logs from the NSC indicate that a document dated October 20 was generated from Gregg's office. This material strongly supports Gregg's claims of noninvolvement. It does not represent incontrovertible evidence, however, since Gregg was a professional intelligence officer who would have understood the importance of creating a false paper trail to conceal his participation in a sensitive operation. Not even these documents, however, were introduced at the trial.

In the case of *The United States of America* v. *Richard J. Brenneke,* the government needed only to positively locate, at the height of a presidential campaign, vice-presidential candidate George Bush or campaign manager William Casey or NSC staff member Donald Gregg anyplace but in Paris and Brenneke would have been subject to a prison sentence. As Brenneke put it:

> I was looking at a five year jail term and a ten thousand dollar fine. To a man who's just filed bankruptcy, ten thousand dollars might as well be a million dollars; and five years of my life, given my health . . . I didn't think I'd survive that! But I turned down a deal. I elected to go to trial. I elected to go to court and say what I knew to be the truth. . . . I had to be found not guilty on all five charges by twelve people. In other words, the vote had to be 60–zero—my favor.[7]

Although the case was no model of prosecutorial prowess, the result was unambiguous: A jury of his peers found Richard Brenneke not guilty on all counts. That fact does not prove that Brenneke's account was true in every respect, but neither can the verdict be dismissed as irrelevant. Brenneke had the courage of his convictions. He stood his ground against some formidable opposition, and he prevailed. It would be foolish to accept his word alone as sufficient proof, but it would be equally absurd to contend that anything he has said must be false.

■ ■ ■

Over the course of the next two years, during the research and writing of this book, I would meet many men like Richard Brenneke. To my frustration, Brenneke's idiosyncrasies and character flaws were too often representative of the general nature of the sources. These men were denizens of a shadowy yet flamboyant subculture who expected absolute discretion in dealing with outsiders but tolerated boasting and exaggerated tales of past exploits among the members of the fraternity. They took pains to conceal key facts from an obvious outsider, and when they chose to talk they routinely embellished the facts and inflated their own importance.

Such characters are a researcher's nemesis; they are meant to be. When the CIA or other intelligence agencies need to hire a "contractor," who may be required to carry out tasks that are potentially dangerous and of questionable legality, they look for three things: a specific and useful skill (a knowledge of money-laundering, for example); a romantic streak that glorifies both the secrecy and the risk; and a propensity for exaggeration and trouble.[8] One former CIA officer, David MacMichael, has said that the agency looks for these free-lancers at small community airports and gun ranges—places where men go to escape the boredom of everyday life. Looking for adventure, these men are fascinated by the imagined glamour and excitement of the world of espionage. MacMichael said that often, after one or two assignments, the agency will put a contractor on a case in which he runs afoul of the law. The contractor finds himself in a compromising position—nothing so major as to put him permanently out of commission, but significant enough that if he ever starts telling tales out of school about covert operations, his record will discredit his testimony.[9]

Essentially, such a free-lancer is a skilled Walter Mitty, who delights in possessing arcane knowledge and who imagines himself the instrument that secretly drives events from behind the scrim of history. It is a profile, alas, of a less-than-credible witness. Intelligence agencies understand this very well, and bank on it. A free-lancer is inherently difficult to control; if he wanders off the reservation and begins blabbing, it is helpful if no one believes him. A retired CIA covert-operations officer, when asked about the extravagant behavior of a former contract employee, said: "The agency likes things that way. . . . The wilder and crazier and sillier the story, the more they like it. The agency indulges people to come up with that. It's the best defense." MacMichael confirmed that the agency permits contractors to become entangled in a legally compromising position, so that if an operation goes awry they can be cut loose. "When a contractor gets caught," he said, "all their 'friends' disappear. It happens over and over again."[10]

In a story in which the principal actors have no desire for the facts to come out, one does not have the luxury of choosing one's sources. The "respectable" people who plotted and carried out a covert operation refuse to comment or, at worst, fabricate stories to protect themselves and their reputations; because of their "respectability," most people are inclined to believe them. The contractors who were hired to do the dirty work are not "respectable" at all, and if they decide to tell their story, most people assume they are lying.

And sometimes they are. These free-lancers, on occasion, are deliberately recruited as front men for disinformation campaigns. In 1988, when stories about possible Republican tampering with the hostage issue began to emerge in the national media, Oswald LeWinter said he was contacted by some people he had known through his intelligence background. They were concerned, he said, that the United States was once again facing the possibility of a Watergate-type scandal that risked tearing the country apart, discrediting the candidacy of George Bush, and electing a Democratic candidate who was unsympathetic to the intelligence community. He claimed to have been offered $40,000 to undertake a disinformation campaign designed to discredit the stories about the 1980 elections and the Paris meetings. He agreed, and for several months he spoke to journalists and others who were investigating the allegations of an "October surprise."[11] He said he used the pseudonym "Razin," and refused to be interviewed in person. Instead, he spoke to reporters only by telephone, offering a few bits and pieces of accurate information laced with fanciful inventions and false leads. His purpose, as he now freely admits, was to throw dust in the air, to invent tantalizing leads that would eventually prove to be false, and thereby to generate so much fruitless commotion that the story would be discredited and abandoned.

To get at the truth, one must listen to those who know something about what happened and who are willing to talk, even if they exaggerate and embroider the truth. Then every significant statement must be carefully weighed against the known facts—dates, places, times, identities—and other witnesses. A bald assertion, however intriguing, must be regarded as false unless it can be corroborated independently, and not just from one of the source's cronies who may have compared stories. When the allegations of Casey's participation in the secret talks with the Iranians surfaced in 1988, the CIA director's defenders swore up and down that Casey had not traveled abroad on the dates that the Madrid meetings were said to have taken place. However, one of my researchers found an obscure item tucked away in the second section of *The New York Times* of July 30, 1980, in which the following sentence appeared: "A spokesman at Reagan head-quarters said that the national campaign chairman, William Casey, would begin negotiations with the Right to Life group when he returns today from a trip abroad." Suddenly, the denials were less convincing.

Casey died of a brain tumor on May 6, 1987, making it impossible to get his side of the story. Nevertheless, he had made several public statements which I now viewed in a new light. For example, when he was questioned in the 1984 Senate investigation into the mysterious theft of President Carter's briefing book four years earlier, he described his knowledge of the hostage crisis at the time as follows: "Information about negotiations for the release of the hostages in Iran came to me from many sources, including bankers involved in loans to Iran and frozen Iranian funds."[12] That Casey admitted, under oath, that he was privy to inside information about the negotiations between the government of the United States and the govern-ment of Iran is itself revealing.

Some of the individuals who chose to talk to me were courageous and were to be taken seriously, despite their difficult personalities and checkered careers. Take Jamshid Hashemi, for example. In the spring of 1980, I had briefly met Jamshid and his brother Cyrus, an Iranian banker with offices in New York and London. As the National Security Council staff member for Iran at the time, I was generally aware that the Carter administration was in contact with the Hashemis, although I did not know then the extent or nature of the intelligence relationship. In October 1990, I flew to Lon-don and spent several days with Jamshid. We were talking in his tiny office near Victoria Station when he suddenly and without explanation began describing in convincing detail a meeting he said he had attended in

Madrid in July 1980 with William Casey, Donald Gregg, and Hojjat ol-Eslam Mehdi Karrubi, a senior cleric in the tiny circle of revolutionaries around Ayatollah Khomeini.

In a soft voice, with the heavy bazaari Persian accent of the merchant class, for almost two hours Jamshid told a Scheherazade-like tale in which he went over the times and places that the Republicans and the Iranians had negotiated the fate of the hostages. He told me of his brothers, Cyrus and Reza, and of how together they had played a dangerous game, sometimes winning and sometimes losing. It was possible to check much of what he claimed to be true. For there was a lengthy paper trail.[13]

When the Reagan administration terminated the FBI surveillance of Cyrus Hashemi in February 1981, a substantial amount of information about his illegal arms dealings was left in the hands of the Customs Service, which had initiated its own surveillance of several of the principal suppliers who had been working with Cyrus and Reza Hashemi. The Customs surveillance continued even after the FBI surveillance had ended. On the morning of November 12, 1981, several Customs agents arrived at the New York offices of Cyrus Hashemi, presented him with a search warrant, and then proceeded to go through his files, telephone books, telexes, correspondence, and other records.

Then, for three years, nothing happened. Although the evidence was in Washington's hands, and the Hashemi brothers were continuing their arms-sales efforts on behalf of Iran, no charges were made.

On July 18, 1984, an eighteen-count indictment against Cyrus Hashemi was handed down, charging him with conspiring to sell arms illegally to Iran, and an arrest warrant was issued. Reza Hashemi was named as an unindicted co-conspirator together with a number of other figures involved in the case. At the time of the indictment, Cyrus Hashemi was in London. On the day before the indictment, Jamshid Hashemi was told by his former CIA contacts to get out of the country immediately. He bought a ticket to Zurich, where he was awakened the following day by his nearly hysterical wife, informing him that everything had fallen apart.[14]

Reza was less fortunate. He was enticed to a meeting in Bermuda, and when his plane from Europe touched down in New York he was arrested. Reza was eventually convicted, but after he agreed to sign a statement promising never to disclose his associations with intelligence operations, he was assigned to a country-club prison where he continued to practice as a civil engineer during his short sentence.[15] (He has refused my repeated requests to discuss the events of 1980, citing this document.)

Cyrus Hashemi engaged several high-powered lawyers to plead that his case be dropped on the grounds that he had performed invaluable services for the U.S. government. In addition to his legal efforts, he established contact with William Casey, now the director of Central Intelligence, through John Shaheen, his usual intermediary.[16] Although the existence of this channel is documented, the substance of Cyrus's messages to Casey in 1985 is not known. Shaheen served again as go-between in the early days of the Iran-Contra Affair, when Cyrus reported to Casey that Iranians were trying to make contact in Hamburg with a scheme to free the hostages in Lebanon.[17] Shaheen died of cancer at age seventy, on November 1, 1985. Among the mourners at his funeral were Casey and Roy Furmark, a former employee of Shaheen's[18] and the man who may have introduced Casey to Jamshid Hashemi at the Mayflower Hotel in March 1980.

Despite the indictment hanging over him, Cyrus Hashemi was never tried. Instead, he went to work for the Customs Service in a sting operation intended to round up a ring of arms dealers. This highly dangerous enterprise resulted in the arrest of a large number of international businessmen, including Americans and Israelis, who were charged on April 22, 1986, with buying arms for Iran.[19] It also may have made Cyrus Hashemi a marked man.

It has been suggested that the 1984 indictment of Cyrus Hashemi raises doubts about his involvement in the hostage episode with Casey, since Hashemi would have held "the royal flush of all blackmail hands" against the Reagan administration if the charges of election tampering were true.[20] But Hashemi was not in a strong bargaining position. He was a known arms dealer with a remarkably checkered past. His word, against the predictable denials of senior officials of the U.S. government, was no contest. Years later, when his brother Jamshid finally decided to speak out about his own participation, his revelations were met with disdain by the White House and profound skepticism by most of the media.

The Hashemis had an almost superstitious awe of the power of the U.S. government and its intelligence organizations. They were prepared to play dangerous games on the margins of power, but they would have considered a head-to-head confrontation with someone like Casey as nothing less than suicidal. The fact that Cyrus Hashemi would decide to keep his mouth shut and take the best offer he could get was in keeping with his character.

On July 21, 1986, Cyrus Hashemi died in London after a mysterious two-day illness that was diagnosed as acute myeloblastic leukemia, a rare disease. His death came two days after he played a vigorous game of tennis and within a week of a thorough medical examination. Many of his friends and relatives suspected foul play, though no evidence was ever found. The autopsy showed "injection sites on both elbows with surrounding bruising," but the examining physician found no reason to dispute the diagnosis of leukemia as the cause of death.[21] Hashemi died without ever giving an interview about his role and his knowledge of what happened in the Paris meetings. Although his brother Jamshid did not attend the Paris meetings, he claimed to have been told about them, at least in general terms, by both Cyrus and Hushang Lavi. Several other sources also placed Cyrus at one or more of the Paris meetings.

One of these sources was Ari Ben-Menashe, whom I first met in November 1990 in New York, where he was being tried for allegedly seeking to sell U.S.-made arms, owned by Israel, to Iran. Ben-Menashe claimed to have seen Israeli intelligence reports about the Madrid meetings, and he offered specific details about the meetings that amplified Jamshid Hashemi's account. He also claimed to have been part of the Israeli team at the Paris meetings of October 1980.

Ben-Menashe, by his own admission, remained actively involved in the Israel-Iran covert arms relationship until the mid-1980s. In 1986, he was nearly arrested in the Cyrus Hashemi sting operation, which he regarded as an attempt by Casey and North to neutralize a competing arms network. He then decided to play some hardball of his own. He contacted Raji Samghabadi, a reporter for *Time* magazine, and revealed to him many of the details of secret U.S.-Iranian contacts. Samghabadi wrote up these stories in 1986, but *Time* was unable to verify them and decided not to publish. Months later, the story was printed by a Lebanese magazine and ignited the firestorm over the Iran-Contra Affair.[22]

Ben-Menashe was arrested on November 3, 1989, in California, on charges of plotting to sell three U.S.-made, Israeli-owned C-130 transport aircraft to Iran for $36 million. He was held without bond for nearly a year. On November 28, 1990, he was acquitted of all charges. Bitter at the treatment he had received and at the failure of the Israeli government to assist him, he began talking to reporters while in jail.[23] After his release, he gave dozens of interviews describing covert operations, arms sales, and Israeli intelligence operations in the United States and many other countries around the world.

Hushang Lavi also placed Cyrus Hashemi and William Casey at the Paris meetings in October 1980. Lavi became a lawful permanent resident of the United States in March 1981. He joined the parade of arms dealers who began promoting arms sales to Iran after Ronald Reagan's inauguration. In December 1981, he went to Israel to promote the sale of F-14 parts to Iran with Israel's assistance. General Efraim Poran, the military assistant to Prime Minister Menachem Begin, vouched for him and arranged for him to shake hands with Begin in the Knesset, where they had their pictures taken together.

As a result of this visit, Lavi entered into a relationship with Abraham Shavit, a former Israeli intelligence officer who ran a company named ASCO with headquarters in Belgium and a branch in Malta. Several sources identified ASCO as associated with Israeli intelligence. One of the Iranian contacts used by Lavi and ASCO for its arms deals in the early 1980s was Mehdi Kashani, Ben-Menashe's Iranian contact, who reportedly came to Israel in early 1980 to help arrange some of the early arms shipments.[24] Through ASCO, Lavi participated in some of the extensive arms trade to Iran. After several years, Lavi concluded that ASCO had conducted a major arms deal with Iran without informing him or paying him his commission. ASCO denied the charge, and Lavi sued unsuccessfully.

Lavi participated with Cyrus Hashemi in the Customs sting operation that resulted in numerous arrests of arms dealers in 1986. He was convinced that Hashemi had been murdered because of his participation in the sting, and he tried to bring the case to public attention. For Lavi, as for Hashemi, this case was a disaster. After working with Customs, he was permanently tainted in the world of arms dealers and was never again able to practice his profession. Lavi, who at one time had been a very wealthy man, ended his days bitter, angry, and deeply in debt. He died of a chronic heart ailment in December 1990, at the age of 55.

■ ■ ■

In July 1990, on one of my research trips to Europe, I met Ahmed Heidari, who had been described to me as a man who had located and purchased military equipment on the European black market and then arranged arms shipments to Iran, evading the U.S. embargo. It was also a matter of public record that in 1981, Heidari had been involved in a scam against the government of Iran itself, in which Iran paid $56 million for arms that were never delivered. The Iranian government pursued him in the French courts but never managed to get its money back.[25] There was a huge scandal in Iran about the lost $56 million. An Iranian general was imprisoned in Tehran and attempted to commit suicide in his cell.[26] But Heidari escaped unscathed. It was said in Iran that Heidari had threatened, if he was arrested or harmed, to implicate Ayatollah Beheshti by revealing the payments that had been made to Beheshti's private bank accounts. Today, he lives in grand style, dividing his time between Paris, Geneva, and the French Riviera, where he owns one of the finest restaurants in a region of fine restaurants.

Heidari confirmed many of the accounts I had heard from others, especially regarding the arms transfers from Israel to Iran in 1980 and 1981. He also told me that after William Casey became director of Central Intelligence in 1981, the United States made a major effort to acquire a Soviet T-72 tank, including approaches to both Iran and Iraq, though without success.[27] Heidari claimed to have been contacted on this subject by U.S. intelligence in Paris.[28] The man who approached him about the T-72, he said, was Oswald LeWinter, the member of the "clean-up team" at the Paris meetings a year earlier who would later participate in the Republican disinformation campaign of 1988. (The intervening years were not to be kind to LeWinter. After retiring from intelligence work in the early 1980s, he was arrested in West Germany in 1984, in what was at the time one of the largest drug busts in European history. While his associates received twenty-year prison terms, LeWinter was extradited to the United States after eight months and served only a short sentence. He said that while he was in the Manhattan Correctional Center in New York in 1985, he was employed by the authorities to spy on his fellow inmates. When his activities were discovered, he was badly beaten and had to be moved.)[29]

While in France, I also met with Abol Hassan Bani-Sadr, the former president of Iran. Bani-Sadr was a man with a grudge. He believed that he was removed from office by an illegal maneuver that thwarted the expressed will of the Iranian people in a free election and that he would one day be restored to power in Iran. Like all politicians in exile, he lived for the moment of return. He was constantly aware of the phantom politics of an imagined future and shaped his words accordingly. When I met him in May 1990 in his modest villa in Versailles, he spoke freely about the circumstances surrounding his ouster and the secret deal to delay release of the American hostages. However, speaking of his own role in politically sensitive issues such as covert relations with Israel or the United States, he chose his words carefully and was less than candid.

I would not be human if I did not confess that I have at one time or another awakened in the middle of the night with the thought: What if all of these people are lying to me? Is it possible that all of these accounts are themselves a conspiracy of lies?

In the early stages of the research, when the description of these events relied on only a handful of admittedly unreliable sources, I had to take that possibility seriously. But as time went on and the number and diversity of sources increased, the likelihood of a concerted, organized disinformation campaign dwindled. At some point, I had to ask myself why all of these individuals might have decided to propagate false statements, and how they had managed to coordinate their stories. Most of these men did not know one another, and those who had met or talked at some point in the past frequently distrusted one another. Most of them did not come forward of their own accord to publicize this story. On the contrary, most of them were discovered only as the result of persistent digging by journalists and researchers. To believe that there was an orchestrated effort to plant these individuals in Europe, the United States, and the Middle East, and that each was supplied with the same false story, required a considerable leap of imagination—a grand conspiracy theory to counter a conspiracy theory. Is it easier to believe that all of these sources surreptitiously coordinated their stories to create trouble for the Reagan and Bush administrations, or, alternatively, that each of these sources may be telling the truth (or pieces of the truth) as perceived on the basis of his own personal background and particular experience? The answer seems obvious: The chance that these sources are telling their versions of the truth is much higher than the chance that they are all lying in concert. These sources seemed to be describing the same event, albeit from different perspectives, rather than merely improvising a description based on sketchy published accounts.

In the absence of convincing corroboration, however, I have reserved judgment. For example, several reports have surfaced claiming that vice-presidential candidate George Bush was present at least briefly in Paris during the course of negotiations in October. I have always been uncomfortable about this allegation. There was little reason for a vice-presidential candidate to take such an extreme risk at the very peak of a political campaign. Besides, it would have been difficult for any candidate to slip away from his campaign responsibilities, not to mention his Secret Service protection, for a transatlantic flight. Even if the Iranians insisted on very high-level personal assurances as part of the final agreement, which would be entirely characteristic of Iranian bargaining style, surely someone could have been found to stand in for the candidate.

I was also aware that the allegation about Bush might have been deliberately floated in order to discredit the story. An effective way to divert attention away from what really happened is to invent a sensational story and send the media scurrying off on a wild-goose chase. That is essentially what happened in the Iran-Contra Affair, where all journalistic resources and public attention were fixated on the question of whether the President knew about the diversion of Iranian arms-sales profits to the Nicaraguan contras. When that could not be proved, because the original memos with identifying signatures had been destroyed and because Admiral Poindexter testified that "the buck stopped here, with me," the entire congressional case came to an end. Other important constitutional and legal issues simply faded into the background or were shunted off to the special prosecutor's office.

When the "October surprise" story first received wide publicity in 1988, much of the media attention was devoted to the question of whether or not George Bush had been in Paris. When the evidence proved to be ambiguous, and especially after Bush won the 1988 presidential election, the entire story was shelved.

President Bush has denied, emotionally and unequivocally, that he was in Paris for these meetings. The White House has provided some background information about his schedule on the days in question.[30] Vice President Dan Quayle provided other information about Bush's schedule to television station WXYZ in Detroit, which broadcast it on April 24, 1991. Unfortunately, the matter was not really laid to rest.

Quayle said that Bush spent the entire day of October 19, 1980, at his residence in Washington without Secret Service protection, preparing a speech that he delivered that evening. The information leaked by the White House said that Bush had brunch that day with Supreme Court Justice Potter Stewart at the Chevy Chase Country Club and then visited a friend in the afternoon before delivering a speech in the evening. Justice Stewart is dead, and the friend was not identified. If there was a brunch at the Chevy Chase Country Club, Bush (who, unlike Stewart, was not a member) would have required Secret Service protection, contrary to the information given by Vice President Quayle.

The FBI in early 1990 tried to verify Bush's presence at the Chevy Chase Country Club on that date as part of the preparation for the government's prosecution of Richard Brenneke, but was unable to do so. In the Brenneke trial, one of the charges that the government attempted to prove was that Richard Brenneke was lying when he indicated that Bush may have been in Paris on the weekend of October 19. In that case, the government was unable to prove to the satisfaction of a jury that Brenneke was lying.

Despite the attention that has been devoted to this issue, the stories have been incomplete and contradictory. It should not be difficult to establish the whereabouts of a vice-presidential candidate in the final weeks of an election campaign. Yet no significant records have ever been made public, and the General Accounting Office, in an independent investigation of these charges, was not permitted to interview the Secret Service agents who were on duty during the days in question.

George Bush insists adamantly that he was not in Paris. The available evidence seems to point the same way. Yet there are several sources who maintain just as strongly that he was in Paris.[31] Hushang Lavi, for example, told family members that he had some contact with Bush during the period of the Paris meetings. He mentioned Bush in his telephone call to Mitchell Rogovin on October 21, 1980, concerning events in Paris.

On the date in question, George Bush was the vice-presidential nominee of the Republican Party, in the final fortnight of the election campaign. It was a Sunday, but in the course of the day he must have spoken—if only by telephone—to someone who is still alive. The most puzzling aspect about this part of the story is not whether Bush was in Paris but why he has been so reluctant to produce evidence that would completely and finally prove that he was not.

Some of the participants in the Paris meetings clearly believed that George Bush was associated with those events. Perhaps they were mistaken, perhaps not. If it is difficult to believe that Bush flew off to Paris in the midst of a presidential campaign, it is equally difficult to believe that something of this magnitude could occur without his knowledge. This part of the story remains, stubbornly, an open question.

As for the question of Ronald Reagan's knowledge of or participation in the secret deal, the only evidence we have is a statement Reagan made on a golf course in California in June 1991:

> REAGAN: I did some things actually the other way, to try to be of help in getting those hostages—I felt very sorry for them and getting them out of there. And this whole thing that I would have worried about that as a campaign thing is absolute fiction. I did some things to try the other way. . . . The only efforts on my part were directed at getting them home.
>
> QUESTION: Did that mean contacts with the Iranian government?
>
> REAGAN: Not by me. No.
>
> QUESTION: By your campaign perhaps?
>
> REAGAN: I can't get into details. Some of those things are still classified.[32]

Even making maximum allowances for the informality of the golf-course setting and the ravages of time, Reagan seemed to understand the question very well, and he stated, three times in quick succession, that there were efforts on his part during the 1980 campaign to get the hostages out of Iran. The meetings in Madrid and Paris, as described by every source, were indeed an independent effort to get the hostages out, and they might well have been presented to candidate Reagan in a positive light.

In the end, it is irrelevant whether Bush went to Paris or whether Reagan approved or knew of the deal. The critical question is whether representatives of a political party out of power secretly, and illegally, negotiated with representatives of a hostile foreign power, thereby distorting or undermining the efforts of the legitimate government. Even today, more than a decade later, it is still difficult to imagine that an opposition political faction in the United States would employ such tactics, willfully prolonging the imprisonment of fifty-two American citizens for partisan political gain. Nevertheless, that is what occurred: the Reagan-Bush campaign mounted a professionally organized intelligence operation to subvert the American democratic process.

We are accustomed to the petty scandals of Washington politics: A candidate for high office is a lush or a compulsive womanizer; a member of Congress diverts campaign funds to a private account; an official lies to cover up an embarrassing policy failure. These are misdeeds on a human scale, and those miscreants who are unfortunate enough or careless enough to get caught are pilloried and punished by the press and their peers in periodic cleansings. We regard such rituals with a certain satisfaction, evidence of our democracy at work.

There is another category of offenses, described by the French poet André Chenier as "*les crimes puissants qui font trembler les lois,*" crimes so great that they make the laws themselves tremble. We know what to do with someone caught misappropriating funds, but when confronted with evidence of a systematic attempt to undermine the political system itself, we recoil in a general failure of imagination and nerve.

We understand the motives of a thief, even if we despise them. But few of us have ever been exposed to the seductions of power on a grand scale and we are unlikely to have given serious thought to the rewards of political supremacy, much less to how it might be achieved. We know that groups and individuals covet immense power for personal or ideological reasons, but we suppose that those ambitions usually will be pursued within the confines of the laws and values of our society and democratic political system. If not, we assume we will recognize the transgressions early enough to protect ourselves.

Those who operate politically beyond the law, if they are deft and determined, benefit from our often false sense of confidence. There is a natural presumption, even among the politically sophisticated, that "no one would do such a thing." Most observers are predisposed toward disbelief, and therefore may be willing to disregard evidence and to construct alternative explanations for events that seem too distasteful to believe. This all-too-human propensity provides a margin of safety for what would otherwise be regarded as immensely risky undertakings.

Illegitimate political covert actions are attempts to alter the disposition of power. Since all of politics involves organized contention over the disposition of power, winners can be expected to maintain that they were only playing the game, while those who complain about their opponents' methods are likely to be dismissed as sore losers. Even if suspicions arise, the charges are potentially so grave that most individuals will be reluctant to give public credence to allegations in the absence of irrefutable evidence. The need to produce a "smoking gun" has become a precondition for responsible reporting of political grand larceny. The participants in political covert actions understand this and take pains to cover their tracks, so the chance of turning up incontrovertible documentation of wrongdoing—such as the White House tapes in the Watergate scandal—is slim.

This leads to a journalistic dilemma. In the absence of indisputable evidence, the mainstream media—themselves large commercial institutions with close ties to the political and economic establishment—are hesitant to declare themselves on matters of great political gravity. The so-called alternative media are less reluctant, but they are too easily dismissed as irresponsible. By the time the mainstream media are willing to lend their names and reputations to a story of political covert action, the principal elements of the story have almost always been reported long before in the alternative media, where they were studiously ignored.

When the Iran-Contra scandal exploded in 1986, both the Congress and the media pulled up short. Neither had the stomach for the kind of national trauma that would have resulted from articles of impeachment being delivered against a popular President who was in his last two years of office. So, when it could not be proven conclusively that the President saw the "smoking gun" in the case—a copy of a memo to Reagan reporting in matter-of-fact terms that proceeds of Iranian arms sales were being diverted to the Nicaraguan contras—the nation seemed to utter a collective sigh of relief. (The original memo, bearing the signatures of those who had seen it, had been deliberately destroyed.) The laws trembled at the prospect of a political trial that could shatter the compact of trust between rulers and ruled, a compact that was the foundation upon which the laws themselves rested. The lesson seemed to be that accountability declines as the magnitude of the offense and the power of those charged increase.

The ultimate dilemma, which Chenier captured so perfectly in his comment on the revolutionary politics of eighteenth-century France, is the effect of very high stakes. A run-of-the-mill political scandal can safely be exposed without affecting anyone other than the culprits and their immediate circle. A covert political coup, however, like the one engineered by Casey in 1980, challenges the legitimacy of the political order; it deliberately exploits weaknesses in the political immune system and risks infecting the entire organism of state and society. Such a virus of secrecy and subterfuge would permeate the Reagan administration and would culminate in the Iran-Contra Affair, the contours of which bore an uncanny resemblance to Casey's 1980 deal to swap arms for hostages. One of the more puzzling aspects of the Iran-Contra Affair was the Reagan administration's dogged pursuit of a deal in the face of repeated Iranian demands. Yet Reagan's men refused to take no for an answer. The reason now seems plain: The same parties had cut a deal once before.

A PERSONAL NOTE

My involvement in the story of the secret deal began in earnest after the election of President Bush in 1988. Martin Kilian, a Washington correspondent for *Der Spiegel*, the German weekly newsmagazine, contacted me in late 1988 about the evidence he had been collecting. He had taken an interest in the story when it began to emerge in 1987–88 and had been steadily cultivating relationships with many of the sources. Kilian, a historian by training, had begun to assemble the evidence in a systematic way and had gone much further than any of the American reporters I had met. He had, for example, uncovered several credible sources in Europe who confirmed some of the key facts, but there were two complications. Their version of the story suggested that what had occurred in October 1980 was far more complicated than just a quick deal in Paris. An entirely new set of events and actors needed to be checked. These sources also insisted on absolute anonymity. Neither Kilian nor I was willing to publish such serious accusations on the basis of anonymous sources. Kilian began calling me at my home in Manhattan after each new interview or whenever he picked up some nugget of information from the small network of individuals who continued to delve into the elusive story. During these long-distance chats, I became familiar with the names and identities of the key actors who were thought to have taken part in the secret deal.

I also came to know and like Martin Kilian. Now forty years old, he had come to the United States from Germany as a young man to complete a Ph.D. in American history. He then settled in Thomas Jefferson's hometown of Charlottesville, Virginia, before joining *Der Spiegel* and coming to Washington in 1987. He was in love with all things American. He collected jazz and blues recordings; he sought out reporting assignments that took him into small-town America; and he believed passionately in the Jeffersonian democratic tradition. It was the apparent violation of those values that prompted him to spend much of his spare time investigating the curious circumstances of the 1980 election.

Kilian and I did not meet for five months after he first contacted me, but when we finally sat down to a sumptuous dinner at the MacPherson Grill in Washington, D.C., it was like a reunion of two old college friends. Despite our disparate backgrounds and a sixteen-year age difference, we were kindred spirits, and the restaurant's comfortable surroundings seemed perfectly suited to our rambling discussions. It became our chosen rendezvous point in Washington.

My own interest in the story was still almost entirely passive. Because of my experience with the hostage crisis in the White House, I could serve as a useful sounding board for Kilian. I was intrigued with the information he was discovering, but I regarded it as his story, not mine. I was then in the midst of final negotiations with the Twentieth Century Fund for a book I planned to write about U.S.-Iranian relations during the Reagan administration. I expected to focus largely on the Iran-Contra Affair, and my proposal to the Fund, which was approved at the end of 1988, made no allusion to the events of the 1980 campaign. I soon learned, however, that I could not evade the issue.

The first step in my research was to compile a comprehensive chronology of events from 1980 to 1988, greatly expanding a computerized set of historical files that I had been developing for some years. As I went back over the historical record of 1980, I kept stumbling across bits of information that had never seemed important to me but now assumed new meaning in light of my conversations with Kilian. By April 1989, the rough outlines of a pattern began to emerge. I decided to run some data-base searches to check some of Kilian's information, and in June I began conducting interviews and actively pursuing several leads that were available to me because of my White House connections.

The computer was an integral and irreplaceable element of the inquiry. I ransacked data banks, adding huge hunks of information directly to my storage disk. I developed a set of elaborate chronological files, biographical files, and transcripts of interviews, and a running account of conversations, questions, meetings, and working hypotheses. All of this information could be retrieved or cross-checked within seconds. I kept virtually no paper. Documents too bulky to enter were cross-referenced on the computer disk. My network of contacts expanded exponentially, and as time went on, my expanding set of reference files became an essential tool for everyone involved in the research. In effect, I became the archivist of the project. If a new name or place or date showed up in an interview, I was able to check quickly for all previous references. My file of names associated in some way with the events of 1980 ballooned to nearly fifty pages of densely packed type and became too cumbersome to print, since it changed and grew almost daily.

I relied heavily on research done by others. Those actively involved in this investigation were remarkably trusting and uncompetitive. Our common objective was to get to the bottom of the matter, but our resources were so limited that we could not afford the luxury of concealing information from each other. Anyone who could make a contribution to the work was welcome to join in, but those who only seemed interested in milking us for a quick story were unceremoniously cut out. We were not inclined to rush into print.

Throughout 1990, I had been in occasional touch with Jamshid Hashemi, the Iranian businessman and arms dealer who, with his brother Cyrus, had been closely associated with the 1980 hostage episode. In our early meetings, he confirmed in general terms that the Reagan-Bush campaign had concluded a deal with Iran to delay the release of the hostages, but he warned me to drop the subject because it was dangerous. In our first meeting at his home in a Washington suburb, he warned me: "This story cannot be done without stepping on the toes of some very powerful people. I know people who would think nothing of spending a million dollars to have something happen to you." I decided to ignore his warning.

While working on this story, I was often told by investigators and reporters to "follow the money." I also chose not to follow that advice. I had no reason to question its wisdom, but I had every reason to doubt that it would work for me. My eyes glaze over at the sight of a balance sheet, and complicated descriptions of money laundering always lose me about halfway through. The names of offshore banks and front companies all sound the same to me, which presumably is the intent of those who invent blandly generic titles. If I tried to follow the money, I feared, I would probably only fall asleep. Fortunately, not everyone suffers from this affliction, and I gratefully salute those who delved into the numbers and who valiantly attempted to make me understand their significance.

I did try to follow the weapons trail, however, and that effort led me into several bizarre situations. Some of these—including midnight meetings in seedy bars—were pure Hollywood cliché. Others, such as my rendezvous with Ahmed Heidari, were more original.

By all accounts, Heidari, one of the principal Iranian arms agents operating at the time, was a sinister figure. On several occasions, according to a 1981 memorandum written by Jacques Montanès, Heidari had attended meetings accompanied by a silent, muscular fellow named Michael who was described as a "hit man." In 1990, Heidari was said to be living in great luxury in the south of France. I decided to try to interview him in person.

I wrote letters to several of my European contacts asking their help in locating Heidari. To my surprise, I received a response almost immediately from a young Iranian journalist in Paris who knew someone he believed could arrange a meeting. He was as good as his word. He called later with detailed instructions for a rendezvous: I was to be at the reception desk of the Loews Hotel and Casino in Monte Carlo at nine o'clock in the evening on Tuesday, July 17. There I would be met by a Mr. Aalam, who would recognize me. He would take me to meet Heidari at an unspecified location.

I gulped and hesitated. Was this safe? He laughed and assured me it was. There was a good reason for the strange directions, he said, and I should not worry. Would he be willing, I asked, to accompany me to the meeting? No, he replied, he could not get out of Paris on that date.

I discussed my intentions with several people, including a professional investigator, who advised me not to go. Nevertheless, I decided to trust my new associate in Paris, and I booked a flight.

I arrived in Nice on July 16, rented a car, drove to Monte Carlo and checked into a pleasant but unfashionable seaside hotel on the outskirts of town. That evening I took the hotel bus to the city center and wandered around the casino, surveying the lay of the land. The next day, ignoring the sunshine and the beach, I sat in my hotel room with a portable computer, reviewing my notes and wondering about the evening that lay ahead. That night, at nine o'clock sharp, I was standing a bit awkwardly in the ornate lobby of the casino, where a huge backgammon tournament was in progress, when a lively, dark-haired man came up to me and introduced himself. Rashid Aalam turned out to be a cousin of the mysterious Heidari. A frustrated academic with a Ph.D. in sociology from the University of Southern California, and the president of the French backgammon association, he was in Monte Carlo with his cousin to participate in the tournament. They could not meet before nine o'clock, because they had expected to be competing until then. Luck, however, had not been with them and both had been eliminated in early rounds.

I was taken to a suite on the sixth floor of the hotel, where Heidari and Aalam's wife were waiting, anxious to be off to dinner. Heidari proved to be a pleasant man in his mid-forties, wearing a rumpled suit, with the well-rounded look of a successful shopkeeper. He seemed shy and uneasy in both French and English, although he was quite competent in both languages. When he wanted to emphasize a point, he would whisper it in Persian to Aalam, who would then translate. There were awkward pauses. It was clear from the first few minutes of small talk that I would learn very little of real interest that night. He wanted to size me up before saying anything serious.

We had a glass of wine in the room, then went downstairs to the Jockey Club for one of the more extravagant meals I have ever eaten. The four of us had a large room to ourselves. A flock of tuxedoed waiters fluttered in the background, poised like a SWAT team to deliver us from the peril of a fumbled fork or an empty bread plate. Heidari obviously enjoyed showing off his wealth. Over dinner, we had a thoroughly conventional discussion of the Iranian revolution. Heidari asked me questions about key events and personalities, weighing my answers against his personal experiences. We disagreed on several fine points, but I had the impression that I had passed my oral exam. Over a strawberry soufflé, I presented him with several pages of questions I had intended to ask. He invited me to join him again the following night, promising to talk some more.

The next evening we met in his suite for a solid hour of questions and answers with my tape recorder, then it was off to another restaurant for another Falstaffian extravaganza. At the end of the second evening, he finally ventured to ask me the question that apparently had been most on his mind. How much would it cost to maintain his life-style in New York City? I did not know, but my estimate was high enough to make him gasp.

He gave me answers to most of my questions. On technical matters he was voluble and precise, but on sensitive issues of politics he mumbled generalities. I did not get everything I wanted, but I did learn a lot about his business. I also probably learned more than he wanted me to know about the volatile mixture of political rivalry and military avarice in revolutionary Iran.

By early 1991, I realized that my colleagues and I had assembled only scattered clues about an extremely complicated picture. I also knew that many bits of evidence, with the answers to some of the most important questions, would probably remain permanently beyond the reach of our small, loosely knit group of researchers, working largely on our own time and with pitifully few resources. It was surprising, in fact, that we had made as much progress as we had. We had been engaged in political archaeology, and in archaeology there comes a time when you must stop digging and present your evidence for public scrutiny and debate.

For several months in late 1990 and early 1991, Robert Ross and Robert Parry had been working on a documentary on the October surprise for the PBS-TV investigative series *Frontline*. I had met Bob Parry, an experienced investigative reporter, a year earlier through Martin Kilian. He was one of the small group of journalists who stubbornly persevered in tracking this story, often on their own time, after their colleagues and editors had lost interest. Ross was a television producer who had lived in Iran and spoke Persian. I had no affiliation with *Frontline,* but I compared notes with Parry and Ross at every stage of their work, since we were all working on the same story, with the same sources. We had informally agreed that it would be useful to have an article in the print media at about the same time as their television special. Although I had been working on the story for more than two years and had discussed it in television and newspaper interviews, I had not written a word for publication. When they got an air date of April 16, 1991, I decided that the moment had come.

Kathleen Quinn, an editor on the op-ed page of *The New York Times,* had contacted me a year earlier to ask if I planned to write something on the October surprise. I told her I was not ready, but we stayed in contact after that. In April I called her and said that if they were still interested, I was now ready to write an article. It appeared on April 15, under the headline, "The Election Story of the Decade," one day before "The Election Held Hostage" aired on *Frontline.*

The combination of the two reports ignited intense interest and controversy. President Bush and the White House spokesman made some disparaging remarks about me, which added fuel to the fire, and the Congress began preparing to investigate the events of the 1980 elections. I had always intended to write a book, but unfortunately when the article and television special appeared in mid-April I had only a few draft chapters in hand. As a result, most of this book was written over the summer of 1991.

This book, more than most, owes its existence to the help of others who provided information, interpretation, encouragement, support, or simply tolerance. Many of my collaborators are identified in the book and in the comments above. Those remaining are almost too numerous to name, but too important to ignore.

My wife, Karlan, learned to do without my company on weekends, as seven-day work weeks became the norm. When our apartment became a full-time office and the dining room filled up with books and papers, she worked around the mess with remarkable good humor. When our daughter, Gyneth, came home from Italy for a visit, and our musician son, Jeffrey, and his wife, Abigail, joined us for a rare family reunion, even that turned into a week-long copy-editing session. The book profited from their comments and suggestions, and we had our family visit despite it all.

The Twentieth Century Fund, and especially its president, Richard Leone, gave me extraordinary financial and moral support as the conventional book I had promised them turned into something quite unconventional and risky. Without them, it never could have been done.

Three other journalists were particularly generous and helpful. Tara Sonenshine of ABC-TV's *Nightline* took an early interest in the story, introduced me to some key sources, and, with her superb team of researchers, broke several parts of the story. Stephen Pizzo provided me with documents and insights drawn from his own extensive research into the savings-and-loan scandals, which overlapped at several key points with the October surprise. Frank Snepp shared with me some important documents, and I benefited greatly from his research published in the *Village Voice*.

In the final two months, I had the full-time assistance of Suzanne Charlé, a writer and editor, and Beth Silverman, a talented researcher and a former student of mine at Columbia. They worked endless hours in less-than-ideal circumstances. Adam Gould joined us briefly in August. We became a real team, and the book is both richer and more accurate because of their contributions. Cheryl Moch tracked down and organized the photographs that appear in this book.

Stacie Bradford of Facts on File arranged for me to download huge hunks of material from their data base to my own computer. That saved me dozens of visits to the library and helped me construct a comprehensive and accurate chronology.

Others who gave freely of their time and expertise to assist me at various stages include Bob Barnett, Robert Bernstein, Tom Blanton, Selma Brackman, Malcolm Byrne, Richard Cottam, Garry Emmons, Mansour Farhang, Alton Frye, Claudio Gatti, Christopher Hitchens, Leslie Janka, Carole Jerome, Farhad Kazemi, Moorhead Kennedy, William Miller, Ali Mohammedi, Baqer Moin, Edmund Muskie, Maurice Paprin, Tony Pell, Mansur Rafizadeh, Steen Ramsgaard, Bill Royce, Shmuel Segev, Jonathan Silvers, Behrouz Souresrafil, William Vanden Heuvel, Nicholas Veliotes, William Wachtel, and Andrew Whitley. To them, and to others who would prefer to remain nameless, my warmest thanks.

Barbara Honegger deserves special mention. Although we did not work together and did not see eye to eye on many points of evidence and interpretation, she was nevertheless one of the earliest and most dedicated researchers on this story.

My agent, Jim Stein, of William Morris, provided discreet and always effective assistance.

Finally, I wish to thank Peter Osnos of Random House and publisher of Times Books, and Steve Wasserman and Paul Golob, editorial director and editor of Times Books, respectively. A crack team of editors extraordinaire, Wasserman and Golob took what I thought was a pretty good piece of work and made it better.

Whatever faults or errors may remain are solely my responsibility.

G.S.
New York City
September 1991

NOTES

1. AN ELECTION HELD HOSTAGE

1. Sixty-six Americans were taken at the embassy on November 4. Most of them were U.S. diplomatic officials, although several private Americans who were visiting the embassy at the time were also trapped and held. Three diplomats at the Foreign Ministry at the time of the attack were held there throughout the crisis. Of those captured, thirteen women and blacks were released on November 17, 1979, leaving a total of fifty-three hostages during most of the crisis. Six other diplomats were outside the embassy at the time of the attack and managed to escape on January 29, 1980, with the assistance of the Canadian Embassy. One hostage, Richard Queen, was released on July 11, 1980, because he was severely ill. The remaining fifty-two hostages were released on January 20, 1981, after 444 days of imprisonment.

2. *Gharbzadegi*, an invented word, was the title of a famous essay by the well-known Iranian writer Al-e-Ahmad, which was banned under the shah because it criticized the superficial ways of the West.

3. The evolution of U.S.-Iranian relations and their effects on the revolution are examined in: Shaul Bakhash, *The Reign of the Ayatollahs: Iran and the Islamic Revolution* (New York: Basic Books, 1984); James A. Bill, *The Eagle and the Lion:*

The Tragedy of American and Iranian Relations (New Haven, Conn.: Yale University Press, 1988); Richard W. Cottam, *Iran & the United States: A Cold War Case Study* (Pittsburgh: University of Pennsylvania Press, 1988); Nikki R. Keddie, *Roots of Revolution: An Interpretive History of Modern Iran* (New Haven, Conn.: Yale University Press, 1981); Barry Rubin, *Paved with Good Intentions: The American Experience and Iran* (New York: Oxford University Press, 1980); and Gary Sick, *All Fall Down: America's Tragic Encounter with Iran* (New York: Random House, 1985).

4. *The New York Times,* November 21, 1980.

5. In fact, the early success of the news show at eleven-thirty P.M. spurred ABC executives to create a regular late-night news program, *Nightline,* which focused on major news events, including the hostage crisis. For a more detailed discussion, see "Siege Mentality: ABC, the White House and the Iran Hostage Crisis," a case study by Howard Husock and Pamela Varley for the Kennedy School of Government, Harvard University, 1988.

6. *The Washington Post,* December 17, 1979.

7. Jimmy Carter, *Keeping Faith: Memoirs of a President* (New York: Bantam Books, 1982), p. 463.

8. It was neither a new idea nor a new complaint. When Jimmy Carter was a candidate in 1976, he used the term "Rose Garden strategy" to describe President Gerald Ford's practice of campaigning largely through presidential news conferences. See Nelson W. Polsby, "The Democratic Nomination," in Austin Ranney, ed., *The American Elections of 1980* (Washington, D.C.: American Enterprise Institute for Public Policy Research, 1981), especially pp. 37–49.

9. Carter, *Keeping Faith,* p. 519.

10. Interviews with former President Carter, Atlanta, September 15, 1990, and Zbigniew Brzezinski, Washington, D.C., June 6, 1990. On April 27, 1980, I was called to Brzezinski's office with General William Odom, his military assistant. Brzezinski, grim and determined, said the President had authorized him to begin planning a new rescue mission. "We must go back in," he declared. The previous mission, he said, had been far too complicated and too dependent on high technology; the new plan should correct these weaknesses.

My response did not please him. In the meeting, and later in a more detailed memorandum, I argued that the first mission had changed everything. Admittedly, we should have the capacity to act in extremis, if the lives of the hostages were in imminent danger, but otherwise the chances of success of a second mission were slim; a second failure would only make things worse. Brzezinski never acknowledged my memorandum and never mentioned the subject to me again.

11. Hamilton Jordan, *Crisis: The Last Year of the Carter Presidency* (New York: G.P. Putnam's Sons, 1982), pp. 285–86.

12. Michael K. Deaver, *Behind the Scenes* (New York: Morrow, 1987), p. 99.

13. Interview with Robert Neumann, Washington, D.C., April 4, 1990.

14. Joseph C. Goulden, *The Death Merchant: The Rise and Fall of Edwin P. Wilson* (New York: Simon and Schuster, 1984), p. 15.

15. "The Election Held Hostage," PBS-TV *Frontline*, April 16, 1991.

16. Interview with Richard V. Allen, Washington, D.C., November 24, 1989.

17. Interview with Robert Garrick by Robert Parry and Robert Ross of *Frontline*, September 22, 1990. See also "Unauthorized Transfers of Nonpublic Information During the 1980 Presidential Election," report prepared by the Subcommittee on Human Resources of the Committee on Post Office and Civil Service, House of Representatives, Committee Print (Washington, D.C.: U.S. Government Printing Office, May 17, 1984), p. 36. This investigation, which was conducted from July 1983 to April 1984 by the Subcommittee on Human Resources, under the direction of its chairman, Don Albosta, will henceforth be referred to as the Albosta Report. A separate investigation of these events was also conducted by the FBI.

18. Interview with Richard V. Allen, Washington, D.C., November 24, 1989.

19. Ibid.; interview with Zbigniew Brzezinski, Washington, D.C., April 16, 1991.

20. See the Associated Press's advance report of Anderson's allegations, August 16, 1980.

21. Associated Press, August 19, 1980.

22. Telephone interview with Jack Anderson and Dale Van Atta, August 14, 1991.

23. The certification of the mission meant that it was ready to proceed at any time. It could not proceed, however, unless the hostages were assembled in Tehran at the embassy or some other location that was accessible to the team. From the perspective of the mission commanders, reliable intelligence on the location of the hostages would be the trigger to launch the operation.

24. Associated Press, August 20, 1980.

25. Albosta Report, pp. 1076–79.

26. Interview, August 8, 1990. This person, who himself opposed Carter's re-election, spoke to me on condition of anonymity.

27. Albosta Report, pp. 1152–55. Garrick, in his affidavit to the subcommittee, said he could not remember the names or locations of this network. His memory

later improved, and he described the operation in some detail to Robert Parry and Robert Ross of *Frontline* in an interview on September 22, 1990.

28. See the account of the proceedings in the Albosta Report.

29. Interview with Richard V. Allen, Washington, D.C., November 24, 1989.

30. ABC-TV *Nightline*, April 15, 1991.

31. See Sick, *All Fall Down*, p. 314; Jody Powell, *The Other Side of the Story* (New York: William Morrow, 1984), pp. 252ff.

32. Interview with Richard V. Allen, Washington, D.C., November 24, 1989.

33. *The New York Times*, October 7, 1980.

34. Interview with Robert Neumann, Washington, D.C., April 4, 1990.

35. Interview with Richard V. Allen, Washington, D.C., November 24, 1989.

36. Interview with Jody Powell, Washington, D.C., March 20, 1990.

37. Interview with Ronald I. Spiers, former assistant secretary of state for intelligence and research, New York, September 6, 1991.

38. Casey simply was too large a character to hide behind an alias. In his excellent biography of Casey, Joseph Persico describes a telling incident that took place at the Rolling Hills Sheraton in Worcester, Massachusetts, just before the crucial New Hampshire primary in the 1980 campaign. Casey had only recently accepted the position as Ronald Reagan's campaign manager. The change was still a secret from most people—particularly John Sears, who was about to be dumped. Casey and Richard Allen, Reagan's foreign-affairs adviser and an old Casey friend from the 1968 Nixon campaign, were taking an elevator up to Reagan's suite when a young woman got in and greeted Allen. Trying to hide Casey's identity, Allen responded by introducing his friend as "Frank Williams." "Aaah, c'mon," the veteran OSS officer said, putting out his hand, "My name is Bill Casey." The elevator doors opened, the woman headed off and a distracted Allen whispered: "Jesus, Bill. You blew your cover. She's one of Sears' people. Now he'll know why you're here." *Casey: From the OSS to the CIA* (New York: Viking, 1990), p. 179.

39. Interview with Jamshid Hashemi, London, October 13, 1990.

40. Persico, *Casey*, p. 192.

41. For an alternative view, see Carter, *Keeping Faith*, pp. 502–4; Jordan, *Crisis*, pp. 242–45; Powell, *The Other Side of the Story*, pp. 214–19; Sick, *All Fall Down*, pp. 275–78.

42. *The New York Times*, April 22, 1980.

43. Interview with Jamshid Hashemi, London, October 15, 1990.

44. Many of the jobs on the NSC staff are regarded as nonpolitical and are filled by civil servants and military officers seconded by their respective agencies.

45. The details about Donald Gregg's career were drawn from his testimony at

the trial of Richard Brenneke. *United States of America* v. *Richard Brenneke*, CR No. 89-189-MA, April 24, 1990, Portland, Oregon; vol. I, pp. 74–95 and 234–91.

46. Interview with a former CIA colleague of Gregg, who spoke to me on condition that he not be identified, Washington, D.C., March 20, 1990.

47. Interview with Jamshid Hashemi, London, October 13, 1990.

48. We talked on the understanding that I would not reveal his name, even on internal U.S. documents. I reported my conversations in full to Zbigniew Brzezinski, the national security adviser, but no one else was aware of these meetings.

49. Interview in Europe with a former senior Defense Department official and personal friend who spoke to me on condition of anonymity. This individual acknowledged his own opposition to Carter's policies and his preference for Reagan's election, but he denied any direct involvement in electoral politics.

2. THE QUEST FOR ARMS

1. This account is based on a series of interviews in 1990 with former American hostage Colonel Charles W. Scott and on his excellent book, *Pieces of the Game* (Atlanta: Peachtree Publishers, 1984), especially pp. 278–303.

2. The September offer omitted the demand for withdrawal of U.S. military forces. Abol Hassan Bani-Sadr, Iran's new president, had told French correspondent Eric Rouleau on February 11, 1980, that Iran no longer insisted on the return of the shah. That was not confirmed by other officials, however, and no new negotiating position was conveyed to the United States, either formally or informally, until September.

3. In A.D. 680, Husayn, the grandson of the Prophet Mohammed, who is revered by Shi'i Muslims as the legitimate successor of the Prophet, was martyred by the False Prophet Yazid in a battle on the plain of Karbala. Husayn was buried nearby in Najaf. Both sites are now marked by magnificent mosques. This was the pivotal event in the evolution of Shi'ism as a separate school of Islam, and it is celebrated each year on the tenth of Muharram by frenzied displays of mourning and self-flagellation.

4. Abol Hassan Bani-Sadr, *My Turn to Speak: Iran, the Revolution & Secret Deals with the U.S.* (New York: Brassey's [U.S.], Inc., 1991), p. 23.

5. Interview with General Hassan Toufanian, Washington, D.C., July 10, 1990.

6. Ibid.

7. Interviews with Ahmed Heidari, Monte Carlo. July 17 and 18, 1990.

8. Bakhash, *The Reign of the Ayatollahs*, pp. 41–42.

9. Interview with a former senior official of the Islamic Republic of Iran, who spoke to me on condition of anonymity, New York, October 30, 1990.

10. Ibid. Interview with Mansour Farhang, former Iranian ambassador to the United Nations, New York, December 28, 1990.

11. William H. Sullivan, *Mission to Tehran* (New York: W.W. Norton & Co., 1981), p. 200ff.; Sick, *All Fall Down,* pp. 132–38.

12. Interview with a former senior official of the Islamic Republic of Iran, who spoke to me on condition of anonymity, October 30, 1990.

13. Karim Minachi should not be confused with Naser Minachi, an associate of Mehdi Bazargan, who was the minister of information in Bazargan's first provisional government and who was briefly arrested in early 1980 on espionage charges raised by the students holding the U.S. Embassy.

14. Interviews with Ahmed Heidari, Monte Carlo, July 17 and 18, 1990.

15. Keddie, *Roots of Revolution,* p. 158.

16. His official name was Mohammed Ali Hashemi. Jamshid was a name used within the family, but not on his original Iranian passport. In addition to the Hashemi family name he also sometimes used Balanian, a name derived from the family's village of origin. In later years he mixed these and other names in a seemingly endless string of aliases.

17. The information on the Hashemi brothers was derived from court documents and press reports, as well as interviews during 1989 and 1990 with Jamshid Hashemi, former U.S. government officials, and a number of associates of the Hashemis who requested anonymity.

18. Mark J. Gasiorowski, *U.S. Foreign Policy and the Shah* (Ithaca, N.Y.: Cornell University Press, 1991), pp. 166–69.

19. Interviews with Ahmad Madani, New York, November 4 and 27, 1990.

20. The Clark mission is described in Sick, *All Fall Down,* pp. 207–15. Interview with Ramsey Clark, New York, November 15, 1990.

21. Interview with Jamshid Hashemi, Washington, D.C., March 8, 1990.

22. The U.S. intermediary spoke to me in a series of interviews in New York, 1989–90, on condition that he not be identified.

23. Habibi was quite an interesting choice. Hasan Ebrahim Habibi was born on March 6, 1937, and studied theology in Iran before taking a Ph.D. in sociology and law in France. He was involved in student activities against the shah in the 1960s and became a member of the Revolutionary Council after the shah fell. A lawyer, he was one of the architects of the controversial draft constitution of 1979 that provided for clerical supremacy. After the failure of his presidential bid, he became minister of justice in 1984 and was reapproved in 1985 with the second-

highest vote total of any Cabinet minister. In 1989, President Rafsanjani appointed Habibi first vice president and head of the presidential office, the second-highest-ranking position in the executive branch. He came to be regarded as relatively moderate in his political views and as more of a technocrat than an ideologue.

24. Interview with Jamshid Hashemi, London, October 13, 1990.

25. Madani was badly hurt in the final days of the campaign by allegations, published by the students holding the American Embassy, that he had contacts with the CIA. Madani was considered as a possible prime minister by Bani-Sadr and was elected to the first Majles in 1980, but was forced to resign on July 10. Shortly thereafter he went into hiding and eventually escaped the country on September 20, just two days before the Iraqi invasion. His abortive association with the United States was widely reported in Europe and Iran and was eventually confirmed publicly by Madani himself (see his interview with Agence France Presse on December 11, 1986, cited in *Foreign Broadcast Information Service*, the same date). For another partial account, see Amir Taheri, *Nest of Spies: America's Journey to Disaster in Iran* (New York: Pantheon Books, 1988), p. 143.

26. The Foreign Military Sales contract signed by every country that purchases military equipment from the United States contains a clause that prohibits the transfer or resale of any U.S.-origin equipment to a third country without formal permission from the United States. That prohibition does not extend to matériel that is manufactured by the recipient country for its own use, even if it is designed to be used on a U.S. weapons system.

27. Interview with Ahmed Heidari, Monte Carlo, July 18, 1990.

28. Ibid. The underground railroad for Iranian Jews indeed began to function very well about this time. Over the following years, as many as 30,000 to 50,000 members of the Iranian Jewish community were permitted to leave quietly, a clear sign that the leaders of the Islamic Republic chose to look the other way.

3. THE DOCTRINE OF THE PERIPHERY

1. Cyrus's decree and subsequent Jewish relations with his successors, Darius and Xerxes, are recounted in the Book of Ezra.

2. Uri Bialer, "The Iranian Connection in Israel's Foreign Policy, 1948–1951," *Middle East Journal*, vol. 39, no. 2, spring 1985, pp. 292–308.

3. See Michael Bar-Zohar, "Ben-Gurion and the Policy of the Periphery," in Itamar Rabinovich and Jehuda Reinharz, eds., *Israel in the Middle East: Docu-*

ments and Readings on Society, Politics, and Foreign Relations, 1948–Present (New York: Oxford University Press, 1984), pp. 164–71.

4. Interview with Arieh Eliav, Tel Aviv, March 17, 1989.

5. Although it was an open secret, neither Israel nor Iran ever acknowledged this arrangement publicly. It was first revealed in detail in the U.S. Embassy documents captured by Iranian students in November 1979 and subsequently published as the "Documents from the Den of Spies" in Tehran, especially volume 63. For this citation and other background information, I am indebted to Daniel Raskas, whose unpublished research paper on Israeli-Iranian relations (Harvard 1989) was very helpful to me.

6. See Samuel Segev, *The Iranian Triangle: The Untold Story of Israel's Role in the Iran-Contra Affair* (New York: The Free Press, 1988), pp. 29–62.

7. For an analysis of SAVAK's relations with the CIA, see Mark J. Gasiorowski, "Security Relations Between the United States and Iran, 1953–1978," in Nikki R. Keddie and Mark J. Gasiorowski, eds., *Neither East Nor West: Iran, the Soviet Union, and the United States* (New Haven, Conn.: Yale University Press, 1990), pp. 145–65.

8. The most authoritative source on the Kurdish secret war from the U.S. perspective is the report prepared by Representative Otis G. Pike of the House Select Committee on Intelligence, which was leaked to the *Village Voice* and appeared in special supplements on February 16 and 23, 1976. It was also the subject of several columns by William Safire in *The New York Times* (see *Safire's Washington* [New York: Times Books, 1988]). Henry Kissinger, in the first volume of his memoirs, said he would address the subject of the Kurdish war in the second volume. The second volume contains no mention of the subject.

9. The notes of General Toufanian's meetings with Israeli Defense Minister Ezer Weizman in July 1977 were published in volume 19 of the "Documents from the Den of Spies." The documents were reported in *The New York Times* on April 1, 1986, p. 17. See also Segev, *The Iranian Triangle*, p. 99.

10. Interview with General Toufanian, Washington, D.C., July 10, 1990.

11. Ibid.

12. Interview with a senior Israeli military official who was in Iran at the time and attended the briefing. He asked that his name not be used.

13. See Sick, *All Fall Down*, p. 37.

14. For the following remarks, I rely in part on Victor Ostrovsky and Claire Hoy, *By Way of Deception: The Making and Unmaking of a Mossad Officer* (New York: St Martin's Press, 1990). Ostrovsky spent four years as a Mossad trainee and, briefly, as an operative. He left the Mossad after an altercation and wrote a

book critical of the Mossad and Israel. The Israeli government made a highly publicized effort to suppress the book, thereby turning it into a best-seller. Although some of the cases Ostrovsky described were admittedly based on evidence acquired indirectly or through hearsay, there was reason to believe that his descriptions of tradecraft and operating procedures as taught in his training courses were accurate, if unflattering.

15. Pollard, a passionate Zionist, had top-security clearance and access to sensitive compartmentalized information about intelligence-gathering systems. For seventeen months, until his arrest on November 15, 1985, he delivered over a thousand classified documents to Israel's Bureau of Scientific Liaison, known by its Hebrew acronym, Lakam, which gathered secret scientific and technological intelligence. Pollard's trial and conviction in 1987 made headlines in the United States. The scandal of Israeli espionage in America was highly embarrassing to Israel, but had little effect on long-term relations between the two nations. See Wolf Blitzer, *Territory of Lies: The Exclusive Story of Jonathan Jay Pollard: The American Who Spied on His Country for Israel and How He Was Betrayed* (New York: Harper & Row, 1989); and Ian Black and Benny Morris, *Israel's Secret Wars: A History of Israel's Intelligence Services* (New York: Grove Weidenfeld, 1991), esp. pp. 416–26.

16. In the 1980s, the Mossad reportedly had a total of only about 1,200 employees and only about thirty to thirty-five case officers operating around the world, compared with thousands in the CIA and KGB (Ostrovsky and Hoy, *By Way of Deception*, p. xi). Israeli intelligence, of course, focused on a narrow set of issues directly related to the country's own security, while the services of the two superpowers had truly global responsibilities. That alone, however, could not account for the much greater efficiency of the Israeli service.

17. The portrait that follows is based on many hours of interviews with Ari Ben-Menashe in 1990 and 1991, with some occasional helpful contributions by his mother. Key elements of the story were independently confirmed by Iranian, Israeli, and American sources.

18. Dennis Rohan, a twenty-eight-year-old sheep shearer from Australia, came to Jerusalem in 1969. Interior voices had told him that the Messiah was coming and a new temple had to be constructed. He decided on the site of the Dome of the Rock, a golden-domed shrine that is the third-holiest site of Islam. Tradition has it that the al-Aqsa Mosque was built on the site of a temple planned by King David and built by his son, Solomon. Rohan managed to set fire to the mosque, but only the pulpit was fully destroyed. Rohan quickly confessed when Israeli police tracked him down at the kibbutz; at a trial, he was found guilty and sentenced to

life confinement. The al-Aqsa fire was believed by many Arabs to be a Zionist plot. See Abraham Rabinovitch, *Jerusalem on Earth: People, Passions and Politics in the Holy City* (New York: The Free Press, 1988), pp. 23–44.

19. Interview with Ari Ben-Menashe, New York, January 12, 1991. There was no evidence presented at the trial of connections between Rohan and the Jewish Defense League.

20. Interview with Ari Ben-Menashe, New York, November 25, 1990.

21. Interview with Ari Ben-Menashe, New York, January 12, 1991.

22. See Richard W. Cottam, *Nationalism in Iran* (Pittsburgh: University of Pittsburgh Press, rev. ed., 1979), esp. pp. 150–57; Bill, *The Eagle and the Lion,* esp. pp. 69–72.

23. There is some confusion over names. Ben-Menashe described in detail a man whose background can be positively identified as Ahmed Kashani. According to Ben-Menashe, however, this man used the name Mehdi Kashani in his dealings with him. Mehdi Kashani's name also showed up in Israeli-related arms deals in the early 1980s. Jamshid Hashemi told me in an interview in New York on August 29, 1991, that a man who used both the names Ahmed and Mehdi Kashani visited Israel in the early 1980s and was associated with Israeli arms sales to Iran. However, according to Hashemi, he was not related to the famous ayatollah.

24. Written communication from a former senior aide to Israeli Prime Minister Menachem Begin, June 10, 1991. This same information and timing were volunteered by several other high-level Israelis, who asked not to be named.

25. Interview with Ari Ben-Menashe, New York, January 12, 1991. Other authoritative Israeli sources confirm that Iran was particularly interested in F-4 tires and that a delivery was made during this time period.

26. Interview with Ari Ben-Menashe, New York, December 28, 1990.

27. Ibid. This information was confirmed by many senior U.S. and Israeli officials with firsthand knowledge of these events. They declined to be identified by name.

28. Interview with Ari Ben-Menashe, December 28, 1990. Ben-Menashe's account was subsequently confirmed by a number of high-level Israelis.

29. The source insisted on anonymity.

4. THE DIE IS CAST

1. Quoted in *The National Journal,* July 26, 1980, p. 1215.

2. For a discussion of the conventions, see Michael J. Malbin, "The Conven-

tions, Platforms, and Issue Activists," in Austin Ranney, ed., *The American Elections of 1980,* pp. 99–141.

3. Associated Press, July 15, 1980.

4. Abbie Hoffman and Jonathan Silvers, "An Election Held Hostage," *Playboy,* October 1988, p. 152, citing an interview by journalist Morgan Strong with Bassam Abu Sharif. Abu Sharif was interviewed again on this subject in November 1990 by Robert Ross and Robert Parry of the *Frontline* television program. On that occasion he again repeated the story in almost exactly the same terms, but he refused to identify the individual who approached him.

5. Bassam Abu Sharif, interview by Ross and Parry, Tunis, November 1990.

6. Sick, *All Fall Down,* pp. 224, 225.

7. Bassam Abu Sharif, interview by Ross and Parry, Tunis, November 1990.

8. This episode was first publicized by Simon O'Dwyer-Russell in *The Sunday Telegraph* (London), September 17, 1989, p. 1. An associate of Nixon told O'Dwyer-Russell, "We will neither confirm nor deny this story. We have nothing to say." When I mentioned this incident on the ABC-TV *Nightline* program on November 3, 1989, Nixon protested vigorously to ABC. Bristow has never denied the accuracy of the report, though he was embarrassed by the flurry of attention it attracted and has steadfastly refused to discuss the matter further. Bristow refused to meet with me, despite repeated requests.

9. The account of this meeting is based on a series of interviews with Jamshid Hashemi in London and Washington from October 1990 to June 1991.

10. Roy Furmark refused to see me, but in an interview with *Der Spiegel* reporter Martin Kilian in 1990, he denied that he introduced Casey to Jamshid Hashemi.

11. Interview with Bradford Shaheen, John Shaheen's younger son, New York, August 1, 1990. See also Shaheen's obituary in *The New York Times,* November 4, 1985, and Theodore Draper, *A Very Thin Line: The Iran-Contra Affairs* (New York: Hill and Wang, 1991), p. 440.

12. Telephone interview with Ahmad Madani, November 27, 1990.

13. Interviews with Jamshid Hashemi, Washington, D.C., 1991.

14. Just before his death, Khomeini named Mehdi Karrubi as one of two personal "attorneys" to dispose of unclaimed assets available to the *velayat-e faqih* (the unique position of supreme clerical leader established in Iran after the revolution). In 1989, at age fifty-two, Karrubi was elected speaker of the Majles.

15. Interview with Harold Saunders, former assistant secretary of state for Near Eastern and South Asian affairs, Washington, D.C., March 21, 1990.

16. I knew of the meeting because of my position within the National Security

Council at the time. The details of the meeting and the identity of the participants are still classified, and they must remain classified since their revelation could be dangerous to those individuals who were willing to take a considerable risk in the effort to find a resolution of the hostage problem. Cyrus Hashemi is now dead, and his brother Jamshid has revealed to a U.S. news organization his own role in arranging this meeting. The other participants, however, have never been identified publicly in connection with the events of 1980.

17. Bani-Sadr, *My Turn to Speak*, p. 29.

18. Personal communication from former President Carter, September 19, 1990.

19. The detailed description of these meetings that follows is based primarily on my interviews with Jamshid Hashemi in late 1990 and early 1991.

20. Tracking Casey's movements during these crucial days was a research effort in itself. My researchers and I discovered an obscure reference that established that he had traveled outside the country. The rest of the credit must go to Tara Sonenshine and the investigative staff of ABC-TV's *Nightline*.

21. Karrubi's statement of July 28, 1991, was reported in Foreign Broadcast Information Service, *Daily Report: Near East and South Asia*, July 29, 1991, p. 61.

22. Spain later became an important center for Iran in its efforts to acquire European military equipment, and Ambassador Behnam was deeply involved in that process. Interview with Ahmed Heidari, Monte Carlo, July 18, 1990.

23. Four years after the Madrid meeting, on November 20, 1984, Hassan Karrubi and Manuchehr Ghorbanifar met former CIA officer Theodore Shackley in Germany for a discussion that eventually ripened into the Iran-Contra Affair. For a detailed account of this meeting, see Draper, *A Very Thin Line*, pp. 126–27.

24. Jamshid Hashemi remembered the meetings being in July and August, but he was unable to reconstruct the precise dates. The dates cited here were derived from research by the ABC-TV *Nightline* investigative team. On the basis of Plaza Hotel records, in which Jamshid and Cyrus Hashemi appeared using lightly disguised names ("Jamshid Khalaj," "Abdullah Hashemi"), the dates of their visit to Madrid could be narrowed to the week of July 25–August 2, with July 25–29 as the most probable dates of the meetings.

25. This was presumably a reference to the negotiations that Bani-Sadr and his foreign minister, Sadegh Ghotbzadeh, had conducted with Washington through private intermediaries during the early months of 1980.

26. Interview with Ahmad Madani, New York, November 4, 1990.

27. Interviews with Ari Ben-Menashe, New York and Washington, 1990–91.

28. Interview with Arif Durrani by Robert Ross and Robert Parry, January 4, 1991.

29. Interview with Heinrich Rupp by Robert Ross and Robert Parry, Colorado, December 8, 1990.

30. Babayan made this comment to a visitor, who asked not to be identified.

31. "The Iran Hostage Crisis: A Chronology of Daily Developments," report prepared for the Committee on Foreign Affairs, U.S. House of Representatives, by the Foreign Affairs and National Defense Division, Congressional Research Service, Library of Congress (Washington, D.C.: U.S. Government Printing Office, March 1981), p. 257. Henceforth CRS Chronology.

32. Segev, *The Iranian Triangle*, p. 120.

33. Records from the Plaza Hotel, where Cyrus and Jamshid Hashemi stayed, show that the brothers, again using slightly disguised names ("Ali Balanian," "Parsa Jamshid"), were in Madrid on August 8–13. These dates overlap with the 1980 Democratic National Convention, which took place on August 11–14.

34. Interview with Ari Ben-Menashe, New York, November 1990. His mention of four meetings in Madrid originally struck me as most unlikely. It was only months later, when Jamshid Hashemi gave me a detailed description of the sequence of meetings, that Ben-Menashe's account was corroborated.

35. According to Jamshid Hashemi, the contact point for the Israeli front company in 1980 was also Mr. Yehoshua Nishri. An Israeli General Talem [phonetic] represented the Israeli Military Industries in the deal.

36. *London Observer*, November 2, 1980, cited in CRS Chronology, p. 370.

37. The text of this letter was subsequently published in Bani-Sadr's newspaper *Enghelab Eslami* on September 11, 1980. It attracted no attention at the time. A copy of the original text was given to me by Bani-Sadr in June 1991.

38. Professor Richard Cottam of the University of Pittsburgh was in frequent contact with Ghotbzadeh during this period. He recalls that Ghotbzadeh was insistent about the Republican plot to play politics with the hostages. Ghotbzadeh, however, was an inveterate conspiracy theorist; and since he offered no hard evidence, neither Cottam nor anyone else took his claims seriously.

39. CRS Chronology, pp. 269–70.

40. Bani-Sadr, *My Turn to Speak*, p. 29.

5. IRANIAN INTRIGUES

1. Bakhash, *The Reign of the Ayatollahs*, pp. 112, 113.

2. See, for example, Taheri, *Nest of Spies*, pp. 137–38. According to Taheri, Ghorbanifar operated at this time under the name Manuchehr Suzani.

3. Report of the President's Special Review Board, henceforth Tower Commission Report (Washington, D.C.: U.S. Government Printing Office, February 26, 1987), p. III-5.

4. *The New York Times*, August 9, 1991.

5. Significantly, the unfilled Cabinet posts were the most important: foreign affairs, economics and finance, planning and budget, labor and social affairs, oil, education, and commerce. Bani-Sadr and Raja'i did agree, reluctantly, on a non-ideological air force colonel, Javad Fakuri, as defense minister.

6. Tabatabai's willingness to skirt the law eventually landed him in serious trouble. In 1983 he was convicted by a court in Düsseldorf of attempting to smuggle 3.75 pounds of opium into West Germany. He was sentenced to three years in jail, but the sentence was quashed when the West German Foreign Ministry intervened on his behalf, claiming that his negotiating efforts on behalf of Iran gave him quasi-diplomatic status. A new warrant for his arrest was issued in 1986, but he continued to make occasional visits to Germany, where his wife lived, through at least the end of 1990. (See Reuters, August 20, 1986.)

7. For additional details, see Sick, *All Fall Down*, pp. 309, 310, and Warren Christopher, et al., *American Hostages in Iran: The Conduct of a Crisis* (New Haven, Conn.: Yale University Press, 1985), esp. pp. 297–306, by Roberts B. Owen.

8. In January 1986, when the Reagan White House was considering an arms-for-hostages agreement with Iran, Manuchehr Ghorbanifar, speaking on behalf of Iran, told his American contacts that Khomeini was going to step down on February 11. Lieutenant Colonel Oliver North and others accepted this story, and it appeared in North's "time line" describing a hostage-release scenario. When Khomeini did not step down, no one seems to have noticed or to have held Ghorbanifar to account. See Draper, *A Very Thin Line*, pp. 277–79, and the Tower Commission Report, p. B-73.

9. The following account is based on a review of the West German role in the hostage crisis that was prepared for West German Minister of Foreign Affairs Hans-Dietrich Genscher by Gerhard Ritzel, West Germany's ambassador in Iran, in early 1981. I am indebted to Steven M. de Vogel of the magazine *Vrij Nederland* in Amsterdam for sharing this information with me.

10. Although West German diplomacy was successful in setting aside the trou-

blesome demand for an apology, the last-minute deletion of this condition apparently caused some confusion in Tehran. For several days thereafter, Rafsanjani continued to insist publicly that Khomeini's failure to call for an American apology was an inadvertent omission and that "there are more conditions."

11. See Roberts B. Owen, "Final Negotiation and Release in Algiers," in *American Hostages in Iran*, pp. 301–6, for a more detailed description of the meetings; see also Sick, *All Fall Down*, pp. 309–11.

12. There was another body of military equipment in U.S. hands which had been produced for Iran under contracts signed by the shah's government. Iran had never paid for, and did not own, this equipment, whose total value fluctuated constantly. New items were still being produced and other high-value items were being sold off to the U.S. military and other purchasers to cover the costs of canceling some $12 billion in military contracts by the shah's government. This matériel never played any role in the hostage negotiations.

13. These three categories were regarded as bargaining chips in the negotiations over the following six weeks, until the election. In the first meeting, Warren Christopher referred to the first category. About three weeks later, the Carter administration added the items in category two. Finally, it was agreed that all three categories would be returned to Iran after the hostages were safely out of Iran. That decision was announced publicly by President Carter on October 28 in his nationally televised debate with Governor Reagan.

14. CRS Chronology, p. 284.

15. Interview with Sadegh Ghotbzadeh by Ram Suresh of Reuters, Tehran, September 16, 1980. Also CRS Chronology, p. 295.

16. Interviews with Richard Cottam of the University of Pittsburgh, who was the principal contact point between the U.S. government and Ghotbzadeh and who had numerous lengthy telephone conversations with him during this period; and Carole Jerome of the Canadian Broadcasting Company, whose close personal relationship with Ghotbzadeh was described in her book, *The Man in the Mirror* (London: Unwin Hyman, 1987).

17. *The New York Times*, September 14, 1980.

18. Agence France Presse, June 29, 1991.

19. Interview with Colonel Charles Scott, Los Angeles, February 1, 1990. Interviews with Rosen and Kennedy, New York, March 29, 1990. See Kennedy's account of his experiences in *The Ayatollah in the Cathedral: Reflections of a Hostage* (New York: Hill and Wang, 1986), esp. pp. 132–33; and Barbara and Barry Rosen with George Feifer, *The Destined Hour* (New York: Doubleday, 1982), esp. p. 246.

20. Scott, *Pieces of the Game*, pp. 340, 341.

21. For a useful summary of military developments in the war, see Edgar O'Ballance, *The Gulf War* (New York: Brassey's [U.S.], 1988), p. 30.

22. Discussion with a U.N. diplomat who had direct knowledge of this exchange, New York, October 1980.

23. CRS Chronology, p. 309.

24. *The New York Times*, September 24, 1980.

25. This meeting took place on September 25. See *The New York Times*, September 26, 1980.

26. Washington was deeply concerned that such an attack would lead to Iranian retaliation against the Arab shaikhdoms, thus widening the scope of the war and threatening to close down all oil operations in the Gulf. When this danger was drawn to the attention of Gulf rulers, they reversed their original decision and refused to permit Iraqi military operations from their territory. This incident led Saudi Arabia to consider the vulnerability of its oil installations to an Iranian strike. As a result, the Saudis requested emergency air-defense assistance from the United States, leading to the deployment of U.S. AWACS early-warning aircraft to Saudi Arabia before the end of the month.

27. For a version of this theory, see Bani-Sadr, *My Turn to Speak*, p. 70.

28. Brzezinski later characterized reports of his supposed meeting with Saddam Hussein as "absolutely false." In a letter to *The Wall Street Journal*, dated June 18, 1991, he wrote: "It is also false to suggest that the Carter administration in any fashion whatsoever, directly or indirectly, encouraged Iraq to undertake a military adventure against Iran." I worked very closely with Brzezinski and traveled with him during this period. My own experience accords entirely with this denial.

29. See the transcript of Saddam Hussein's meeting with U.S. ambassador April Glaspie on July 25, 1990. This document, which was released by Iraq, was published in *The New York Times*, September 23, 1990, p. 19.

30. On September 26, just four days after the war began, former Iranian Prime Minister Bakhtiar announced in Paris that he planned to establish an Iranian government-in-exile. He also disclosed that he had visited Iraq five times over the previous year. Military groups associated with former Iranian General Gholam Ali Oveissi and Admiral Madani (who had just escaped from Iran) were also hatching plots at this time. Bani-Sadr said that he received reports on a series of such plots on September 27. Bani-Sadr, *My Turn to Speak*, p. 79.

31. Zbigniew Brzezinski, *Power and Principle: Memoirs of the National Security Adviser, 1977–1981* (New York: Farrar, Straus & Giroux, 1983), pp. 568–69. Deputy Secretary of State Warren Christopher warned Baghdad on September 28

that the U.S. "could not condone" the seizure of Iran's oil-producing Khuzistan province. Christopher also cautioned the Soviet Union against taking advantage of Iran's weakness. "I think the Soviets understand that the United States would regard any effort by them to move into Iran with utmost gravity."

32. Shortly after the war began, an individual with close contacts to the Iranian leadership told Washington that the "hostage crisis is now front burner again."

6. SCRAMBLING FOR POSITION

1. Interview with Ali Reza Nobari, former head of the Central Bank of Iran, Paris, August 11, 1990.

2. The following account is based primarily on an interview with Jacques Montanès in his office in the freight terminal of Charles de Gaulle airport outside Paris on May 18, 1990. It draws heavily on a memorandum written by Montanès in July 1981, which was described in a series of special reports by Pierre Salinger on ABC-TV in late 1981. (Henceforth Montanès memo.) I am indebted to Pierre Salinger for sharing the memo with me and for introducing me to Jacques Montanès.

3. Ibid.

4. Count De Marenches, quoted in Christine Ockrent, *The Evil Empire: The Third World War Now* (London: Sidgwick & Jackson, 1988), p. 30.

5. Ibid., p. 142.

6. Testimony of Richard Allen at Brenneke trial (transcript pp. 433ff). Interviews with Richard Allen and Albert Jolis by Robert Ross and Robert Parry, October 1990.

7. De Marenches, quoted in Ockrent, *Evil Empire*, p. 159.

8. The De Marenches rendezvous with Reagan is reported in Bob Woodward, *Veil: The Secret Wars of the CIA 1981–1987* (New York: Simon and Schuster, 1987), pp. 39–41.

9. Montanès memo, July 1981, in the author's possession.

10. Interview with Ahmed Salamatian, Paris, May 17, 1990.

11. These meetings were independently reported by a European intelligence official, a European arms dealer, and a man with close ties to Israeli intelligence. These individuals were not acquainted with each other. All three agreed on the general dates, location, and purpose of the meetings.

12. Hamid Naqashan was the chief arms-procurement officer for the Iranian

Revolutionary Guards. See also Martin Kilian, "Alle haben riesige Angst," *Der Spiegel*, August 12, 1991, pp. 127–36 for an account of this meeting.

13. Israel radio as reported in British Broadcasting Company Summary of World Broadcasts, September 28, 1980. The same report was carried by Reuters. At this time, Zippori was effectively the acting defense minister since Prime Minister Menachem Begin had failed to appoint a defense minister and was technically responsible for that portfolio, among others. Begin, who was involved in a prolonged and complex political battle, delegated almost total responsibility to Zippori.

14. Reuters, September 19, 1980. Although Begin did not mention it, the United States had also been involved in this covert action intended to destabilize the Iraqi government.

15. Interview with a former Iranian official who requested not to be named, Washington, D.C., June 12, 1991.

16. Associated Press, Vienna, October 1, 1980.

17. Interview with a former senior official of the Israeli Foreign Ministry, New York, November 10, 1989; interview with a former senior official of the Israeli Defense Ministry, Tel Aviv, March 17, 1989. Both requested anonymity. The same information was provided by Ari Ben-Menashe in late 1990.

18. Interview with Jacques Montanès, May 14, 1990. Montanès Memo, July 1981.

19. Montanès memo, July 1981.

20. Interview with Ahmed Heidari, Monte Carlo, July 18, 1990.

21. Ibid. Montanès memo, July 1981.

22. For a vivid and detailed account of some of these operations, see Ostrovsky, *By Way of Deception*, pp. 1–28.

23. Interview, Washington, D.C., June 12, 1991. The former Iranian official asked not to be named.

24. Interview with a former Iranian general, who asked not to be identified, London, October 5, 1990.

25. Interview with Bani-Sadr, Versailles, May 18, 1990. Bani-Sadr insisted that the raid was due to a targeting error by the F-4 pilot.

26. Alfonso Chardy, "Reagan Aides, in 1980, held hostage talks: Advisers met figure claiming to represent Iran, but deny making deals," *The Miami Herald*, April 12, 1987. Allen had probably told the story earlier, to Bob Woodward and Walter Pincus of *The Washington Post*, who published the bare outline of the story on November 29, 1986, citing an unnamed source.

27. Interview with Richard Allen, Washington, D.C., November 24, 1989.

28. Chardy, *The Miami Herald,* April 12, 1987, citing a written communication with McFarlane.

29. Laurence Silberman, letter to the editor of *The Miami Herald,* September 1, 1987; telephone interview with Silberman, May 23, 1991.

30. Telephone interview with Laurence Silberman, September 10, 1990; letter from Laurence Silberman, April 17, 1991.

31. Interview with Richard Allen, Washington, D.C., November 24, 1989.

32. Interview with Hushang Lavi by David Marks, April 14, 1989.

33. Ibid.

34. The basis for this firm judgment is somewhat obscure since neither Allen nor Silberman had ever laid eyes on Lavi to the best of their knowledge. Silberman told me that Lavi (an Iranian version of Levi) was a Jewish name and would have registered with him.

35. Parviz Lavi identified the handwriting to ABC-TV *Nightline* investigators.

36. Transcript of Jonathan Silvers interview with Hushang Lavi, Plainview, Long Island, April 21, 1988; Lavi repeated this same claim in his interview with David Marks on April 14, 1989.

37. I was aware of the offer to Anderson because of my position in the National Security Council at the time. Several internal U.S. government memorandums relating to this offer, dated October 2, 3, 9, 14, 15, 21, and 29 of 1980, were later declassified and released. Contained in *An Election Held Hostage? A Compendium,* prepared by David Marks (New York: The Fund for New Priorities in America, June 1991).

38. Interview with Ari Ben-Menashe, New York, May 20, 1991.

39. Ben-Menashe said that Lavi's note was part of a set of papers that he had assembled years later as background information for Amiram Nir, the Israeli counterterrorist specialist who played a prominent role in the Iran-Contra Affair in 1985–86. Ben-Menashe, who said he was close to Nir in the years before Nir's mysterious death in November 1988 in a plane crash in Mexico, was never willing to produce the other papers that he said he compiled for Nir.

40. Letter from Laurence Silberman, April 17, 1991.

41. Interview with Alton Frye, April 30, 1991. See also the interview with Rogovin on *Frontline,* April 16, 1991.

42. This account is based on a secret, now declassified memorandum from an official of the CIA to David Aaron, dated October 3, 1980. In Marks, *An Election Held Hostage? A Compendium.*

43. Interviews with Ari Ben-Menashe and Jamshid Hashemi, late 1990. The

same information was provided by an American with close ties to Israel, in New York, June 6, 1990. He asked that his name not be used.

44. Declassified memorandum from unnamed CIA official to David Aaron, October 3, 1980. In Marks, *An Election Held Hostage? A Compendium.*

45. Department of State memorandum, "Approach on Iranian Spares," October 9, 1980, Secret, Eyes Only, now declassified. In Marks, *An Election Held Hostage? A Compendium.*

46. State Department memorandums for the record, "Exchanges with Regovin [sic] and Lavi," October 14 and 15, 1980, Secret/Sensitive, now declassified. In Marks, *An Election Held Hostage? A Compendium.*

7. INDIAN SUMMER

1. Associated Press, October 1, 1980.

2. See "The Election Held Hostage," a PBS-TV *Frontline* special, April 16, 1991.

3. Bani-Sadr, *My Turn to Speak,* pp. 30–31.

4. Carter, *Keeping Faith,* p. 560; Sick, *All Fall Down,* pp. 311–12.

5. Bani-Sadr, *My Turn to Speak,* p. 83; also CRS Chronology, pp. 301–2 and O'Ballance, *The Gulf War,* pp. 47–49.

6. Interview with a former senior Iranian official who asked not to be identified, Washington, D.C., June 12, 1991.

7. Ibid.

8. Brzezinski, *Power and Principle,* p. 504.

9. Carter, *Keeping Faith,* p. 560.

10. "The Hostage Seizure in Tehran: Notes of the Federal Republic of Germany's Ambassador in Tehran," by Gerhard Ritzel, February 5, 1981. This paper, a lengthy description of Ritzel's actions and observations during the hostage crisis, was written for the German Foreign Ministry. I am obliged to Steven M. de Vogel of the Dutch magazine *Vrij Nederland* for drawing it to my attention. It was translated by Eve Schaenen.

11. The text of Ritzel's letter to Khomeini was provided by Steven M. de Vogel.

12. CRS Chronology, pp. 137–41, 147; Sick, *All Fall Down,* pp. 271–73.

13. Interview with a member of the rescue mission team who asked not to be identified, Washington, D.C., December 6, 1989.

14. CRS Chronology, p. 324.

15. Carter, *Keeping Faith,* p. 560.

16. Personal communication from Jimmy Carter, September 19, 1990.

17. Albosta Report, p. 1079.

18. This conversation, which reportedly occurred during a meeting of campaign advisers, was noted in Allen's personal log. Affidavit of Richard V. Allen, April 13, 1984, Albosta Report, pp. 1078–79.

19. Albosta Report, p. 1498. Emphasis in original.

20. Ibid., p. 1113. Codevilla later declared that he did not recall speaking to Richard Allen on this subject.

21. Ibid., p. 1939.

22. Carter, *Keeping Faith*, p. 591.

23. Personal communication from Jimmy Carter, September 19, 1990.

24. As reported by John Wallach in the *Los Angeles Herald Examiner*, October 16, 1980. Reproduced in the Albosta Report, pp. 1494–96.

25. This memo is reproduced in the Albosta Report, pp. 1490–91. Also interviews with Richard V. Allen, November 24, 1989, and John Wallach, July 18, 1991. Edmund Muskie, in an interview with me on January 8, 1990, had no specific recollection of his meeting with Wallach but had no reason to doubt the accuracy of the account.

8. CLOSING THE DEAL

1. CRS Chronology, p. 316.

2. The following account is based on a series of interviews I had with Ari Ben-Menashe from late 1990 through mid-1991. Throughout our conversations, Ben-Menashe refused to identify any active Israeli intelligence agents by name, though he did provide the names of some policy-level individuals who had since retired. He never identified, directly or indirectly, the other members of the group who went to Paris in October 1980.

3. Reported by the Associated Press, October 18, 1980.

4. Hushang Lavi had been in and out of Washington from September 29 to October 15, in almost constant contact with Mitch Rogovin and Harold Saunders of the State Department concerning his proposal for a swap of F-14 parts for the hostages. On the fifteenth Lavi was informed that the State Department was checking his story directly with Bani-Sadr. Lavi then disappeared from sight for about five days. An examination of Lavi's telephone calls during this period indicates none of his usual business calls from the afternoon of October 16 until midday on the eighteenth, and again from the evening of the eighteenth to at least the twenti-

eth and possibly the twenty-second. There were a number of telephone calls on the eighteenth, but other members of the family also had access to the same home telephone, so his location cannot be positively confirmed. (Personal examination of some of Hushang Lavi's papers, August 1991.) Lavi gave numerous interviews starting in 1988 until his death in December 1990. His description of the Paris meetings remained consistent throughout. For the following account, I have relied on the transcript of an interview by David Marks on April 14, 1989, and on notes of multiple interviews by Robert Parry and Martin Kilian in 1989 and Robert Parry in 1990.

5. Interviews with a close relative of Hushang Lavi, New York, August 1991.

6. Oswald LeWinter, interview with Martin Kilian, September 4, 1988; Jamshid Hashemi, interview with Tara Sonenshine of ABC-TV's *Nightline*, Washington, D.C., June 11, 1990.

7. Interview with Hushang Lavi by Robert Parry and Robert Ross, November 1990.

8. Based on entries in Shaheen's personal diaries. See Martin Kilian, "Alle haben riesige Angst," *Der Spiegel*, August 12, 1991, pp. 127–36.

9. Frank Snepp, "Brenneke Exposed," *Village Voice*, September 10, 1991, pp. 27–31.

10. Interview with Richard Brenneke, Washington, D.C., May 19, 1991.

11. See *United States of America* v. *Richard Brenneke*, CRS No. 89-198, esp. pp. 74–95 and 234–84. Donald Gregg was a principal witness in the Brenneke trial. During the course of his testimony, he denied under oath that he had participated in any improper political activities or had been in contact with George Bush in the course of the 1980 election.

12. For much of the following information, I am indebted to Martin Kilian of *Der Spiegel*, who spent many hours with LeWinter, both on the telephone and in Germany, where LeWinter returned to take up residence in the 1980s. I also acquired some of LeWinter's academic records, and I spoke at length with several individuals who had known him for more than twenty years.

13. Oswald LeWinter, *Shakespeare in Europe* (New York: World Publishing Co. and Meridian Books, 1963).

14. When LeWinter was awaiting sentencing in June 1985 for having transported chemicals from Germany to the United States that were used in making drugs, Saul Bellow sent a letter to the presiding judge on LeWinter's behalf.

15. Interview with German intelligence sources by Martin Kilian, Fall 1990.

16. Interview with Oswald LeWinter by Robert Ross and Robert Parry, Germany, October 28, 1990.

17. See Martin Kilian, "Alle haben riesige Angst," *Der Spiegel*, August 12, 1991, pp. 127–36.

18. "The Election Held Hostage," PBS-TV *Frontline*, April 16, 1991.

19. Telephone interview with François Cheron, August 11, 1990; telephone interview with François Cheron by Carole Jerome of the Canadian Broadcasting Company, July 21, 1990. These negotiations are described in Warren Christopher, et al., *American Hostages in Iran*, esp. John E. Hoffman, Jr., "The Bankers' Channel," pp. 235–80; Harold H. Saunders, "The Beginning of the End," pp. 281–96; and Roberts B. Owen, "The Final Negotiation and Release in Algiers," pp. 297–324.

20. Interview with Durrani by Lawrence Lifschultz, December 7, 1989. I am indebted to Lifschultz for sharing with me his extensive research on the Durrani case. For additional information, see Lifschultz, Steven Galsten, and Rabia Ali, *Bordering on Treason: The Trial and Conviction of Arif Durrani* (East Haven, Conn.: The Pamphleteer's Press, 1991).

21. "The Election Held Hostage," PBS-TV *Frontline*, April 16, 1991; also interviews with Durrani by Martin Kilian, May 12, 1990; by Lawrence Lifschultz, June 8, 1990; and by Robert Parry, January 3, 1991.

22. See Martin Kilian, "Alle haben riesige Angst," *Der Spiegel*, August 12, 1991, pp. 127–36.

23. Interviews with William Herrmann, 1989–91. See also "The Election Held Hostage," *Frontline*, April 16, 1991.

9. REVERSAL OF FORTUNE

1. Telephone interview with Katherine Keough, July 26, 1991.

2. Statement of October 20, 1980. See *Facts on File*.

3. *The New York Times*, October 21, 1980.

4. Brenneke trial transcript, pp. 481, 822. At the time of this phone call, it would have been 1:30 P.M. in Paris.

5. Interview with Richard V. Allen, Washington, D.C., May 3, 1991.

6. Interview with Robert Garrick by Robert Ross and Robert Parry, September 22, 1990.

7. The telephone call was referenced in a court document: Affidavit for a Search Warrant, United States District Court, Southern District of New York, undated but about August 1981.

8. Interview with Jacques Montanès, May 14, 1990. Montanès memo, July 1981.

9. Montanès memo, July 1981.

10. Ibid.

11. "The Election Held Hostage," PBS-TV *Frontline*, April 16, 1991.

12. Ibid.

13. State Department Memorandum for the Record, October 21, 1980, Secret/ Sensitive, now declassified. In Marks, *An Election Held Hostage? A Compendium.*

14. Indictment, 84 Crim. 480, *United States of America* v. *Cyrus Hashemi, et al.,* U.S. District Court, Southern District of New York, July 18, 1984.

15. Interview with Harold Saunders, Washington, D.C., March 21, 1990.

16. CRS Chronology, p. 348; Sick, *All Fall Down,* p. 315.

17. *The New York Times,* October 22, 1980.

18. Ibid.

19. Ibid.

20. Scott, *Pieces of the Game,* pp. 347ff. Interview with Scott, February 1, 1990.

21. CRS Chronology, p. 349.

22. Ibid. p. 350.

23. Interview with Ahmed Salamatian, Paris, May 17, 1990.

24. This event was first reported in Sick, *All Fall Down,* p. 315, and n. 10 on p. 359. The expanded account that follows is based on interviews with former U.S. government officials, including Jimmy Carter, Zbigniew Brzezinski, Harold Saunders, Samuel Lewis, and others, including intelligence officers. Interviews were also conducted with the Iranian arms dealer Ahmed Heidari and two senior Israelis who were in a position to know about this event in 1980 but who spoke on condition of anonymity. Details about the aircraft movements, manifests and invoices are from the July 1981 Montanès memo.

25. The following account is from the Montanès memo, July 1981.

26. Personal communication from Jimmy Carter, September 19, 1990; interview with Zbigniew Brzezinski, Washington, June 6, 1990.

27. Albosta Report, pp. 1487–88.

28. Interview with Robert Garrick by Robert Ross and Robert Parry, September 22, 1990.

29. Benjamin Fernandez, campaign adviser on minority issues, cited in *The New York Times,* October 24, 1980. A spokesman for Ronald Reagan denied that this represented Reagan's position.

30. Unidentified campaign official, cited in Associated Press wire report October 24, 1980.

31. Reuters news service, October 25, 1980.

32. This is from personal observation at the time. I first met Richard Allen on

December 18, 1980, during the transition period between the Carter and Reagan administrations. He dropped by my office for an informal discussion, as he did with other NSC staff members. He asked me if the hostages would be out of Iran before Reagan's inauguration. At that point, negotiations seemed to be making slow progress, and after a long pause I said yes, I thought so. He then asked me to tell him "what really happened with the October surprise." I told him there never *was* an October surprise or any secret plan to spring the hostages at the last minute before the election. He obviously did not believe me, so I offered to send him a memo summarizing everything that had happened to the best of my knowledge. A few days later I did send him a long memo, based on my own files, describing in great detail the events of September and October. I have no idea if he ever read it. I never saw the memo again and we never discussed it further. On the basis of this conversation, however, there was no doubt in my mind that Allen and the Reagan-Bush campaign genuinely expected some last-minute desperation move by Carter.

33. Associated Press wire report, October 25, 1980.

34. CRS Chronology, p. 354.

35. Ibid., pp. 355–56.

36. Brzezinski, *Power and Principle*, p. 505.

37. Interview with Harold Saunders, Washington, D.C., March 21, 1990.

38. Albert Hunt, "The Campaign and the Issues," in *The American Elections of 1980*, pp. 165–66.

39. Elizabeth Drew, *Portrait of an Election: The 1980 Presidential Campaign* (New York: Simon and Schuster, 1981), p. 317.

40. In fact, when results of the 1980 elections were tallied, the Republicans had a margin of 10 points. William Schneider, "The November 4 Vote for President: What Did It Mean?" in *The American Elections of 1980*, p. 217.

41. Drew, *Portrait of an Election*, p. 321.

42. Memorandum from Harold Saunders to Warren Christopher, "Two Related Items on Iranian Military Supply," October 29, 1980, Secret, now declassified. In Marks, *An Election Held Hostage? A Compendium*.

43. See Sick, *All Fall Down*, pp. 314–15.

10. CARTER UNDONE

1. Jordan, *Crisis*, p. 361. See also Sick, *All Fall Down*, for a more complete account of the events within the White House during those days.

2. Jordan, *Crisis*, p. 365.

3. Scott, *Pieces of the Game*, pp. 360–62.

4. CRS Chronology, p. 395.

5. For the texts of these negotiating documents and a more complete description of the various maneuvers of both sides in the following months, see Sick, *All Fall Down*, pp. 320–38. This same period is also described in Christopher et al., *American Hostages in Iran*, in the chapters by Robert Carswell and Richard J. Davis, "Crafting the Final Settlement," pp. 209–29, and Roberts B. Owen, "Final Negotiation and Release in Algiers," pp. 306–23.

6. John Wallach, "Carter Aide Contradicts Reagan," Hearst News Service, July 4, 1991.

7. Carter, *Keeping Faith*, pp. 575–76. Interviews with Jimmy Carter, Atlanta, September 15, 1990, and Samuel Lewis, Washington, D.C., April 15, 1991.

8. Interview with Ari Ben-Menashe, New York, January 12, 1991.

9. Interview with General Yehoshua Saguy by Robert Ross and Robert Parry, November 16, 1990.

10. Indictment, 84 Crim. 480, *United States of America* v. *Cyrus Hashemi, et al.*, U.S. District Court, Southern District of New York, July 18, 1984. I obtained copies of the affidavits by FBI and Customs agents produced in about August– November 1981 and filed with the court papers in the Southern District of New York. The following information is based on those documents.

11. Affidavit for a Search Warrant, United States District Court for the Southern District of New York, date unreadable but approximately August 1981, p. 12.

12. Telephone interview with Lloyd Cutler, April 15, 1991. For a description of the "banking channel" negotiations, see Christopher *et al.*, *American Hostages in Iran*, esp. John E. Hoffman Jr., "The Bankers' Channel," pp. 235–80.

13. This incident was first discovered and reported in a copyrighted story by reporters Jeff Neismith and Scott Shepard, "Reagan Adviser Meese, Iranian Linked in '80 Report," *Atlanta Journal-Constitution*, June 20, 1991. According to Shepard, Meese's office was contacted repeatedly both before and after this article was published, but he never returned the calls or offered any comment.

14. Indictment, 840 Crim. 480, *United States of America* v. *Cyrus Hashemi, et al.*, U.S. District Court, Southern District of New York, July 18, 1984.

15. CBS, *Face The Nation*, July 7, 1991.

16. *The New York Times*, December 25 and 29, 1980.

17. Bani-Sadr, *My Turn to Speak*, p. 47.

18. Interview with Ali Reza Nobari, Paris, August 10, 1990.

19. Interview with Christian Bourguet by Martin Kilian, Paris, May 1989.

20. Interview with Jamshid Hashemi by Tara Sonenshine, Washington, D.C., January 1, 1990.

21. *United States of America* v. *Richard J. Brennecke,* CR No. 89-198-MA, U.S. District Court, District of Oregon, p. 442.

22. Interview with Customs agent who spoke on condition of nonattribution, New York, January 10, 1990.

23. Bani-Sadr, *My Turn to Speak,* p. 48.

24. Ibid., pp. 49–51.

25. Iran's military assets were moved from McGuire Air Force Base to a warehouse in Vienna, Va., in January 1986. See John Wallach, Hearst News Service, *San Antonio Light,* January 22, 1986. Talks about the disposition of this equipment were still in progress at The Hague in 1991.

11. QUID PRO QUO

1. A Reuters report from Iran on January 20 just prior to the departure of the hostages noted that Iran "appeared to be trying to time the takeoff to coincide with the inauguration of Ronald Reagan." CRS Chronology, Addendum of events January 1–25, 1981, p. 29.

2. Public Papers of the President 41, January 27, 1981 (Washington, D.C.: U.S. Government Printing Office, 1981).

3. Public Papers of the President 55, January 29, 1981 (Washington, D.C.: U.S. Government Printing Office, 1981).

4. See "Public Report of the Vice President's Task Force on Combatting Terrorism" (Washington, D.C.: U.S. Government Printing Office, February 1986).

5. Bani-Sadr, *My Turn to Speak,* pp. 49–51.

6. Interview with Richard Allen, Washington, D.C., November 24, 1989. The issue was raised publicly by Secretary of State Haig and President Reagan in their maiden press conferences of January 28 and 29, 1981, respectively.

7. The announcement was made on February 17 at the opening of congressional hearings on the agreements. President Reagan signed Executive Order 12294 implementing the agreement on February 24, 1981. Public Papers of the President 158, February 24, 1981 (Washington, D.C.: U.S. Government Printing Office, 1981).

8. Telephone interview with David Newsom, under secretary of state for political affairs during the Carter administration and acting secretary of state prior to the confirmation of Alexander M. Haig, Jr., August 12, 1991.

9. *The New York Times,* January 29, 1981.

10. Interview with a former Reagan administration official, Washington, D.C., December 18, 1989.

11. Bob Woodward and Walter Pincus, "Israeli Sale Said Allowed by Haig in '81," *Washington Post,* November 29, 1986. McFarlane and Kimche would both play important roles in the Iran-Contra Affair in 1985–86. Richard Allen told me that he had also been approached on the same subject of Israeli arms shipments to Iran by Morris Amitay, then the director of the America Israel Public Affairs Committee, in December 1980. Interview with Richard V. Allen, Washington, D.C., November 24, 1989.

12. John Wallach, "Iran-Israel Arms Deal Began in 1980," Hearst News Service, *Albany Times Union,* March 7, 1987.

13. "The Election Held Hostage," PBS-TV *Frontline,* April 16, 1991.

14. Interview with former Defense Department official, who spoke to me on condition of anonymity, August 8, 1990.

15. Interview with Avraham Tamir, Israel, March 17, 1989.

16. For the Arens interview and response to the State Department, see the *Boston Globe,* October 21 and 23, 1982. Arens repeated the same points in an interview in late 1986. See *The Washington Post,* November 29, 1986.

17. Interview with Alexander Haig by Robert Parry and Robert Ross, January 9, 1991.

18. Interview with a former CIA officer who spoke on grounds of anonymity, Washington, D.C., March 20, 1990.

19. "The Election Held Hostage," PBS-TV *Frontline,* April 16, 1991.

20. United States Court of Claims: *Gary Howard and Ronald Tucker v. United States of America,* 386–87 C; affidavit of William Warren Northrop, November 14, 1988.

21. Ibid. See also Samuel Segev, *The Iranian Triangle: The Untold Story of Israel's Role in the Iran-Contra Affair* (New York: The Free Press, 1988), p. 5. Both of these sources, who derived their information from Israeli intelligence information, agree on the dollar totals, the participants, and the nature of the equipment in this deal.

22. Tass news agency reported on July 23, 1981, that the plane collided with a Soviet plane and burned.

23. Interview with a former Reagan administration official who spoke on condition of anonymity, Washington, D.C., September 28, 1991. See the State Department press briefing of August 21, 1981, in *American Foreign Policy Current Documents, 1981 Supplement* (Washington, D.C.: U.S. Government Printing Office, 1985), 1737:5.

24. Interview with Jamshid Hashemi, New York, August 29, 1991. United States Court of Claims: *Gary Howard and Ronald Tucker* v. *United States of America*, 386-87 C; affidavit of William Warren Northrop, November 14, 1988.

25. I was given a copy of this contract by a former official of the Reagan administration.

26. These invoices were published in *Le Canard enchaîné* in March 1984. Cited in Bani-Sadr, *My Turn to Speak*, p. 194.

27. It will be recalled that his official name was Mohammed Ali Hashemi, and he often used the additional name of his family's village of origin, Balanian. Court records referred to him as "Djamshid Hashemi, a/k/a 'Mohammed Ali Balanian,' and 'Mohammed Ali Balanian Hashemi.' " Indictment, *United States of America* v. *Cyrus Hashemi, et al.*, U.S. District Court, Southern District of New York, July 18, 1984, p. 9.

28. Interview with Bani-Sadr, Versailles, May 18, 1990. See also Bani-Sadr, *My Turn to Speak*, p. 194.

29. Montanès memo, July 1981; interview with Ahmed Heidari, Monte Carlo, July 18, 1990.

30. Interview with William Herrmann, New York, November 6, 1989; interview with William Herrmann by Robert Parry and Robert Ross, about December 1990.

31. Interview with Arif Durrani by Robert Parry and Robert Ross, January 4, 1991.

32. Ibid.

33. "The Election Held Hostage." PBS-TV *Frontline*, April 16, 1991.

34. Ibid.

35. Indictment, 84 Crim. 480, *United States of America* v. *Cyrus Hashemi, et al.*, U.S. District Court, Southern District of New York, July 18, 1984.

36. Ibid.

37. Affidavit for a Search Warrant, U.S. District Court, Southern District of New York, undated but about August 1981.

38. Adel Darwish and Gregory Alexander, *Unholy Babylon: The Secret History of Saddam's War* (New York: St. Martin's Press, 1991), p. 124.

39. Interview with Ari Ben-Menashe, New York, November 20, 1990.

40. Interview with a former Reagan administration official who spoke on condition of anonymity, Washington, D.C., December 18, 1989.

41. Interview with Bani-Sadr, Versailles, May 18, 1990.

CONCLUSION

1. Admiral Poindexter was the assistant to the President for national-security affairs at the time. This original "finding" was replaced by a slightly revised version on January 17, 1986. See the Tower Commission Report, pp. B-63–B-65. Brenneke's statement to the DIA official was submitted as part of the court records in *United States of America* v. *Samuel Evans,* the court case that followed Cyrus Hashemi's participation in a Customs Service sting in 1985.

2. Sue Lindsay, *Rocky Mountain News,* October 2, 1988. Also see Barbara Honegger, *October Surprise* (New York: Tudor Publishing Company, 1989). The Bush campaign issued an absolute denial, saying Bush was on the campaign trail at the time and was not in Paris.

3. See U.S. District Court, District of Colorado, *United States of America* v. *Richard Brenneke,* Criminal Case 89-CR-152, May 12, 1989, Indictment, U.S. Code, Title 18, Section 1623(a), paragraphs 4 and 5.

4. For a detailed description of the trial, see Cameron Barr, "Stranger Than Fiction," *The American Lawyer,* December 1990, pp. 70–72. See also the trial transcript, *United States of America* v. *Richard J. Brenneke,* CR No. 89-198-MA, U.S. District Court for the District of Oregon, April 24, 1990.

5. Frank Snepp, "Brenneke Exposed," *Village Voice,* September 10, 1991, pp. 27–31.

6. These documents were made available to ABC News *Nightline* in June 1991.

7. Robert Ross and Robert Parry, interview with Richard Brenneke, September 24, 1990.

8. A former agency officer put it as follows: "There's a pattern . . . in a number of these cases that I call 'disposable assets.' These are people, typically U.S. citizens, that are developed to be used by those who run these clandestine games. They are never officers or members of the organization. . . . Typically, the profile is a young man with some technical skill, frequently a pilot, but with a bent for adventure. These will be guys who are involved in skydiving, stuff like that." Interview with David MacMichael, July 1991.

9. Ibid.

10. Quoted by Paul Muolo and Stephen Pizzo in "The Banks and the C.I.A.: Cash and Carry," *Penthouse,* November 1990, p. 123.

11. In interviews with Martin Kilian of *Der Spiegel,* LeWinter would only discuss his disinformation efforts in the most guarded terms. These efforts were confirmed independently by two individuals who saw LeWinter almost daily during this period.

12. Casey affidavit dated March 2, 1984. Albosta Report, p. 1102.

13. The account that follows is drawn from information contained in the court documents submitted in the federal government's case against Cyrus Hashemi. See especially the indictment in *United States of America* v. *Cyrus Hashemi, et al.,* U.S. District Court, Southern District of New York, July 18, 1984.

14. Interview with Jamshid Hashemi, Fall 1990.

15. Ibid.

16. A series of secret (now declassified) CIA internal memorandums in the author's possession documents Cyrus Hashemi's efforts to engage Casey on his behalf. These include: Memorandum from the Director of Central Intelligence to Chief, Near East Division, DO [Directorate of Operations], "Release of Hostages," dated June 17, 1985; Memorandum for the Record, "New Developments on the Shaheen-Hashemi Indirect Channel to Iran," dated July 9, 1985; and Memorandum for the Record, "Hashemi Tries to Play Hard Ball," dated July 15, 1985.

17. See Draper, *A Very Thin Line*, pp. 134–36, and Persico, *Casey*, pp. 448–51.

18. Draper, *A Very Thin Line*, p. 440.

19. This case, which was dubbed the "merchants of death" case, received extensive publicity. For a good summary of the issues, and its relation to the Iran-Contra Affair, see William Rempel, "Iran Arms Dealers May Use Secret CIA Links as Defense," *Los Angeles Times*, August 4, 1988.

20. Lloyd Cutler, "The 'October Surprise' Made Unsurprising," *The New York Times*, May 15, 1991.

21. Medical report of examination of the body of Cyrus Hashemi, July 23, 1986, by Dr. Iain Eric West, Guy's Hospital, London. Report dated August 6, 1986. A copy of this document was kindly provided to the author by New York attorney William M. Kunstler.

22. Interview with Raji Samghabadi, New York, January 4, 1991. The existence of these stories from Ari Ben-Menashe, giving detailed information about the Iran-Contra Affair long before it became public knowledge, was privately confirmed to me by other members of the *Time* magazine staff. Samghabadi says he still has the original copy.

23. One of the first reporters to interview him in the Manhattan Correctional Center was Robert Parry.

24. Mehdi Kashani's name appears as the addressee on a pro forma invoice from ASCO for aircraft parts, dated January 21, 1983, in author's possession. There is some confusion of names between Ahmed and Mehdi Kashani.

25. Montanès memo, July 1981; interview with Ahmed Heidari, Monte Carlo, July 18, 1990.

26. Interview with Ahmed Heidari, Monte Carlo, July 18, 1990.

27. There was a second attempt to get a T-72 from Iran in 1986, during the Iran-Contra Affair. It was also unsuccessful. A T-72 was reportedly acquired later from a country in Eastern Europe.

28. Interview with Ahmed Heidari, Monte Carlo, July 17 and 18, 1990.

29. Interview with Francesco Pazienza, Rome, May 21, 1990. Pazienza was an Italian businessman who was arrested in the United States and held briefly in New York before extradition to Italy. He was LeWinter's cellmate for part of that time. LeWinter later confirmed the accuracy of this account to Martin Kilian in late 1990.

30. L. Gordon Crovitz, "Bush Had Lunch With Potter Stewart, Not with Iranians," *Wall Street Journal,* May 8, 1991.

31. The sources for this allegation are Ari Ben-Menashe; the French SDECE intelligence officer, a deputy of Alexandre de Marenches; Oswald LeWinter; Richard Brennecke; and Heinrich Rupp.

32. Author's transcription of complete tape of radio broadcast of Ronald Reagan's impromptu press conference on the golf course, Thousand Oaks, California, June 15, 1991.

INDEX

ABOUT THE
AUTHOR

G ARY SICK served on the National Security Council staff under Presidents Gerald Ford, Jimmy Carter, and Ronald Reagan. He was the principal White House aide for Iran during the Iranian revolution and the hostage crisis and is the author of *All Fall Down: America's Tragic Encounter with Iran*—voted one of the eleven best books of 1985 by *The New York Times* and *The Wall Street Journal*. He is a captain (ret.) in the U.S. Navy, with service in the Persian Gulf, North Africa, and the Mediterranean. Mr. Sick, who holds a Ph.D. in political science from Columbia University, was the deputy director for International Affairs at the Ford Foundation from 1982 to 1987, where he was responsible for programs relating to U.S. foreign policy. Mr. Sick is the chairman of Middle East Watch and a member of the Executive Committee of Human Rights Watch in New York. An adjunct professor of political science and a Fellow of the Research Institute on International Change at Columbia University, he currently works as an independent writer, speaker, and consultant on Middle East issues.